W9-DEB-446

ONE

INCREDIBLE

JOURNEY

ONE
INCREDIBLE
JOURNEY

Clayton
Klein

Verlen
Kruger

WILDERNESS HOUSE BOOKS

Library of Congress Catalog Card Number 84-090233

ISBN: 0-9611596-1-8

Cover photos by
Verlen Kruger and Valerie Fons

Typesetting by
Word Processing Services
Okemos, Michigan 48864

Published by
Wilderness House Books
9350 Gregory Road
Box 968
Fowlerville, Michigan 48836

Manufactured in the United States of America

To my ever-loving wife,
JENNY
without whose loyal cooperation and moral support
this journey would never have been
more than just a dream。

Also in grateful, heartfelt acknowledgement
to my
LORD AND SAVIOR, JESUS CHRIST
without whose abiding comfort and presence
at all times
and whose faithful help in times of need
the trip would never have been completed。

Other Books

by

Clayton Klein

COLD SUMMER WIND   *1983*

Note

MEN THAT DON'T FIT IN

There is a race of men that don't fit in,
A race that can't stay still;
So they break the heart of kith and kin,
And they roam the world at will.

They range the field and they rove the flood,
And they climb the mountain crest;
Theirs is the curse of the Gypsy blood,
And they don't know how to rest.

— Robert Service

CONTENTS

MAPS

ACKNOWLEDGEMENTS

Our dreams for the book **One Incredible Journey** became a reality because of the cooperation and hard work of the following people:

Special thanks to Bernice M. Chappel, author of **Bittersweet Trail, In the Palm of the Mitten** and various other books and articles, for her most valued counsel and suggestions.

Special thanks to Marjorie Nash Klein for her assistance in preparing the maps, typing the material and suggesting improvements. Thanks also to Debbie Klein for assisting in typing directly from Verlen's diaries.

Thanks to Clinton Waddell in supplying details of the journey from his memory and point of view.

Thanks to Jenny Kruger for all of her help in supplying facts, photos, and the necessary details to help make this book a reality.

Thanks to both Tom and Pat Boufford of Word Processing Services of Okemos, Michigan, for their superb assistance in helping to produce **One Incredible Journey.**

Thanks also to Valerie Fons and Cliff Jacobson for the kind words they have said on the dust jacket of our book.

Thanks to Phil Pemberton for his fine photos.

INTRODUCTION

Life would be enriched for everyone if we would all share what we are, what we have and what we do. There is no man so insignificant as not to have some influence upon another, for better or worse.

In the course of giving nearly three hundred unsolicited 35-millimeter slide travelogue talks of our "big" trip, many people have asked, "Why don't you write a book about it?" Apparently there are a few who would like the whole story. I feel the obligation to share this "once in a lifetime" experience with those who may be interested.

As a boy, down on a sharecropper's farm in Pulaski County, near Francesville, Indiana, I loved to read about Huckleberry Finn, Robinson Crusoe, Daniel Boone, Kit Carson, and such men of daring and adventure. I lived their experiences and exploits right along with them. As the years went by, I was particularly fascinated with stories of the mountain men, wilderness travelers and venturesome explorers.

More recently, I have been excited by tales of canoe-related adventures, such as the fur traders and long-distance wilderness canoe journeys, of both past and present. I have always appreciated those few who wrote and shared their experiences. Then I'd hear about other outstanding canoe trips which were not written up and I had wished that they could have been. There is a real satisfaction in the fellowship of like spirits and like experiences.

There are already many excellent books on the

market on canoeing, canoe tripping, equipment, etc. I expect to touch upon such subjects, but only as related to this trip. I will be giving my own personal preferences, observations and analysis of **how** and **what** and **why**. You may detect that at times I have strong and convincing opinions, as time and experience tend to give confidence and settle doubts. Don't be surprised if your conclusions differ from mine. You are entitled to your opinion -- just as I am entitled to mine! The world should be all the more interesting because of it.

The writing of **One Incredible Journey** began in 1972. I worked on it for many months during the next couple of years. Progress was slow and I found the work tedious. Finally, I gave it up. Canoeing was much easier and more enjoyable to me than writing. I decided to try and find someone else to finish the story.

Talking with numerous writers, the search continued for the next ten years. Then shortly after Steven Landick and I finished our 28,000-mile journey known as the Ultimate Canoe Challenge in December of 1983, I found my co-author.

I had known Clayton Klein for several years. He is the author of the best-selling true life adventure book, **Cold Summer Wind**, an excellent story of canoeing in the wilderness of the Canadian Barrens. He and his son Darrell had canoed more than 3,000 miles in the Far North. After reading **Cold Summer Wind**, I knew that with his background, he would certainly have the feel for our kind of adventure.

Fortunately Clayton Klein was willing. I supplied him with a copy of my writings, diary, photos and route maps in February of 1984. Working with him on **One Incredible Journey** has been a pleasure.

My canoeing experience had its beginning in 1963 when my wife Jenny and I bought an aluminum canoe and took a five-day October canoe trip in the "bush" country of Ontario. I was "bit by the bug" from the beginning. It was the first hobby or sport that I had ever engaged in. It seemed to fit my long-suppressed dreams and disposition perfectly!

We took several more trips together, and the "canoe fever" got stronger. From the start, Jenny was, and still is, my favorite companion in a canoe. We have had dozens of great, exciting journeys. Each October we try to make a "bush" trip together. That "last trip of the year" has always been reserved for just ourselves. Early in my canoe-racing career, she and I participated in a few mixed races. The first race that I ever won was when teamed up with her.

In the spring of 1965, I was introduced to Clint Waddell, who was with the U. S. Forestry Department, on temporary duty in Lansing, Michigan. Clint was very involved in the professional canoe-racing circuit, and he, along with several of his canoe-racing buddies, taught me the tricks of canoe racing.

I was then not interested in canoe racing but was immensely interested in learning what I could from them. I had read all the books I could find about canoeing and still didn't think I knew much. I found this was true as I started working out with them regularly on their training schedules and learned how the long-distance marathon canoe racers handled a canoe. It was quite a revelation. Their efficiency and technique in use of power and energy was not remotely covered in the books I had read.

Next, I bought a used racing canoe and was trying to talk Clint into teaming up with me for a particular canoe race. I was still telling myself that I was not interested in canoe racing, but there was one wild cross-country canoe race that really turned me on, probably because it was a true wilderness-type canoe race. It was the International Canoe Derby, out of Atikokan, Ontario, across Quetico National Park, day and night to Ely,

ONE INCREDIBLE JOURNEY

Minnesota, and back again day and night. It took about a week to complete. I still consider it the roughest, toughest canoe race there ever was. It has since been discontinued. It was just too rough and not many racers managed to even finish the course.

I still don't know why Clint let a forty-three-year-old greenhorn talk him into something like that, as at that time I had not yet seen a canoe race. In spite of being poorly prepared and making too many mistakes, we survived through the first day and night and were somehow in first place, mostly through good navigation, I think. Then Clint took sick and we had to drop out at a lodge. I had tried to feed him some special "moose juice" concoction that probably would have killed a horse!

The next year, with better planning and preparation, we came back and won it! It was an upset victory against most of the winners from previous years, including a team that was then considered the U. S. National Professional Champs, both also previous winners. That was high wine for a new paddler.

By September, 1968, I was beginning to get ideas, dreaming dreams and starting to make plans for a big cross-continent canoe voyage, but having doubts about what could be done.

I came up with an idea to test ourselves and at the same time attempt to set a Boundary Waters Canoe Area (B W C A) record. The International Boundary Route from International Falls to Grand Portage, Minnesota covers 262 miles, including 37 portages, and is a night and day, non-stop run. It would be an interesting experiment.

At that time I hadn't selected a partner for the "big" journey. I was well aware of the critical psychological problem two people would have on such a long journey, and was being very cautious about who my partner would be. After much thought

Introduction

I arrived at the conclusion that the main over-riding qualification would be to select the person who most wanted to go. It needed to be someone who was a fanatic about it. It had to be someone who wanted to go badly enough to put up with me for six months. I had Clint in mind, but was not yet sure how desperate he was to go.

It didn't take much to talk him into going on this marathon test race in the Boundary Waters Canoe Area. That was a good sign. It took us just eighty hours and forty minutes from the start at International Falls to the time we walked into the stockade at Grand Portage. It was an interesting and satisfying experience.

In his book, **Canoe Trails Through Quetico,** published in 1959, Keith Dennis tells of some speed records in the Quetico Canoe Country. He states that the customary travel time on this route was fifteen to seventeen days. Apparently, Sir George Simpson had the fastest known time through the Quetico.

> George Simpson, Governor-in-Chief of the Hudson's Bay Company, was noted for the swiftness of his movement over the waterways of Canada — the trip from Fort William to Fort Frances took from May 25th to noon June 1st; just six and a half days. These astonishing trips were made with picked crews of five to eight paddlers who were undoubtedly familiar with the route and directed by leaders who had the ability to obtain the full cooperation of the men. Their records still stand.

But not any more! Clint and I took care of that in 1969 with our 262-mile, record-breaking, eighty hour and forty minute dash. That was less than three and one-half days of total time from beginning to end and our time was witnessed by officials.

ONE INCREDIBLE JOURNEY

The main outcome of our B W C A marathon trip was that Clint and I accepted one another as partners for the proposed cross-continent journey.

So it was to be, that a six-foot tall, one hundred and eighty-five pound, good-looking, blond Viking type would supply the power in the stern of the canoe. Clint Waddell, a thirty-six year old, U. S. Forestry Department Biology Technician from Minneapolis, Minnesota, is an outstanding outdoorsman and canoeist. In every way, he was a good choice for a partner on a venture such as this. He is one of that quiet kind that knows a lot more than he lets on. He is knowledgeable in the ways of the wilderness, skilled around a campfire, skilled at navigation and a true expert in a canoe. But the one thing far above all else that qualified him for this particular endeavor was his fanatical desire to make the trip.

I would supply as much power as I could from the bow of the canoe. At that time, I was a forty-nine year old, self-employed plumbing contractor from DeWitt, Michigan. I stood five and one-half feet tall and weighed about one hundred and sixty pounds. My family consisted of a loving wife, Jenny, and nine healthy children. My love of the outdoors, and especially the unspoiled wilderness, was all the more enhanced by my love for God, the creator of it all.

It was with considerable elation that we were now making definite plans. The planning would be a large part of the fun. Only once in a lifetime could we reasonably expect to put together an endeavor such as this, and our plans and preparations had to be extremely thorough. Our success or failure hung on these preparations.

Organizing the project and putting it all together was done by myself, with Clint contributing valuable assistance. We lived nearly seven hundred miles apart, which made working together rather difficult, but we did get together as often as we could to share ideas and to keep the fire burning. We shared an unusual accumulation of mutual interests, dreams and ambitions that led our paths along the same lines. This finally pushed us to the point at which we were able to break loose from all the usual excuses and conventions that keep people bound to a lifestyle that does not totally fulfill. The drive within, the urgent desire to fulfill a lifelong dream——the challenge of attempting the impossible—— had to be strong enough in both of us to overshadow any combination of problems, frustrations, pressures and aches or pains that might develop, including the most difficult problem of all, which was how to get along with another human being when so closely bound together for such a long time.

The canoe was to be our home for six months if all went according to our plan, as we paddled and portaged the long way, northwest, across the North American continent——just two men alone in a twenty-one foot homemade canoe, against very improbable odds. We would follow the old historic fur trade canoe route out of Montreal to its extreme end at Fort Yukon, then on beyond that another 1180 miles across Alaska to the Bering Sea. Hopefully this would be an all-time record breaking, long distance voyage, never before accomplished in less than one year. It would be a "once in a lifetime" experience, a realization of dreams and ambitions since boyhood, with the added excitement and challenge of attempting the impossible.

We tried to anticipate and prepare for every problem that might come up. One of the major questions in which we could get no answer was, "Is it physically possible to make this trip?" There would be long hours sitting in a canoe seat, possibly for more than thirty-six hours at a time. Would our backs hold up? How about blisters and sore bottoms or circulation in the legs? Could we stand the cold, wet and fatigue, not to mention sickness or accidents? Would our bodies wear down under the hardships, or would they toughen up to meet the demands made of them? From all that we could learn from books and personal experiences of others, we were led to believe that we would simply wear out under the pace. The experts said that we were attempting the impossible. No one had ever done it before or even come close. Even the journeys of the fur traders were not more than one-half of this distance. At first, I tended to believe them and had accordingly planned shorter versions of the trip. But as planning and personal experience developed, I was spurred on by the challenge of the impossible. I slowly began to believe that "if the good Lord was willing," we just might be able to pull it off. It was for sure that an awful lot of things had to go just right.

I eventually competed in just about every major canoe race there was on the North American continent, not winning very many but gaining a lot of satisfaction and invaluable experience. Canoe racing never was my first love--I have always thought of myself as a wilderness canoeist, a voyageur, a traveler. I was born two hundred years too late! How I would love to have searched for that mysterious northwest passage that lured so many early explorers across the far reaches of this great continent.

We had a lot going for us in our experience and training as long-distance professional canoe racers. Undoubtedly, this helped us overcome psychological and physical barriers that prevented others from believing that it could be done. I can remember when twenty miles was a long ways in a canoe. A one-hundred mile canoe trip was outstanding and still is to most. Not many people who get in a canoe ever make a one-hundred mile trip in a lifetime. Five hundred miles puts you in a very special class of traveling canoeists. A one-thousand mile journey would make you eligible for

Introduction

the very exclusive One Thousand Mile Canoe Club.

This statement may be hard for some to believe, but I want to emphasize that we did not plan it as a stunt, nor would we be out to break any records. We would be trying to fulfill dreams and ambitions of a lifetime -- doing our own thing, at our own pace, in a way that was most satisfying to us personally. We did not feel we were pushing ourselves excessively.

We happened to be strongly motivated by challenges. The force of a challenge was usually stronger than the desire for comfort, thereby dictating our actions. Sometimes there would be a conflict between a desire to linger at a particularly enjoyable spot, and the drive within to move on. We did what we most wanted to do. I don't recall that there ever were any conflicts between us about it. Apparently, Clint and I were marching to the same tune.

I have frequently heard people say that they would rather go slower and enjoy it more. Then I think that's the way they should do it. I'd go slower too if I enjoyed it more! I don't agree with the logic that you get more out of nature, or learn more or see more or enjoy more by going slowly and leisurely. Neither do I intend to put down those who prefer to go more slowly. I may have missed a lot, as some say, by going too fast through the country but I more than made up for it by seeing and enjoying more of the country in a day's time. What I may miss here, I gain there.

Early in the planning stages the idea developed that a book should be written. Consequently, I started an information file with that in mind. On the trip, Clint and I both kept a complete day-by-day journal. I, for one, did not want to trust my memory when it came to facts and details.

Perhaps of even greater value in keeping the record straight and in the many satisfying hours spent in reliving the adventures, has been in the more than three thousand 35 millimeter color slides that I took during the trip with the main idea of recording the journey. If a picture is worth a thousand words, then we are off to a good start! These pictures along with the journal have been of inestimable value in sharing with you the true, exact and unembellished account of **Cross Continent Canoe Safari.**

In all of our extensive research we found that if we could pull it off this would be a world record of the most miles by canoe ever paddled in less than six months' time. Never had this entire route been covered in one season. Never before had anyone paddled this many miles in less than one year. So we had goals and purposes which would more than compensate for the inconveniences. The satisfaction of attempting to accomplish an impossible dream was far more meaningful to us than any pleasures we missed. A far more important factor is enjoying what you are doing and the sum total of your awareness and appreciation of all that is around you.

This, then, is the unusual story of two men alone who would attempt to paddle and portage the long way across the North American continent, during the summer of 1971.

TWO YEARS
OF PLANNING

The strong life that never knows harness;
The wilds where the caribou call;
The freshness, the freedom, the farness —
O God! How I'm stuck on it all.

— *Robert Service,*
The Spell of the Yukon

In the two years of serious planning and research prior to take-off, I eventually read a stack of books taller than my canoe paddle. I tried to obtain every journal and diary about the voyageurs, fur traders and early explorers that was available, including some microfilm copies. History and geography have always been two of my favorite subjects, and this made research an exciting part of the whole thing.

Our research revealed that in the year of 1610 Henry Hudson discovered Hudson Bay. In 1611, Samuel DeChamplain, exploring up the St. Lawrence River, came to a large unnavigable rapids and sent his men on shore to build a small fort. That fort today is called Montreal. From there the North West Company and many other aggressive independents eventually began operations. Also in the year 1611 the King James Version of the Bible was published, with even greater historic consequences.

Then in 1670, the Hudson's Bay Company was formed in London. In the early days they were officially known as "The Governor and Company of Adventurers of England Trading into Hudson's Bay." More recently, they were often referred to as "The Company" or the "H.B.C." At the present time they are usually referred to as "The Bay." In 1682, the Hudson's Bay Company established York Factory in Hudson Bay at the mouth of the Hayes River. Ten years earlier, in 1672, they had established posts at the mouths of the Moose and Albany Rivers in James Bay, as well as a warehouse on Charlton Island.

"The Company" adopted a policy of letting the furs come to them at these posts. Then in 1717 a fourth post was built at the mouth of the Churchill River to serve the Indians and Eskimos to the north and west. By the late 1700's, competition from the North West Company forced them to start establishing forts out across the land. In 1821, the Hudson's Bay Company and the North West Company merged into what was to become the present H.B.C.

It was many years before the fur trade highway became very heavily traveled. In 1768 the fort at Grand Portage was built, though a lot of traffic had been coming through there before that. It was 1787 before Peter Pond, the first explorer over Methy Portage, built a fort at what is now Fort McMurray. The volume of the fur trade seems to have reached its peak in the late 1700's.

The peak of exploring interests and activities was sustained a little longer. In 1846, James Bell was the first over McDougall Pass. A year later, Alexander Murray followed through and founded Fort Yukon, at that time in Russian territory. In 1867 the United States purchased Alaska from Russia and took over Fort Yukon. By then the fur trade traffic was dying down and when the railroad opened to the west in the 1800's, the super highway of the voyageur faded into history. In searching through the records we found that the longest distance that the voyageurs traveled in one season was about thirty-five hundred miles. Eric Morse of Ottawa, probably the outstanding fur trade historian and author of our day, in his book **Fur Trade Canoe Routes of Canada, Then and Now,** puts it all together the best of anything I have read. Over a period of many years he has personally canoed most of our entire route and consequently passes on up-to-date information not found in other writings.

In our journey we planned to paddle through a lot of history and geography. We were on the main line of the Super Highway of the fur trade out of Montreal. Today, Trans-Canada Highway 17 closely parallels this route for nearly twelve hundred miles, to the far side of Lake Superior. Just out of North Bay these two highways cross but continue westward, side by side.

More extensive research revealed that only once before had our proposed route been covered by two men in a canoe. That was back in the years of 1936 and 1937 when Sheldon Taylor and Geoffrey Pope covered the entire route and even a little more. The New York Times newspaper account of their fantastic adventure dated Sunday, April 26, 1936, reads as follows:

TWO ADVENTURERS IN 17-FOOT CANOE
START 6,000 MILE VOYAGE TO NOME

Young Men, Both 24 and Tired of Book-keeping, Push up Hudson on 18-Month Journey Through Inland Waters, Pledged to Self-Imposed "Ten Commandments" to Guide Conduct.

ONE INCREDIBLE JOURNEY

Paddles digging deep, two young adventurers pushed off in a seventeen foot canoe from the foot of West Forty-Second Street yesterday morning bound for Nome, Alaska, by way of inland waters.

Bareheaded and with happy smiles upon their faces, the young men, Geoffrey Pope and Sheldon Taylor, both 24, waved good-bye to a group of friends and with an American flag flapping bravely at the stern of their small craft, set out on a venture they had planned for four months.

They have been employed as bookkeepers by MacFadden Publications for three years, but, tiring of "just reading" about the adventures of others, they resigned from their jobs Tuesday after saving nearly $1,000 to make the trip.

Pope, who lives at 19 Bethune Street, is a native of Montreal. Taylor, formerly of San Francisco, lives with his sister, Mrs. Muriel Euchner, at 309 West Fifty-Seventh Street. Both are expert canoeists.

The canoe, named Muriel, after Taylor's sister, boasts a small sail and rudder. It was loaded with provisions, hunting knives, cameras, tarpaulins and a five-pound balloon-silk tent in which the youths will camp along the way.

Confident of an average of twenty-five miles a day——under sail if possible and by paddle when the wind is light——the adventurers plan to reach their destination, 6,000 miles away, in eighteen months, including a seven-month layover at Fort Chipewyan on Lake Athabaska, Alberta, Canada.

Their route, as they eagerly traced it out on a map while waiting for the tide to turn up-river at 10:20 yesterday, follows the Hudson River and Lake Champlain to Montreal.

Two Years of Planning

From Montreal, it runs down the St. Lawrence River to Ottawa, where the youths will purchase firearms and ammunition for their hunting along the banks of rivers and lakes which will lead them to The Pas, Manitoba, and thence to Fort Chipewyan.

"Holing in" at the fort until the spring of 1937, the youths expect to hunt and fish and write about their experiences. With the thaws, they will leave on the last lap of their journey, which is up the Great Slave and MacKenzie Rivers to Fort McPherson; thence across the Great Divide to Fort Yukon and down the Yukon River to Nome. The route is almost entirely by water, and only a few portages will have to be made, the longest fourteen miles. They will return to New York by steamer and train.

Friends have warned the young men that the worst danger about the trip will be "getting on each other's nerves." Pope and Taylor have known each other but seven months, and to offset any arguments that might spring up during the long weeks when they may not see another human, they have drawn up a set of their own "Ten Commandments." They are:

> We shall decide minor disagreements by flipping a coin.

> We shall not try to settle minor points while fatigued, but shall wait until after meals and rest.

> We shall be tolerant of each other's viewpoint in all matters.

> We shall not permit annoyances to smolder, but shall face our difficulties intelligently.

5

> *The day's work shall be evenly divided.*

> *It shall be "we" in all things and never "I."*

> *We resolve not to settle any differences with our fists.*

> *We will not "kid" each other excessively on any one point, as it eventually leads to hard feeling.*

> *We will abide by the law of cleanliness.*

> *We promise faithfully to abide by the first nine commandments.*

At 10:20 the tide turned, and the youths were off amid a burst of cheers and several cries such as "Give my regards to the Eskimos." "See you in two years," they called, hoisting the sail and leaning hard on their paddles to keep the tiny craft upright in the choppy Hudson.

A later account from the same newspaper dated Saturday, July 31, 1937, reads:

NEW YORK CANOEISTS NEAR NOME, GOAL OF LONG TRIP

Bethel, Alaska, July 29. Natives brought word here today that the two New York City youths who set out last year in a canoe for Nome, Alaska, had passed a village on the Yukon River a week ago and were two weeks ahead of schedule.

The adventurers, Sheldon Taylor, 24, and Geoffrey Pope, 23, left New York City April

25, 1936, but a short distance up the Hudson
River off Tarrytown, NY, the 17 foot canoe
overturned.

Undaunted, they set out again, went up
the Hudson to Montreal, thence to Pigeon
River, via the Great Lakes, then by lake and
river to Pas, Manitoba.

They spent the winter at Lake Athabaska,
in northern Alberta.

The Pope-Taylor Journey was one that contributed to our inspiration. We tried to find out more
about it, and were surprised that for such an outstanding journey we could find out so little. If it
was ever written up, we have not been able to find
it. The newspaper account gives the mileage as six
thousand miles. The **1976 Guinness Book of World
Records** gives it as 7,165 miles. Apparently, they
had the same problem we did in computing total
mileage, that obtaining actual mileage figures is
rather difficult, and that when found, it adds up
to more than expected. If they took the same route
we did, which from all information I have been able
to obtain they did, plus their extra miles at the
beginning and the end, then I am sure that in a
more exact computation their total journey would
exceed 7,400 miles.

We needed a name for our trip. We settled on
the "Cross Continent Canoe Safari." We thought the
word "safari" sounded more official. We wanted the
name on our canoe in big letters as well as the
starting and ending destinations, for psychological
reasons. This would also help to explain to people
what we were doing. The theory is that it gave the
canoe the protection of an official status. We
were never to have any problem leaving it unatten-
ded while it was tied up at many strange docks.

A young friend of mine, Steven Landick of
Lansing, Michigan, once started out alone on a five
thousand mile kayak trip from west to east across

the continent with no name on his kayak and had it stolen off a portage. That ended his trip after having come about one thousand miles. I don't think it would have been stolen if it had been heavily labelled.

Our particular route was chosen for a number of reasons besides its wide historic fur trade appeal. Mainly, we chose it because it had unlimited possibilities and was headed in the direction of strongest attraction. The north country is a "siren," who can resist her song? The exciting variety of waterways and the many outstanding challenges guaranteed our continued interest. Another thing that appealed to us was that the nature of the journey would change completely at different stages of the route. It seemed that it would be a combination of many outstanding trips rolled into one great spectacular journey.

Our route was to take us through every imaginable type of terrain and water. The North American continent is blessed with a most unusual and fantastic system of waterways. One half of the world's fresh water surface is to be found in Canada. The river systems and the lakes are closely enough connected that with a little portaging it is possible to travel from almost any city in Canada to the Atlantic or the Pacific or the Arctic Ocean, or even to the Gulf of Mexico.

We wrote letters to everyone who might be of help, to get information and to ask advice. I made a questionnaire form and sent it to two dozen remote villages asking about supplies, the people, the industry, culture, roads, airports, telephone, etc. I also wrote to the Hudson's Bay Company asking for a list of their stores along the route, and then arranged for a letter of credit so we wouldn't have to carry much cash.

In those two years of planning a lot of time was spent poring over maps, laying out the route, figuring out our problems and trying to learn all that the maps could tell us. I kept getting maps and more maps until I had to use the scissors and cut them down to size because the weight was getting to be a problem. It was very important that we have the best maps available. Most were the 1:250,000 series of topographical maps. Taken from aerial photographs, they are highly accurate and give much detailed information.

Mileage was sometimes difficult to compute, especially on crooked rivers. Some rivers are so crooked that it can't all be shown on the maps. We would use whatever source of official information was available, then very carefully measure the rest. Accurate mileage is essential to accurate navigation. After much study and computations, I put together a Time and Distance Schedule that listed about forty major check points, giving the mileage and anticipated travel time between points and the date of arrival, taking into consideration all problems and circumstances involved. It went through many changes and corrections but after all the information was in it turned out to be most helpful in measuring our progress and was amazingly accurate on estimated dates.

We planned our schedule on the basis of a six-day week figuring that a day of rest was essential to the physical man and a time of worship was essential to the spiritual man. We planned to regularly take time to read the Bible and pray and to gratefully worship the Lord. Neither of us had any hardline religious convictions that this day had to be Sunday. So being practical, we let it work out to our times off on windbound days or in towns.

I could never consider a venture of this nature taking a partner who was not a Bible-believing Christian. Some might say that is being biased, to which I would agree. But it is also good thinking. We needed something bigger and better than ourselves to moderate our imperfect dispositions. We needed a power and authority in common, outside ourselves, that we mutually trusted. If successful, our journey would be a tribute to that theory, not to us.

Other people had asked to go along with us on our journey by kayak or by another two-man canoe. We refused to consider more than just the two of us. Previous experience had taught us that numbers slow you down and also increase the odds of sickness, accident, mistakes, etc.

We promised ourselves and our families not to take chances on wild seas or irresistible rapids. With a thousand dollars' worth of cameras, film and equipment, a poor man can't afford that kind of excitement. The name of our game was "get to the Bering Sea." There was no provision in our plans for an upset.

Geographically, our route would skirt the edge of the Canadian Precambrian Rock Shield. Most of the time we were in it, until past the Churchill River. The Precambrian Shield involves much of Canada and seems to center around Hudson Bay. That is the part of the continent where the gigantic ice age ground down and scoured clean every living thing, leaving very little soil and a very rugged rock country behind.

We were to go over a "height of land" into a different watershed many times. Some of the minor ones are only from one river system to another. But there were to be three major "heights of land" that would give us an uphill and downhill effect in elevation. Starting at Lachine the water would be flowing into the Atlantic Ocean. On the BWCA route we would cross the height of land into water that drained into Hudson Bay. At Methy Portage would be the "height of land" that flowed into the Arctic Ocean. At Summit Lake the route would take us over our last "height of land" into the Yukon watershed that flows to the Bering Sea.

In the last half of our route we would be in

Verlen Kruger with his P-51 in Japan in 1947

the land of permafrost and smaller timber. Perma
frost covers almost one-half of Canada. Intermittent permafrost extends as far south as the
southern end of James Bay and the northern end of
Lake Winnipeg. Permafrost is simply permanently
frozen ground. It is found to coincide roughly
with an annual mean air temperature of thirty

degrees Fahrenheit. Those doing construction in permafrost country have learned that the way to handle it is not to disturb it but rather to insulate the construction so that no warmth might melt the frozen ground. The permafrost is one of the major causes of the smaller timber and treeless country of the far North, depending largely on the depth that the ground thaws in the summer.

We wondered about getting above the tree line and having a problem with finding adequate firewood. We need not have worried. Although we were to get above the normal tree line we were to find that wherever the big rivers flow, the trees grow, even into treeless territory. Sometimes it was no more than a fringe of brush along the banks, but there was always something. Even without trees, firewood would have been no problem because there was plenty of driftwood. Even in areas where the natives use it, there is a surprising surplus. We never had to cut down a tree, not even a dead one.

Most important of all was the canoe. Neither Clint nor I thought there was anything on the market which was properly designed for our trip. After many long hours of loving labor, I designed and built a woodstrip Sitka spruce canoe, fiberglassed inside and outside with heavy reinforcement at points of wear. It was built along the lines of a marathon racing canoe. Later I used the same forms and made one that I used in several races. It paddled easily, yet was stable and carried our load with ease. It handled the rough water of the big lakes the best of any canoe I had ever been in. The first one was twenty-two feet long and tested out just great. But it wasn't perfect and I thought I could improve on it. So using the same forms I made another, this time twenty-one feet long by thirty-four inches wide and it weighed one hundred ten pounds. This one I was happy with and was even more pleased with it as the trip progressed, for it proved to be just what we wanted.

The paddles were another problem, as we wanted lightweight yet indestructible ones. I had been to an American Canoe Association Olympic training clinic and saw experimental paddles that gave me ideas. Using a piece from discarded fiberglass polevault shaft and many layers of fiberglass and bright red epoxy, I made Clint and myself some paddles that will last a lifetime yet are lightweight. They were fifty-four inches long by eight inches wide and weighed twenty-five ounces. It was another piece of equipment that turned out just right. Those paddles were to come through the trip looking like they had been used for about a week.

The canoe, with the paddles and gear that was to be carried with it, weighed one hundred forty-four pounds. In addition to this, I would carry my personal bag which varied from twenty-five to thirty pounds. It was my canoe and I trained portaging it, so I would have the dubious honor of carrying it. It isn't the weight that gets to you first, it's the pain. I can personally testify that there are very few things in life more enjoyable than setting the canoe down after carrying a load like that for an hour or more. Train as I might, I found no way to carry that canoe without hurting. I came to the conclusion that the human body is not designed to carry that kind of weight on its shoulders. I succeeded in being able to handle the weight and in being able to endure the pain, but not in being able to eliminate the pain from my mind.

Clint had trained and conditioned himself for the journey by carrying about two hundred pounds of children from his neighborhood in Mora, Minnesota, slung across his shoulders and back.

Our plan was to single haul all the long portages, a total of eighty-three miles. That is, carrying everything in one trip which gave us a minimum load of one hundred seventy pounds apiece and sometimes more. We would double haul (make two trips each) on most of the short portages, making use of the opportunity to stretch our legs and look around. As it turned out a strange thing happened. When we were portaging we looked forward to getting back in the water and when we were in the water we looked forward to portaging -- but not those long ones. It hurt worse carrying it all in one haul but we got over it sooner. Clint would carry the two big bags, one in a tump line and the other stacked on top.

Every piece of equipment from the smallest to the largest would have to be the best we could get. Everything was weighed right down to the ounce and everything was agonizingly evaluated. We couldn't forget that we were going to carry it on our backs for at least one hundred and fifty-three miles. If it wasn't just what we wanted and it wasn't available on the market, then we made our own. Nearly every manufactured item that I had was modified, redesigned or improved upon to meet our particular needs. At that time I couldn't find a tent on the market that I thought was just right, so I made one. I couldn't find a sleeping pad just like I wanted, so I made one. I wasn't totally satisfied with the sheath to my belt knife, so I redesigned it to make it safer and handier.

On a journey such as this the right canoe clothes are a critical matter. The variety of weather and conditions combined with rain and splashing water make it important. We used mostly wool or wool-type synthetics. I have tried down many times, but have never been satisfied. Down and the dampness of canoeing don't seem to mix. The multiple layer system (many layers of light-weight clothing) seems to work best. It gives you the desired flexibility so necessary for changing conditions and exertion levels.

Our strategy of action was to be flexible to weather and conditions. On good days we would put

Verlen and Clinton Waddell in spring of 1971
Photo by Jenny Kruger

in extra long hours to offset bad days. We figured that there were twenty-four hours in a day and we would use them all if need be.

About a month before "D Day," through a mutual friend, Bob McKee of Grand Rapids, Michigan, I was contacted by Phil Pemberton, an independent movie producer also out of Grand Rapids. Phil had heard about our proposed adventure and was excited about making a sixteen millimeter movie of it. Phil is a unique person with a rare combination of imagination and enthusiasm that made him a great photographer for this kind of venture. He was willing to take six months to do nothing else but chase us around to cover the entire journey from beginning to end. After due negotiation, we arrived at an agreement. This didn't change our trip strategy in any way. Bob McKee was to be his able assistant. His experience would be another interesting story as he expected to pursue us all the way across the North American continent, sometimes by motor boat, motor canoe, powered raft, plane, train, bus, car and by hitchhiking. He even made a couple of valiant attempts to canoe along with us overnight. He sometimes lost us for a week or two at a time, but sooner or later he eventually would show up along the route at some odd or remote spot with cameras grinding away.

Dozens of people were asking that we write to tell them how it was going. There was no way I could write that many letters but I did want to share the experience so I came up with a newsletter idea which was a great success. I would write just one letter about every two weeks and send it to a newsletter editor and he would publish and mail it. Darwin Gilbert of Lansing, Michigan, and his daughter, Truda, agreed to take the job, and for a $5.00 subscription fee they sent the letter out to nearly three hundred interested people in thirty-four states and three provinces. Darwin and Truda did an excellent job using many pictures, news clippings and other material, along with the letter I would send them. Sometimes Clint or Phil Pemberton also added their comments.

It was a strong matter of principle to us that we would go all the way under our own power and at no time would we use a motor, sail, guides or a follow-up crew. Neither would we accept help of any kind in paddling, portaging, towing or trucking on land or water. Being true to the elemental spirit of canoeing seemed to give us a more satisfying sense of earned enjoyment.

We were ultra-psyched up about this venture. We had been building up to a psychological and physical peak until it seemed that we were on a continued high that would reduce mountainous problems to molehills. As our "D Day" approached, it was almost as though our adrenalin flowed continuously, the clock around, day after day.

2

ONE LENGTHY PORTAGE

Saturday, 17 April

DAY 1

April 17, 1971, was a bright and sunny day in the Montreal suburb of Lachine, Quebec. At noon on that day, Clinton Waddell of Minneapolis, Minnesota, and I slid our shiny new canoe into the ice-choked waters of the St. Lawrence River.

The river was open except along the shore where crushed ice and ice floes jammed into each little bay. The breeze was light and feelings ran high that cloudless morning as we loaded the food and camping gear off the Coast Guard docks and talked with newspaper and TV people who had gathered to see us off.

"Yes," I said to the media who had been asking questions. "Our 'D Day' has finally arrived. If the good Lord is willing and all goes well, we intend to follow the old historic fur trade route and paddle this canoe all the way to the mouth of the Yukon River this summer. We hope to complete 6,716 miles to the Bering Sea before freeze-up next fall."

"We had planned to leave here on April 10, which is later than the normal ice break-up date," said Clint. "Last year the ice went out on April 2, but this is the latest break-up date in the past ninety-four years, so they tell us."

A newspaper reporter standing nearby said, "There's still a bloody lot of ice around here and also up the Ottawa River. Why don't you chaps hold up another week or two until these rivers open up?"

"Our tight time schedule just does not allow us the luxury to wait even one more day," I replied. "There are more than 6,700 miles between here and the Bering Sea. We're going to have to race the elements, and time is of the essence! We'll have to really hustle all the way to even stand a chance of completing this journey before the Yukon River freezes over next fall."

Several false starts, as well as various poses, were then made for the benefit of the media and movie producer Phil Pemberton. There were more short interviews and much shaking of hands in "farewells" and "best wishes." I turned back a couple of times to hug and kiss my wife, Jenny, and to tell her goodbye, before I finally stepped into the canoe where Clint had been patiently waiting.

Consequently, it was a little after one o'clock when we finally headed west, paddling up the St. Lawrence towards Dorval Island. It was with a deep sense of anticipation that we took those first of several million paddle strokes, heading off into our seemingly impossible dream.

Phil Pemberton followed along in his fifteen

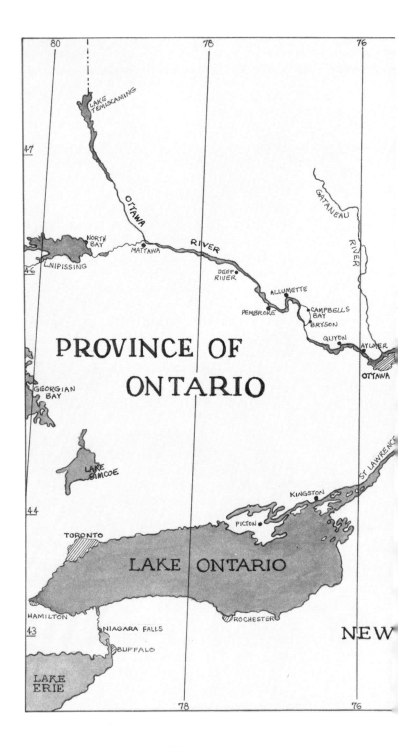

PROVINCE OF ONTARIO

LAKE ONTARIO

LAKE ERIE

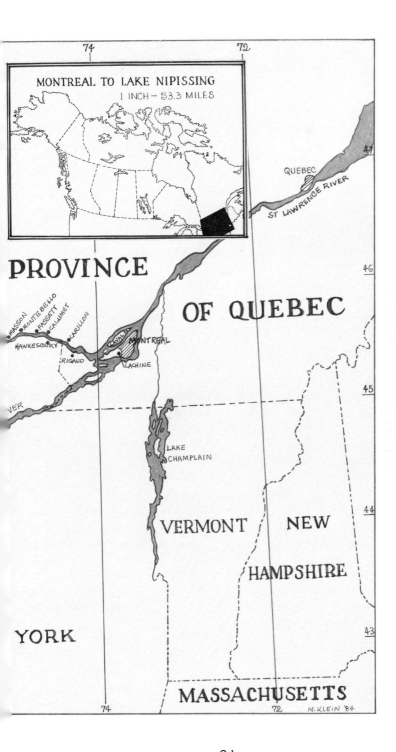

MONTREAL TO LAKE NIPISSING
1 INCH = 53.3 MILES

QUEBEC

ST LAWRENCE RIVER

PROVINCE

MASSON
MONTEBELLO
FASSETT
CALUMET
CARILLON
HAWKESBURY
RIGAUD
LAVALIA
MONTREAL
LACHINE

OF QUEBEC

VER

LAKE
CHAMPLAIN

VERMONT   NEW

HAMPSHIRE

YORK

MASSACHUSETTS   M. KLEIN '84

21

foot Old Town canoe, powered with a small motor. He had contracted to film and produce a movie of the journey and he wanted good coverage of the start of the trip. My youngest son, Philip Kruger, held down the bow as the producer's assistant that afternoon. The motor on the Old Town was not running too well at the start, but even when they finally did get it operating properly and running at full speed they could barely keep up with us. Clint shouted to Phil, "I'd sure hate to have to rely on your motor to get us to the Bering Sea. I don't think we would make it in five years if we had to rely on your outfit."

Less than two miles beyond Dorval Island we came up against solid ice. It looked as though Lac St. Louis was frozen over from shore to shore and that ice was nearly three feet thick. The two Phils were standing on the ice with camera rolling as we came paddling up. Then we attempted to walk on the ice and tow the canoe, but that proved futile as there was more than six inches of soft slush on top of the ice. It was impossible to slide the outfit along as we had hoped.

Putting back into the water again, we headed for the nearest shore that could be paddled to. In a few minutes we were unloading our gear on Brown Point, which is about two miles northwest of Dorval Island. Such was our determination that we must have seemed almost eager as we shouldered our loads and headed off on what was to turn out to be one lengthy portage.

It was going on four that afternoon when we shouldered our loads and started down the sidewalks and streets of Lakeshore Drive. The streets were crooked and winding as we closely followed the north shoreline of Lac St. Louis. We carried the whole load in one haul, as we had planned and trained to do. I carried the one hundred ten pound homemade canoe with the bulky gear inside and my personal bag while Clint carried the two big packs,

Portage along Lakeshore Drive

also as we had planned. Each of us struggled along under a total of one hundred seventy pounds on our tump lines and shoulders.

Very soon we were to learn that portaging on hard concrete is not any fun. We pushed along for the next four hours and progressed nearly seven more miles before we stopped for the night.

Jenny and our children followed along that afternoon with the camper and were waiting at Victoria Street. "There's a nice hotel only a few blocks from here," she called, as we approached. "Why don't you stop for the night?"

"That sounds like a winner!" I responded. Finding a suitable tree branch, I slid the bow of the canoe up and over it. Easing the stern to the sidewalk and slipping out of my backpack, I couldn't help but say, "What a relief! That load seemed heavier today than I ever thought it could be!"

Clint, who had been trailing a few yards behind, agreed that he too was ready to call it a day. We soon checked into the hotel, and shortly thereafter we were soaking those sore and blistered feet, sore shoulders and aching bodies in tubs of hot water.

While eating supper, we decided that Clint's feet came through the first day much better than mine. Clint had been wearing hiking shoes, but I had started out wearing lightweight L. L. Bean rubber-bottomed shoe packs. "At the pace we were pushing, my feet were soon overheated," I remarked. "I now have a real set of blisters and some of those blisters are worn out and bleeding. Late this afternoon I borrowed Phillip's work shoes. They worked better than the Beans, but they gave me a new set of blisters. I'll have to try to get some better hiking shoes as soon as possible."

"How many more miles of this ice do you think we are going to have?" asked Clint.

All was silence for several seconds. Then Jenny chipped in, "We drove west as far as the bridge to Perrot Island this afternoon. There's some open water at the rapids below the bridge but the only thing we could see to the north of the island was more solid ice."

"That's not very encouraging! How much more time are we going to lose because of the ice?" No one had an answer to that question.

In driving to Montreal from our home in De-Witt, Michigan, about a week earlier, we had purposely driven along the Ottawa River to check on the ice conditions above the St. Lawrence. We found that we were in for trouble. None of the lakes and only a few of the fast water spots were open.

Clint and I had faced a tough and agonizing

decision as to whether or not to head off into a torturous overland journey that could best be described as sadistic, self-inflicted torture, or to wait for the break-up. Following much discussion, we decided that we could wait until April 17 but not a day longer, if we expected to have any possible chance of achieving our goal that year.

Many days later Clint reflected, "For some strange reason it never occurred to us that the simple solution would have been to have started the journey above the worst of the ice." I guess we were just too bullheaded and psyched up.

Just below the starting point at the Coast Guard docks that morning was the famous Lachine Rapids of the St. Lawrence. In the days of the fur traders, the lower end of Lachine was as far west as the big ocean-going trading ships could make it. This was where these vessels transferred their trade goods to the large "Montreal" freight canoes before they picked up a load of valuable furs and headed back to Europe.

The "Montreal" canoes then headed west up the Ottawa River, through Nipissing, down into upper Lake Huron, up the St. Marys River and across Lake Superior as far as Grand Portage, Minnesota. At Grand Portage they rendezvoused with the smaller "North" canoes which came down from the "bush" country loaded with furs. The "North" canoes came in out of the fur country from just about every direction, some from as far away as Fort Chipewyan on Lake Athabasca. After making their trades, each would go back to their home forts, the round trip usually taking the whole season. The trade goods at Fort Chipewyan would then get relayed on the following season to the very farthest trading outpost, the most distant of these being Fort Yukon in Russian territory, at the junction of the Yukon and Porcupine Rivers.

In those days transportation was slow. If a fifteen-year-old boy from Fort Yukon ordered a pocket knife from England, he would be a man before he got it! The beaver skin going out and the knife coming back would take five years--if everything went smoothly.

It was the fur trade that slowly unrolled the map of the North American continent. Before the pioneer or the early settlers spread out across the continent, the fur traders had already been there. Before Daniel Boone crossed the Mississippi, the fur traders had already been as far as the Pacific Ocean, and before Meriwether Lewis and William Clark made their epic journey across the continent, the fur traders had been there. They were a special breed of men. The early "Voyageur" was a colorful and notorious character. He was as vital to his time and place in history as was the American cowboy to the West. In the canoe trade, "Voyageur" was a word that soon came to have a special meaning. In ordinary French it simply means "traveler," but in canoe country it meant a canoeman in the fur trade. The average voyageur was a small, sturdy man that could go on and on tirelessly, on cheap fuel and primitive accommodations. Most of the paddlers were Frenchmen whereas most of the Bourguois, or bosses, as well as the explorers, were Scottish or English, of equally hardy and adventurous spirit. In those days the canoe was king. The birch bark canoe adopted from the Indians had its day of glory. It played a most significant part in the blossoming of the continent. It filled a need in a land that nothing else could meet. Before the railroad, before the airplane and before our network of roadways, there was no other practical method of transportation. Not even a horse could get through this country. There are still vast sections of this same land where the canoe is the only practical vehicle. In some of this same country there are even less traffic and less people living now than there were two or three hundred years ago.

Sunday, 18 April

DAY 2

The morning dawned bright and clear. It would have been a great day to be canoeing but no such prospect was in sight. All we could see was ice, stretching along our route to the far horizon.

It was eight o'clock by the time we finished breakfast. We began portaging from the same spot that we left off the night before, along the narrow, winding streets. It was nine miles to the bridge and rapids at Saint Anne. In much sweat and strain we arrived there at twelve thirty. There was a half mile of open water near the rapids at the bridge. Eagerly we put our canoe in the water and paddled up to the bridge, lined the rapids underneath and paddled across to Perrot Island, following tight up to the solid ice above the bridge.

It was tricky and about as thrilling as Russian roulette as we worked our way through thick masses of floating ice and huge ice cubes moving and grinding all around us. Phil thought this was great, laughing in glee as he shot some movie footage!

Jenny and the kids were waiting for us with lunch on the far side of the bridge. We ate with them and then said our final goodbyes as she headed the camper back to Michigan. It was time to get our children back to school.

We continued our portage, going along the edge of Highway Seventeen across Perrot Island, and on across the bridge that spans the west channel of the Ottawa River and on into Dorion. Here we packed northerly on a black top road, heading up toward the Ottawa River. Three miles out of Dorion and just west of Vaudreuil-Sur-Le-Lac we gladly set our loads down for the day. What a relief that was! It had been a long, tough day with sixteen miles of portaging and only about one mile of paddling. Apparently we were pushing at much too fast a pace which was causing severe wear and tear on our bodies. At our steady pace the body did not have time to repair itself. The aches and pains were becoming greatly magnified. My feet continued to get worse. They were requiring constant attention in much changing of socks and replacement of bandages. During the day I alternated shoes between Philip's work shoes and my tennis shoes. The rest of my body was also beginning to protest. Before I set the canoe down that evening, I was hurting all over. Clint's major problem seemed to be his hands swelling from the pack straps cutting off his circulation, but he didn't complain.

Looking out across the Lake of the Two Mountains that evening, there was still nothing to be seen except miles and miles of solid ice. Our only consolation was that we were making good progress but at a great price. The questions that evening were how will we be able to endure another day of this, what more can I do to protect my feet and will we get above all of this ice and into open water tomorrow?

Monday, 19 April

DAY 3

A beautiful, sunny morning. After putting fresh bandages on my feet I flexed my sore muscles and said, "Why couldn't it storm so we wouldn't have to feel guilty to rest a day?"

"No such luck," Clint replied. "We have to get going again in spite of the pain. One good thing about it, with this sunshine the ice will certainly melt more today."

All this mileage on hard pavement was killing my improperly shod feet. I alternated between three different pairs of shoes. As I was portaging past a shoe store in one of those towns I put the bow of the canoe up on an overhanging sign and went in and bought an oversized, comfortable pair of shoes. But by now nothing was comfortable. Six toenails were turning black and several toes were bandaged. The hide was peeling off a large heat blister on the center bottom of both feet. The heels had blisters, overlapping blisters. Before the day was over, they were so swollen and bleeding, and covered with bandaids and moleskin, that the only thing that would fit were Clint's size eleven tennis shoes! They were two sizes over size. This made the fifth pair of shoes for this portage. The pain from my feet seemed to slowly creep up my legs, stiffening the muscles. There were moments when it was hard to remember that we were having fun. A couple times during the day I reminded Clint as I called out to him, "Hey, Clint, just think of all the fun we are having!" He didn't laugh. He was having a bad day too. This was the roughest, toughest day of portage in my life. We were pushing it too hard. It seems strange to me now, in retrospect, that we didn't slow down. We seem to have lost our perspective.

At a rest stop I remarked, "I'm finding it hard to believe that we are on a canoe trip! One thing I've learned, canoeing can be hard on the feet!"

"It's a good thing that we have trained hard in portaging as well as paddling," Clint replied.

Every day has its interesting moments. We met and talked to a lot of people at our rest stops. Some of the old timers told us fascinating stories of the area. At one farm house we had trouble breaking away, as the good people supplied us with several glasses of delicious, cold drinking water. We were still in Quebec, and besides being hospitable I think those French people enjoyed trying out their English on us. Occasionally we tried to talk to someone that we couldn't understand. Somewhere out in the country we were joined by a yellow collie dog. He followed us for hours and we became fast friends. When we stopped for a midafternoon hamburger in one of the way-side towns, we lost him. Not much attention was given that day in the way of tourist sights or scenery. Everything was seen through a red blur of pain, as we continued portaging seventeen agonizing miles northwestward. We portaged through nine or ten towns to a spot a couple miles northwest of Rigaud, Quebec. About sundown we simply slowly ground to a halt. I didn't feel I could in any way pick that canoe up one more time! Today's route paralleled Lake of Two Mountains and most of the time we could see it off in the distance, white with solid ice.

I tried always to make the rest stops so as to put the bow up on something such as a tree limb, fence post, street sign or anything but the ground. It became quite a strain picking that one hundred forty-four pound beast up, especially toward the end of the day. Early in the forenoons I would carry the canoe for fifteen to twenty minutes before stopping to rest for about five minutes, but toward evening I'd do well to carry it five minutes and rest fifteen to twenty minutes! My shoulders were getting rubbed raw and the bones felt permanently rearranged. My back muscles were stiffening in pain and tension. I felt like I was getting a permanent curve in my back. Toward the end of the day when I would lie down on the grass and try to relax during rest stops, it would take several minutes before my back muscles would relax enough to let my shoulders and butt touch the ground at the same time. My left shoulder was becoming exceptionally painful during the afternoon. Clint was concerned that I might be having a heart attack, but I told him not to worry.

It was with considerable joy that we set our load down that evening, especially so as we looked out over the ice of the Ottawa River and could see a small lead of open water in the center where the fast current entered the Lake of Two Mountains. We learned from a "local" that only a few miles up the road the river was open right up to shore and we'd be able to get back in the water. That certainly brightened our day!

We didn't see Phil or Bob all day. They had found something better to do back in Montreal, digging up information for background material for the movie.

3

A MOVING WALL
OF ICE

Tuesday, 20 April

DAY 4

It took a lot of determination to get out of the sack this morning. My body was stiff, sore and non-responsive from head to toe. I dressed my feet carefully in fresh bandages and moleskin and made them as comfortable as I could for the ordeal ahead.

Starting with another haul along the edge of the road, we soon crossed the provincial boundary, leaving Quebec and entering Ontario. In about three miles we found open water close enough to the shore to allow us to re-embark. Man, oh man! You'd have to do it to know the joy of putting that canoe down after the portage we had been through. We were as happy as a couple of kids with a new puppy dog. We had open water with lots of floating ice for six miles, up to the Carillon Dam. What a pleasure it was to be paddling. What should have been just a short portage around the dam turned out to be another five miles portaging down the road. Above the dam, the back water was jammed tight with a solid mass of broken ice. To get the canoe back into water even when we did required pushing and dragging it across two hundred yards of treacherous slush and broken ice, to where there was an open current out in the middle of the river. We cut some poles to push with, and with one foot in and one out, we scooted through slush up to one foot thick.

Clint got his feet wet, and they were turning blue with cold and pain as he hurriedly changed shoes and socks when we were back in paddling water. Then all day long we fought heavy ice jams and huge floes. It was so good to be back in the canoe that we didn't stop for lunch until we arrived at Hawksberry, Ontario, about mid-afternoon.

That night we kept going until about an hour after dark, when we stopped at the small town of Fassett on the Quebec side of the river. It had started to rain and there was so much ice along the shore that we fumbled around quite awhile in the dark before we found a place where we could put ashore.

Why hadn't we simply started our journey a few miles further upstream, around all that ice, and spared ourselves the first forty-four miles of self-inflicted torture? We didn't have a sensible answer to that. None of the reasons that we could think of made much sense. In the first four days out of Lachine we had averaged better than eight hours a day portaging. When we put the canoe back into open water, five miles above Carillon Dam, we had portaged forty-four miles and paddled eleven.

My shoulders felt as though they had been hammered with a two by four. My back was stiff with pain and my feet were killing me. I lost six toenails and several square inches of hide off my feet those first few days. But the human body is an amazing piece of machinery. Within hours after getting back into the canoe, it was all but forgotten in the joy of moving on.

Wednesday, 21 April

DAY 5

We woke up to hear a steady rain coming down. "This should be a good day for canoeing," Clint remarked as he pulled his rain gear over his head.

"Ottawa, here we come!" I replied. "Maybe the rain will let up before long and we can make up for lost time today." We were soon on the river and by mid-forenoon our camera crew appeared as we rounded a bend southwest of Montebello, Quebec.

"We've been looking for you since Monday," Bob McKee called out as we paddled up to them.

"We were beginning to think we had lost you," said Phil. "We'll try to keep better track of you two from now on." Phil shot some footage of us working our way up through a rapids, hugging the brush tight to the shore. We made arrangements to meet at noon on Thursday, at the first portage in Hull, Quebec, as they wanted to do some important movie shooting in the capitol city of Ottawa. It turned out to be a cold, wet day with much fog in the afternoon. Even with rain gear on, we slowly got wet that day from body sweat. As long as we kept moving it wasn't too bad, but whenever we stopped a chill would set in.

We paddled into Masson, Quebec, at about five thirty in the afternoon. It seemed like a good place to stop for the day. We had paddled thirty-three miles up a brisk current and besides, there was no need of arriving in Hull too far ahead of our appointment with the camera crew. So far, all our well-organized plans and schedules were not working out all that well. It seems that about the only thing that you can be **sure** about in canoeing is that you cannot be **sure** about anything! Still, our time and distance schedule was very important to us. We intended to stay as close to it as possible.

That evening, our conversations were to do with our bruised muscles and my sore and aching feet. We also talked about Alexander MacKenzie, the voyageurs and the fur trade. Our conversation started when Clint asked, "Verlen, how much do you suppose this river has changed in the one hundred and ninety some years since Alexander MacKenzie used to travel through here?"

"Quite a bit," I replied. "There were more rapids and fast water before Carillon and these other dams were built. Of course, this river was then the main highway. There were no roads or bridges or power lines crossing the Ottawa River then, and the only people living along these shores were the Iroquois and the Algonquins. Both of those tribes had a village that was located on a point of land along the shore of the Lake of Two Mountains. By MacKenzie's time, both the Iroquois and the Algonquins had a Roman Catholic missionary working with their own tribes. Those priests were even instructing the natives in writing and reading in their respective languages.

"Alexander MacKenzie arrived in Montreal from Scotland during the summer of 1779. He was only sixteen years old at that time. For the next five years he worked as a clerk in the countinghouse for the fur trading firm of Gregory and Macleod. Then in the spring of 1784 MacKenzie set out to seek his fortune at Detroit.

"It was apparent that Mr. Gregory had been

favorably impressed by the talents of his young clerk, because within the year he had recommended that Alexander be admitted as a partner in the firm on the condition that he proceed to the Indian country the following spring. The young man was overjoyed at the opportunity and proceeded almost immediately to Grand Portage, where he joined his associates early in the summer of 1785.

"Competition was keen between the several companies who were then in possession of the fur trade with the Indians. One of the firms' wintering partners was murdered and a clerk received a bullet through his powder horn while in the line of duty. Young MacKenzie's firm really had to struggle to survive until finally in July of 1787 at Grand Portage, the free traders working out of Montreal joined together and agreed to form an association which became known as The North West Company."

Thursday, 22 April

DAY 6

We were out early following a good night of sleep, and were both feeling quite ready to attack the river again. We were about twenty miles down river from Ottawa and Hull. It had turned much colder overnight. During the forenoon we were hit by strong, gusty winds and more rain, interspersed with occasional sleet and snow. It turned out to be one of those mean, miserable canoeing days. We hugged the lee shore closely as we paddled upstream into a strong headwind. This put us on the inside of two mile long Petrie Island, but about a mile down the channel it was frozen over solidly so we had to back track and go around. After that, we were more cautious about getting trapped in small dead current channels. As we approached Ottawa, we

Parliament Hill in Ottawa

could see the huge bridges and large buildings from
several miles downstream.

It was an impressive moment as we passed under
the two-mile bridge on the Ontario side of the
river and stopped paddling a moment under an overlook, with the Canadian Parliament buildings beautifully situated on a high hill above us. Our
windbreakers flapped in a cold wind, driving sleet
into our faces as we looked and thought, soaking up
a little more history. Our canoe was being rocked
by the rough water and an occasional ice floe
jostled us around. Here was the capitol of Canada.
It represented a great country with a lot of geography and history. What a vivid impression that
scene made on us! There were some important people
in those buildings, and they were comfortable and
warm.

ONE INCREDIBLE JOURNEY

Ahead of us, through the cities of Ottawa and Hull, were a strenuous seven or eight miles of rapids, fast water and one dam. These usually required five or six portages, which were all on the Hull, Quebec, side.

It was time to meet Phil at the first portage. He had arranged for TV and newspaper people to be there also. I don't think we found the best take out spot. We took out in a small bay, about one-half mile below the dam. It was partially filled with loose fill rocks, giving us a steep, mean place to unload. The portage started down a paper-mill road and through part of the town of Hull in heavy traffic, across a main highway and finally back in the water above the dam, a little over a mile all together.

It was a busy time of day. Cars and trucks were zipping all around us. It must have looked a little odd to some people seeing this strange canoe waiting at traffic lights. I was getting some funny stares and comments in French. It was probably best I didn't understand. In the heavy traffic and large buildings the gusty winds became alarmingly violent, whipping me and the canoe around as much as one hundred and eighty degrees before I could get it stopped. I became concerned about being blown into the path of a car or truck. I could just see the headlines, "CANOE HITS TRUCK IN HEAD ON COLLISION!"

We stayed close to the right shore as we worked our way through broken ice and several minor rapids. We were able to get far enough up the rapids to cut down the portage to only one quarter of a mile at Brebeuf Park.

We were in the hometown of Eric Morse, author of **Fur Trade Canoe Routes of Canada—Then and Now**, which I considered the best, most informative book on this subject ever written. We had hoped to meet and visit with him, but he was away on a lecture tour. After doing some filming and several news media interviews, Phil took us to dinner.

Local people warned us not to go back on the river that day, as the twenty mile long Lac Deschenes was breaking up and pushing a wall of ice down the river. Lac Deschenes is a widening of the Ottawa River, commencing just above Deschenes Rapids. To us that was good news. It meant the river was now probably open all the way. Looking up the river we could see no wall of ice, so we paddled on to meet it.

With a little hard work we paddled up through Remic Rapids. By hugging tight to shore, sometimes pushing off land with our paddles and even grabbing brush to pull us along against the swift current, and paddling furiously under the bridge, we made it without portaging. Usually we liked portages but had recently developed a portage phobia. Three miles of relatively easy paddling brought us to Deschenes Rapids and a mandatory portage of nearly one-half mile. As we were approaching the rapids we were treated to a rare, spine tingling sight as we saw the first wall of tumbling, crumbling ice raging through the rapids with an awesome roaring sound. It didn't take us long to realize that we were on a collision course. The booming noise of ice grinding over huge boulders added to the roar of the rapids was enough to send chills up and down our spines as we raced to get out of its path. We made it to the protection of the rocky island at the portage take out.

The spring breakup of ice had arrived at this rapids at the same moment that we did. We spent considerable time on the portage, watching in fascination. Above the rapids the wall of ice had pushed up on the shore to a height of as much as twenty feet. Further up the shore it had pushed right up to the doorsteps of some cottages. Phil had arrived on the scene earlier and saw the ice coming, and set up his camera in time to get some spectacular footage. In the excitement of the moment, some chunks of ice pushed so close that they hit his camera tripod, before he finally backed off.

By the time we had completed the portage and had a short visit with the camera crew over a pot of hot tea, the main ice front had passed. We were now able to cautiously put our canoe back in the water amidst heavy ice floes and proceed. As far as we could see up the lake, it was a moving mass of broken ice. There was barely room for a canoe. It required slow, tricky maneuvering for many miles before the ice slowly thinned out, as we threaded our way onward.

Toward evening it started to rain again and along with a cold, blustery headwind it induced us to quit a little early. Most of the land along this shore was privately owned and we couldn't find a place to pitch a tent, so at six in the evening we took out at Alymer, Quebec, where we found a hotel for the night.

Friday, 23 April

D A Y   7

It was still raining early in the morning, so we were slow to get moving. By the time we got the canoe back in the water, the rain had stopped. A strong northwest wind was blowing the length of the lake, whipping up white caps and large waves. From the dock it looked like the Ontario side of the lake, about two miles away, was a little calmer. When we angled across we went through some pretty big stuff, getting wet in the process. It was all to no avail. If anything, it was even worse over there. We angled back across to the Quebec side, which we'd started from, because the map showed a possible protection from the wind by a bend in the shoreline. When we came to the narrows in the lake, the wind was creating such a fuss with the waves that we pulled ashore in a wind-sheltered spot behind the point and enjoyed a couple hours of loafing. We finally paddled on, even though the wind hadn't let up. It was hard, wet going against a cold headwind. After twenty-four miles we quit early at Quyon, Quebec, hoping for a better day tomorrow.

Checking our maps that evening, we discovered that we were camped about six miles down river from Chats Falls Dam. "Verlen, you should have brought your copy of Alexander MacKenzie's **Guide to the Fur Trade Route** along with you, as I keep wondering what this river must have looked like down through here a couple of hundred years ago," Clint commented.

"I may have a surprise for you if I can find it," I replied. Within a short time I pulled those folded pages from my personal pack.

"Wonderful! What does it say about the Ottawa River down through here?"

While finding the right page, I said, "Back in those days this was known as the Utawas River. Here we are. It begins where they enter Lac Deschenes, just this side of the present city of Ottawa. Apparently the lake we paddled up through today was then called the Lac des Chaudieres. This is what it says:

> *We now enter Lac des Chaudieres, which is computed to be thirty miles in length. Though it is called a lake, there is a strong draught downwards, and its breadth is from two to four miles. At the end of this is the Portage des Chats, over which the canoe and lading are carried two hundred and seventy-four paces, and very difficult it is. The river is here barred by a ridge of black rocks, rising in pinnacles and covered with wood, which from the small quantity of soil that nourishes it,*

is low and stinted. The river finds its way over and through these rocks in numerous channels, falling fifteen feet and upwards. From hence two trips are made through a serpentine channel formed by the rocks, for several miles, when the current slackens, and is accordingly called the Lac des Chats.

"That's very interesting," said Clint. It sounds like we may have a big dam to cross in the morning."

Saturday, 24 April

DAY 8

The rain was over and a beautiful day dawned. Chats Falls Dam is made up of a two-mile-long retaining wall stretched across the upper end of a string of five islands. We were prevented from making the usual portage around either end because of a wide band of ice along both shores. We took the only open water available right up the middle, to the foot of one of the islands, and portaged to the other end. We came to an abrupt halt by this fifteen-foot concrete retaining wall that stretched a mile in either direction. How do you canoe over an obstacle like that?

It would be very difficult portaging around. Besides being exceedingly rugged terrain, there were three to four feet of snow in spots. We cut a small popple tree, leaving short stubs of the limbs on it to form a ladder to get on top. Then we cut a couple more long, slender poles to skid the canoe up sideways, by a rope on each end. We then did the same thing in reverse, to get down to a rock ledge near water level on the other side. Another minor victory, and we were on our way.

It was a good canoeing day, but rather uneventful the rest of the way as we paddled steadily on. About the middle of the afternoon we started to hit some fast water several miles before the dam at Portage Du Fort. When we tried to get to the portage take out, we were once again prevented from doing so, by ice. We couldn't get closer than one-half mile to the usual trail, which resulted in nearly a two-mile portage. By the time we were again in the canoe a drizzle of rain began falling and it was time to start looking for a campsite. We had been seeing signs of several logging operations late in the afternoon. When about a mile below Calumet Falls Dam we stopped at a small floating shack, located offshore, on a log boom. Investigating, we found the door open. The shack was empty and there was no one around so we moved in to get out of the rain. Other than the fact that the roof leaked at one end, this unusual little shack on a log boom made deluxe accommodations. Thus ended another day on the Ottawa, a day in which we had progressed thirty-eight miles.

Sunday, 25 April

DAY 9

Intermittent showers continued throughout the night. We were back on the river that morning shortly after daybreak. As we nosed our way along the sun came out and once more we were enjoying a great canoeing day.

We moved along the west side of Calumet Island, paddling through a lot of fast water. We hugged the shorelines to keep in the slower current as much as possible. As we approached La Passe, we noticed an Ontario Provincial Police car parked near the shore with its lights flashing. An officer standing nearby motioned us ashore. He called,

ONE INCREDIBLE JOURNEY

"Are one of you men Verlen Kruger?"

"Yes! I am," I shouted.

"Good! We've been looking all up and down the river for you this afternoon. I have some bad news. Your father died this morning!"

That was shocking news! My dad, Emmet Kruger, had been in the hospital during March but appeared to be recovering at home when I last talked with him in early April.

Trying to think at a time like that was almost impossible. Our camera crew soon arrived, as they had also been trying to locate us. I told them I wanted to go home as soon as possible. Bob McKee offered to drive me back to DeWitt, but he wasn't able to leave until the following morning. That sounded good to me.

Then I decided that inasmuch as Clint and Phil wanted to wait for my return in Pembroke, Ontario, we should paddle on upstream. We thought we could make the remaining forty-eight miles into Pembroke by the following morning. That is what we tried to do. Darkness caught up with us in Lac Coulonge. The rapids into Lower Allumette Lake were difficult to ascend. We couldn't see where we were going in the dark, moonless night. We held onto overhanging bushes and looked around with our flashlights. Then we paddled a short distance, hung onto more bushes, swung the flashlight around, and paddled on again. That process was repeated time after time. The river was at flood stage from the spring run off. We were unable to locate any portage trails, although they were undoubtedly there at normal water levels. That was a real struggle but we finally made it up into Lower Allumette. Then it was good going. Just as dawn was breaking we made the final rapids below Pembroke.

I had told Clint that I would return from Michigan right after my dad's funeral. Bob McKee was ready to go that morning, so we headed for home.

A Moving Wall of Ice

Monday and Tuesday, 26 and 27 April

DAYS 10 and 11

Home for the funeral, and return to Pembroke.

4

HIGHWAY TO
THE INTERIOR

> *The Lord will hear before we call,*
> *And every need supply;*
> *Good things are freely given to all*
> *Who on His word rely.*
>
> — *Laura Lee Randall,*
> ***Thanksgiving Song***

Wednesday, 28 April

DAY 12

Right after my father's funeral, Terry Norris and our oldest daughter, Nancy, his wife, along with Jenny, drove me back to Pembroke, Ontario, in our camper. We arrived early in the morning, and found Clint and our cameraman, Phil, in an uptown hotel. We had breakfast at a restaurant and headed back to where the canoe had been left securely tied up. It was a welcome sight, like seeing an old friend. After three days of inactivity, mostly driving in a car, I was itching for a little physical exertion to let off some steam. After three days of loafing around and seeing every movie in

Pembroke, Clint was as anxious as I was to make up for lost time. So, we agreed to again paddle on through the night, going all the way to Champlain Provincial Park where we hoped to spend some time with Charlie Laberge.

We promised to meet Phil at Mattawa the following afternoon. The Ottawa was big and wide for the next fifteen miles and is called Allumette Lake. After hugging and kissing Jenny goodbye for about the third time, we embarked before nine and headed up the Ottawa River into a light drizzle of rain. We were moving along at a pretty good pace in the middle of the river, nearly one quarter of a mile from shore, and were about to pass Deep River, Ontario. The town sits right on the river, and like all tourists we looked the town over as we paddled by. We noticed a large crowd of people, mostly kids, yelling and waving at us from a grassy park which sloped gently to the river's edge. We stopped paddling but couldn't decide what they were yelling about. Then, off in the background I noticed Jenny's camper. This was a pleasant surprise. Apparently she hadn't gone straight home after all. We hurried over to shore and were met by Jenny, Terry and Nancy, Phil, newspaper reporters and what looked like half the town.

Over a cup of hot tea and cookies, after we were interviewed and photographed, we found out that Phil, Jenny and our children had decided to go on ahead and waylay us at this point as it was on their way home. Phil, being the promoter that he was, notified the newspapers, and being a former school teacher, he stopped at the Deep River school where he was given time to lecture the students on history being made out on the river that very moment! The principal then let the whole school out so the kids could go down to the river and see for themselves! That sure brightened our day! Then about ninety minutes later, much refreshed and encouraged, we paddled on.

Deep River is so named because the Ottawa is extra deep in this stretch. About twelve miles further upstream we came to Des Joachims Dam where we made a mile and a quarter portage on the right, taking out below the bridge and putting back in above the dam. We had quite a mass of logs and ice to go around.

By then it was getting dark, with no moon and with a cloud cover hiding the stars. It was a dark and lonesome night. It got a little tricky with ice floes and masses of slush ice in the river that we would frequently ram into. We would then push, pry, back up and feel our way around them. Most of the time we couldn't see the ice in the dark. Slow progress, but we didn't have a problem with sleepiness! It rained for awhile early in the evening, then again in the morning, followed by a heavy blanket of fog. Such is life on the river!

Thursday, 29 April

DAY 13

About three hours before daylight we stopped, built a big fire and ate a hot meal. Then we huddled around the fire and catnapped for about an hour while sitting on a cold, damp rock.

We had noticed from the water marks at all the dams that the water seemed to be let down below normal, apparently in anticipation of the spring run-off. This meant that the dams were opened, which made the river high and the current fast. But with all these dams, we had it easier coming up the Ottawa than did the early voyageurs. We stopped for breakfast near the town of Hodgson, Quebec. It was hard to find enough dry wood to make a decent cooking fire.

Early that afternoon we arrived at Mattawa, Ontario, where Phil was waiting for us. We paddled up to the Ottawa River railroad bridge on the left side where the water was too fast for us. It looked as though we could have made it on the extreme right, but instead we portaged over the railroad and then paddled through the fast water under the Mattawa River bridge.

At the fork of these two rivers is the town of Mattawa. Here we tied our canoe to a dock. Had we continued on up the Ottawa River we would have soon entered Lake Timiskaming, which was the route of the fur traders as they travelled from Montreal to James Bay.

"This was the junction in the highway of the voyageurs," Clint commented as we walked into town for a hot meal. "But of course there were no towns along here in those days."

From the restaurant we called Charlie Leberge, to let him know that we expected to arrive at his place during the evening. After our late lunch we started paddling up the Mattawa River, leaving Quebec and heading out across Ontario. The Mattawa was very different from the Ottawa. It was much smaller and exceptionally scenic. It would be about forty miles up the Mattawa to North Bay with eight or nine portages. The first one was around a dam on the left, only a couple miles upstream. Then in about five more miles we came to De la Rose Rapids. We tried to paddle on the left but didn't make it, so we tried it on the right and succeeded. There Phil met us with his rubber raft and motor. He wanted to get movies of the beautiful country.

At Samuel De Champlain Provincial Park there is another nice rapids. We played around for nearly one-half hour, trying to get up those rapids. I don't know why we bothered, as we were going to stop there anyway. I guess we just couldn't resist the challenge! We pulled ashore on the left, just below the rapids, where there was a hiking trail through the park. By then it was seven p.m. We had come about one hundred ten miles in thirty-four and one-half hours of steady, hard upstream paddling. I think we got rid of some of that surplus energy we had back at Pembroke! It was good to get out of the canoe and stretch our legs.

We were met at the river and welcomed by Charlie Laberge, the chief ranger of the park. He was an interesting and exceptional man, and we struck up a special friendship right from the start. A French Canadian whose ancestors were one of the early groups of voyageurs, he was about my age and size, short and powerful of build. He looked the picture of a capable voyageur. We were soon to learn that he was quite knowledgeable on the fur trade history, and very involved in it. He relives the voyageur past in many ways, but probably the most outstanding way is in the building of birch bark canoes. He makes them just as the Indians did two hundred years ago, using only materials that he can get from the woods. He has made several huge Montreal canoes, one of which is on display as sort of a museum piece, at the park. It looks exactly like the early picture. It is thirty-eight feet long, six feet wide and would hold three tons of freight, along with fifteen or twenty men. It certainly was an impressive building feat.

Charlie put us up in a dry cabin and found us a shower. He told us the disheartening news that the lakes ahead were still frozen over. There had been no need for us to push it as we did in getting here. I guess I had wanted to keep going to help ease the sorrow at losing my dad. Inside the warm cabin I almost fell asleep during a conversation with Charlie. We decided that it was time to hit the sack.

We had worked harder than usual in getting there, as it was upstream all the way, and the ice and crosswind had put a strain on our muscles and ligaments. We both were having problems with swollen muscles and hands. Apparently the swelling was caused by the cutting off of circulation. It didn't bother us too much while paddling, but several times that night my aching hands got me up to take aspirin and rub the circulation back. This swelling and numbness of our hands and my sore feet turned out to be the only physical problems on the entire trip that either of us had from the strain of the pace and the prodigious amount of hard work and exposure involved. The rest of our bodies seemed to get conditioned to the demands put upon them. Only on those occasions when we paddled all night did our hands become bothersome, but even then it never slackened our pace. We hoped that they would adapt to the situation because this was the pace we were going to have to maintain.

Friday, 30 April

DAY 14

The next two and a half days were time well spent. It turned out to be an interesting educational interlude as we talked and were shown around by Charlie and his assistant, Andy Green, an old time trapper. They demonstrated how they collect the material and build birchbark canoes. Charlie showed us an old fifteen-foot birchbark canoe that he had bartered for, that was supposedly nearly one hundred years old and made by an Indian chief.

It appeared that ice was still our big problem. On the route ahead they told us that Lake Talon, Lake Nipissing and Trout Lake were solid with ice. We were concerned, as it was too far to carry around and we weren't about to accept help from anyone. With conditions as they were, we really shouldn't have started the trip as early as we did. But then on the other hand, we knew that it would have been impossible to make it to the Bering Sea if we hadn't. We had canoed three hundred fifty-six miles to that point, for which we had to pay a pretty stiff price. How much more were we going to have to pay? We had expected the wind to be our major problem, but so far it had been ice.

We talked at length about the voyageurs and the fur trade that day with Charlie and Andy Green. "It was the voyageurs who opened up this great country of ours," said Andy. "The main highway to the interior and the northwest in those days, went through here on this river."

"Who were some of the first fur traders to come up the Mattawa? " Clint asked.

Charlie replied, "As far as we know, the first was Pierre Esprit Radisson, who was carried off from his family by a band of Indians when he was a young boy. He grew up as one of the natives. Back in the early 1660's, he and his friend Sieur des Groseilliers paddled their birch bark canoe up through here. They started near Montreal and continued their journey through Lake Nipissing, along the north shore of Lake Huron and on into Lake Superior. That pair wintered up there with the Indians and while there they traded for a canoe load of furs. That was more fine furs than anyone in the colony of New France had ever seen. Most of their load were skins of the beaver, which were already in great demand in Europe. Some of the pelts were supplied from the colonies which later became a part of the United States. The French had also developed a considerable trade in furs from their towns along the St. Lawrence east of Montreal, Three Rivers and Quebec."

The discussion continued as I said, "I recall reading somewhere that they used to make hats from beaver skins."

"Yes," Charlie replied. "European felt makers had never before seen furs like the ones they were obtaining from the New World. Each fine beaver hair had minute barbs, ideal for making high-grade fur felt. To the craftsmen skilled in the "art and mistery" of felt making it was a miracle. Now they could turn out felt such as they had never before been able to produce. Soon after that the fashion in fur felt hats began to boom. Gentlemen clamored for more and more of those huge, handsome, expensive felt hats which were made in nearly every color of the rainbow. Within a short time there were not enough beaver skins being sent to Europe to keep up with the demand. So by the early seventeenth century, a valuable item of trade had been established between Europe and North America. At about that time a gentleman of fashion was paying as much for his felt hat as a skilled workman was able to earn in six months. So, you see it was a fashion in men's hats that eventually led to the formation of the North West Company and the discovery of our vast northwest."

"That's interesting," Clint remarked. Then he added, "I always thought that Radisson and Groseilliers were connected with the Hudson's Bay Company."

"You're right. They were," Charlie replied. "You see, while they were wintering near Lake Superior, those men came to realize that the potential wealth in furs in the interior was almost unlimited. They also put together scraps of information gleaned from the Indian chiefs whom they met, and they thought about reaching the heart of the continent by an easier route than by going through here. That easier route would be possible if they could travel by ship through the bay which had been discovered by Henry Hudson.

"After returning from Lake Superior with their canoe load of furs, they went to the colonial governor of New France and requested financial backing and ships for their proposed trip into Hudson Bay. It was a magnificent idea, but the authorities of the colony wanted nothing to do with it. They seemed to resent the possible fame and wealth which could come to those two uneducated interlopers.

"Disappointed but still certain that they had a good idea, Radisson and Groseilliers made a trip to Boston in an attempt to find someone who would supply a ship for their proposed trip into Hudson Bay. Eventually they found a vessel, but the ship's captain decided to turn back when they met up with the ice floes of Hudson Strait. As a last resort, the determined pair sailed to England and made their appearance before King Charles II.

"The King of England was excited by the stories of their travels into the interior of the North American continent and their prospects of potential wealth. Many months later the King was able to supply two small ships for the venture. Those ships were almost unfit for crossing the North Atlantic, to say nothing of the forbidding and almost unknown Hudson Bay.

"Fortunately, Groseilliers and Radisson sailed one on each ship, for Radisson's vessel ran into a terrific storm and had to limp back to port. Groseilliers, with better luck, reached the lower end of the bay in 1668, returning the following year to London with pelts finer than the grandest of his and Radisson's hopes.

"So as you know, in 1670 King Charles II granted a charter to a group of speculators headed by his cousin, Prince Rupert. That group has ever since been known as the Hudson's Bay Company. In return for the charter a promise was made to explore the interior of the continent, for which they were granted a monopoly to such lands as they might discover and exploit by way of Hudson Straits."

"That's certainly interesting. Now I understand," Clint quipped.

"I enjoy talking about those early days of my ancestors who were voyageurs," Charlie continued.

"While the Hudson's Bay Company was making its early ventures into the bay, individual Frenchmen along the St. Lawrence were carrying the cross and 'fleur de lis' and a taste for brandy and European trade goods ever farther inland. The northwest had become boom country. Because of its harvest of pelts, ships plying the Atlantic between England and Western Europe carried pay loads both ways.

Some of the more famous Northwesters that used to travel this river were Simon McTavish and his nephew, William McGillivray. Then of course there were Alexander MacKenzie, Simon Fraser and David Thompson. Those men were all of the English-Scotch descent and were the bourgeois of the North West Company."

"Those are familiar names," I said. "I've read about them, but it sure is interesting to hear you talk about the fur trade business."

It was late in the evening when Charlie said, "It's my bedtime, boys. Why don't we call it a day? Then we can talk some more tomorrow."

We all agreed, as Clint and I headed for our cozy cabin.

Saturday, 1 May

DAY 15

This was one of those beautiful, sunny spring days. The temperature was in the seventies and the ice in the lakes ahead of us would be melting.

Our cameraman, Phil Pemberton, made another appearance and took advantage of the good weather by taking several movie sequences. That worked out fine, as we usually begrudge time lost while he is shooting his movies.

Clint and I talked a lot about how we could work our way around the ice in Talon and Trout Lakes, but we were talked out of leaving that day by Charlie, Andy and Phil. This gave us more time to visit during the evening. Our conversation started when Phil said, "Montreal must have been a hustling, bustling town during those years of the fur trade."

"That's for sure," Charlie replied. "According to my grandfather, who used to tell me some of the things that his great grandfather did, Montreal was indeed quite a place. My great, great, great grandfather was one of the voyageurs, who for several years made the round trip each summer from Montreal to Grand Portage. On one of those trips he brought Peter Pond out of the interior and at another time while going west, he had the surveyor, David Thompson, in his canoe."

"Wow! That is interesting!" said Clint.

"Sure is!" quipped Phil.

"I'm proud to be the descendant of a voyageur, but I guess I didn't have to tell you that. They tell me that by the late 1770's, about nine thousand people lived in Montreal and a high percentage of them were connected with the fur trade. In late winter and early spring the traders worked in their warehouses, sorting and baling the trade goods to be shipped during the coming season. Every item was carefully checked against the lists of orders from Grand Portage and the wintering partners of the posts in the interior. In other warehouses, piles of pelts were sorted and re-baled for shipment to London and the fur sales there. Then toward the end of March, visits were made to the little farms along the rivers of the area for canoe building materials and to see about engaging voyageurs for the summer.

"As spring approached, the usual piles of trade goods were assembled at Lachine and small mountains of kegged rum were kept under guard until the canoes would be sent off. By the first of April the last of the trade goods had been sledded the nine miles from the warehouses in Montreal and piled high at Lachine.

They say that nearly everyone in Montreal

moved to Lachine on the day when the first brigade of canoes set out for the northwest. As the voyageurs arrived, each would be dressed in his best cap, shirt and breeches. Most of them would be smoking their short pipes. They definitely were an exciting and colorful group. The language of the trade was French, laced with a few expressive Indian and English phrases. Each voyageur carried his own brightly painted paddle, often a handmade gift from a father who had probably spent the best years of his life as an adventurous voyageur."

"How interesting!" Phil quipped.

Then Andy Green joined the conversation. "The voyageurs were called pork-eaters, you know. That's because they lived mostly on dried corn and fat pork between Montreal and Grand Portage. They were tough men, skilled and indispensable to the fur trade, and I guess they knew it. I've heard that one of them who was past seventy years of age once boasted: 'I could carry, paddle, walk and sing with any man I ever saw. I have been twenty-four years a canoeman, and forty-one in service; no portage was ever too long for me. Fifty songs could I sing. I have saved the lives of ten voyageurs. Have had twelve wives and six running dogs. I spent all my money on pleasure. Were I young again, I should spend my life the same way over. There is no life so happy as a voyageur's life'."

I found myself wondering just how accurate was the boast––and how much was legend.

Charlie again spoke up. "Year after year it happened the same way on the day those big, thirty-six-foot-long by six-foot-wide birch bark canoes set out for Grand Portage. Gradually they were loaded with cases of guns, kegs of ball, shot and powder, bales of calico, kettles, knives, beads, traps, kegs of rum and brandy and other trade goods and supplies for the distant posts. Also, into each canoe went provisions for the ten-man crew. Items such as food, blankets and personal luggage were also loaded. Nearly everything had been bundled into ninety-pound packs during the early spring at a warehouse. In all, the load of goods, supplies and men carried in each Montreal canoe weighed nearly four tons.

"On shore, wives and children, sweethearts and parents, and the merchants and clerks who would carry on the business in Montreal during the summer months called out farewells, 'Bon voyage! God bless you!'

"And then always for a brief moment, every voice hushed. Here and there a young voyageur, already steady in his place in the canoe, caught the eyes of a dark-haired girl in the crowd; a young husband smiled an intimate message to his wife, marking a moment he would always remember. In their places just behind the middle seats, agents and bourgeois pressed their tall beaver hats more firmly on their heads against the strong breeze. Steersmen and bowmen half-kneeled, half-stood in their places, tense and waiting. Then the order rang out. Slowly, proudly each paddle rose, flashed in the sun, and dug deep in the rushing, icy water. Steadily each canoe moved off from the landing place. Arms rose and fell rhythmically. The low craft shot forward. Soon the brigade, part of hundreds of canoes which left each summer, was out in the stream, each craft keeping its position in perfect formation. Space blurred familiar faces on shore. The last farewells died on the wind."

Charlie continued. "Often the voyageurs had to break thin ice at the river's edge in the morning during the first few days of the canoes' trip up the Ottawa, even though mid-day sun might force them to shed their shirts. But no matter how cold, when rapids forced a stop or when the brigade paused for breakfast or nooning or supper, the bowman sprang into the stream at the river's edge to steady the craft, followed by the steersman and the middle-men. Only then did the gentlemen disembark, riding piggy-back on the shoulders of their sturdy voyageurs. The disembarking process occurred often, for there were thirty-six portages between Lachine and Georgian Bay. At a portage the voyageurs carried both canoe and cargo; when they could shoot the rapids or track and carry only the cargo they made what they called a 'decharge.'

"Theirs were long days, starting at dawn when the men woke from their blankets on the ground to the guide's cry of 'Leve! Leve!' and ending with only enough daylight to build their supper fires to cook the great kettle of corn-meal and pork."

"That certainly was interesting. Clint and I can picture all of those huge canoes coming up through here each spring. We understand that those voyageurs often sang as they paddled along."

"Yes. That's true." With a grin on his face, Charlie continued. "I've heard that those who could sing the best were often paid a higher wage than those with weaker voices." Then with a stretch and a yawn, he said, "Boys, it's past my bedtime. Let's call it a day."

Sunday, 2 May

DAY 16

We slept late and spent a leisurely forenoon around Charlie's place. It was another beautiful, warm spring day. Clint and I both were developing a terrific urge to get underway once more, even though we knew that the lakes ahead were still solidly frozen. About noon Clint said, "Waiting here like this just doesn't make sense to me. Why don't we head up the river and go as far as we can? Maybe by the time we get there we can find a way around or through those frozen lakes."

I was ready. We decided to take our time so as to give Phil the opportunity to shoot some

Paresseux Falls on the Mattawa River

footage of us moving through this great canoe country. In less than two miles we came to Rock Portage, so called apparently because of its rocky rapids and portage. It was easy to see how the place got its name. All the portages on the Mattawa are well marked and have good, clean trails, although they are sometimes rugged. Next came a portage on the left around thirty foot Paresseux Falls, presenting a scenic view from below. Then in quick succession followed Prairie Portage, Cave Portage and Perches Portage, with a few riffles between.

It was a lovely, fun kind of day. We were pleased with the smooth efficiency in which we were loading, unloading and making the portages. As a force of habit we were timing ourselves, and we were moving over these portages nearly fifty percent faster now than at the beginning. This is important in country such as the Boundary Waters

Canoe Area where there are thirty-nine portages in two hundred and sixty-two miles. Loading and unloading the canoe can be time consuming.

In the late afternoon we came to Talon Falls which was impressive in high water. Talon drops about forty feet in two cascades, down through a fantastic gorge. It was good to spend some time there, listening to the special music of those falls and soaking up some of their wild beauty and the untamed magic that a wilderness falls or rapids seems to have. Something about it really turns me on! Talon Portage is a rugged and scenic trail. It must have been some sight in the early days to see a brigade of twenty or more large Montreal canoes coming through here!

We paddled into Talon Lake to view an exceptionally impressive sunset while Phil shot more footage. He had followed us in his auto and met us at the important spots during the afternoon. The east end of Talon Lake, for about one-half mile from shore and up Kaibuskong Bay, was free from ice. We were encouraged that maybe the other lakes might be opening up, although the rest of Talon Lake was frozen solid.

Around a pot of hot tea that night back in our little cabin at Charlie's place, after much more discussion we decided that tomorrow we would put back into Talon Lake, go across Kaibuskong Bay, up Kaibuskong Creek to Highway 17, and then portage about seven and one-half miles down the highway to the upper end of LaVase River and try to make it out to Lake Nipissing.

Monday, 3 May

DAY 17

Charlie had to go into North Bay on business so we went with him to check out Lake Nipissing.

The ice appeared to be softening, but was not broken up. At noon we put back into Talon Lake, headed up Kaibuskong Bay about four miles, made a portage around a dam into Sheedy Lake and went about one mile across to another short portage into La Chappelle Lake. From thence we proceeded up small Kaibuskong River about one mile to make another short portage around a falls. On up the river a couple more miles we came to a rapids about one quarter mile from Highway 17.

At about four that afternoon we picked up our gear and started the long portage down Trans Canada Highway 17 to where LaVase River made a bend close to the highway. The portage started with a long hill. There were occasional mean, gusty crosswinds. The only good footing was on the shoulder of the highway. When those big semi trucks came barreling down the road, the swoosh of wind would catch the long canoe and it would try to windmill on my shoulders. This was one of those no fun portages. I never did like portaging on a hard surface road. That old familiar pain in my shoulders and back were my only companions. I would look down the road and it seemed to stretch on endlessly. I could see Clint, a small, lumpy speck bobbing along. I wore my lightweight Bean shoe packs all the way, and my feet again became sore.

About a mile from LaVase River a van drove by and honked, then stopped and backed up. It was Hugh McMillian, President of the present-day North West Company, a descendant of one of the original owners. He had heard about us coming through. He was a good friend of Charlie. I let the bow of my canoe down on his van and enjoyed talking and getting acquainted. He asked all kinds of questions and so did I. He admired the canoe and asked, "How much does it weigh?"

"One hundred and seventy pounds if you throw in my bag."

"Is that special padded yoke comfortable?"

"Boy, is it ever!"

"Can I try it out?" he asked.

"Sure, take it for a mile or two!"

With all of that fur trade blood in his veins, he just had to try it out. He didn't get more than ten feet before a gust of wind caught the canoe, causing him to stumble and twist his knee. He put it back down on the van. It sure would have been nice if he would have carried it that last mile for me. But of course, I wouldn't let him. I wasn't about to let anyone spoil my fun, not after what that canoe and I had been through together. So far up to this point, we had portaged fifty-three miles around the ice, plus nineteen other regular portages.

It was nearly eight in the evening when I set the canoe down near a railroad track at the bend of the LaVase River. Charlie came along and picked us up, to spend one more night at his place, where Hugh McMillian also was staying overnight. It was a most enjoyable evening as we talked and swapped stories. Charlie and Hugh both showed some thirty-five millimeter slides, until after two o'clock in the morning.

I drank a lot of tea while Charlie brought out a jug of "high wine" he had made. That was also a duplicate of the voyageur days. I don't like being discourteous but I wouldn't even taste the stuff, mostly as a matter of principle. I have absolutely no use for alcohol for drinking purposes. After seeing what it does to people it just doesn't make sense. I can get just as high, just as intoxicated, with the wonderful, beautiful, exciting things of life as anyone can with their drugs. In fact you might say I was in the midst of a six-month "high" right then and I wasn't making a fool of myself or destroying someone else's life while doing it.

Meeting people like Charlie and Hugh was one of the highlights of our adventure. I would have loved to have spent more time with them. They contributed much to me as a person and to the experience value of the trip. May our paths cross again someday.

5

NIPPED BY THE ICE
ON NIPISSING

> *To see the world in a grain of sand,*
> *And a heaven in a wild flower;*
> *Hold infinity in the palm of your hand,*
> *And eternity in an hour.*
>
> *— William Blake*

Tuesday, 4 May

DAY 18

At breakfast Charlie said, "You boys had better stay with us until tomorrow. That will give the ice another day to break up. I'm afraid you'll be stopped when you get out to Nipissing anyway."

"No," I replied. "We have to keep at it. Clint and I talked it over early this morning and the good Lord willing, we will keep plugging away. We will do what we can and pray about the rest. As

65

you already know, we have neither the time nor the disposition to sit around and wait until things get just right."

Charlie drove us back to the LaVase River where we had left the canoe the night before. There we said our final good-byes, after again thanking him for all of his help and hospitality. He had been a kind and gracious host.

The river looked especially small and crooked that morning. It was no larger than a roadside ditch. A railroad track paralleled the stream for about ten miles. We portaged down it for a mile before trying the river. The LaVase turned out to be a jumbled mess of tangled brush, with lots of deadfalls and tight corners that the canoe wouldn't fit around. We struggled and fussed for about a mile, more out of the water than in, before we gave up and portaged down the railroad again for another mile. We really had put into the LaVase too soon. It just wasn't big enough that far upstream to be navigable. After the second portage the river became large enough to keep the canoe in the water.

It is always interesting to put into a river at its extreme upper end where it is so small you can jump across it, and then to watch it slowly grow, getting bigger and better as you move on downstream.

By late afternoon it had grown to a fair sized stream. We soon came to a small gorge and a rapids that called for a portage. Then a swampy creek from the north joined up. That again put us on the old voyageurs' highway coming from Trout Lake. A couple more miles brought us to another portage of about a half mile, which took us around two sets of rapids. There the river widened considerably.

A half hour later we were looking across Lake Nipissing into the setting sun. For a hundred yards or so around the mouth of the river the lake was open, but other than that, as far as we could see it was solid ice. We paddled out to investigate and found that the ice was soft and slushy and was about ready to break up. It was too thick to ram the canoe through, yet it was too honeycombed and soft to safely walk on.

Along the north side of the river there was a little roadside park with tables and bathrooms. On the south side was a flat, heavily wooded point of stark, bare trees and brush, with occasional patches of snow. We were always more comfortable away from civilization so we headed for the woods and carved out a campsite, leveled off a small piece of ground and cut a little brush. This made a nice spot for our tent. It had been a tough, tiring day hauling that heavy canoe in and out of the water, wrestling with the gear and fighting tangled brush jams. We went to bed that evening after discussing how we were going to get across Lake Nipissing. Would we lose even more time because of ice?

Wednesday, 5 May

DAY 19

It was a beautiful day! That was always the way I felt as I watched the first rays of the rising sun through the trees. It seemed especially so as I squatted there that morning, turning the first batch of pancakes and enjoying the scene through the slow rising smoke of our early morning campfire.

But there we were—icebound! After breakfast we paddled across the river mouth to the park and found that a bus from North Bay used it as a turnaround. We took a bus into town to see what the ice along the north shore of Lake Nipissing looked like. We were somewhat encouraged to find the north side partly broken up, with great, long open leads in the ice. We also found that, tight along the shore from our camp to North Bay, it was mostly open, with loose masses of ice slowly moving around in the gentle breeze. It was nearly twenty miles across the lake to French River and we couldn't tell if the open leads interconnected enough for us to get across. But hope came alive as we hopped another bus back to our canoe and quickly broke camp.

Then came a busy six miles, sometimes canoeing through heavy slush ice, sometimes forcing our way through masses of broken ice, and continually zig-zagging and using more brute force than paddling. Occasionally we had to get out and walk along the shore, forceably towing the canoe on a long rope through packed ice jams. A few times we found ourselves trapped against solid ice. There we cautiously stepped out on the ice to drag the canoe up and across to open water on the other side.

As we slowly made our way past the city of North Bay, a man and a woman hailed us from shore. It turned out to be a couple of reporters from the **Golden Nugget** newspaper. Somehow they had heard we would be passing by. There was an ice jam between us, and as we couldn't get ashore we were inter-viewed in the midst of the ice jam out on Lake Nipissing. We spent nearly a half hour with them. They said they had been looking for us all morning.

Just beyond town we found an open lead, a narrow rift in the ice, and it headed off toward the Manitou Islands. That was the direction we needed to go to hit the mouth of the French River, so we took it. Hours later, after meandering all over the east end of Nipissing from lead to lead, the wind picked up. It caused the whole lake ice mass to slowly move and shift. Fortunately, just as one lead would close another would open. Clint and I were developing an uneasy feeling. What if our lead closed and there was no opening ahead? We discussed the possibilities. It was a ticklish spot to be in!   What was to prevent us from being crunched in the ice?

We were unable to get anywhere near the Manitou Islands as we worked our way across the lake. We did have a couple of narrow squeaks just managing to get out of one lead and into another as the ice floes came crunching together.   At about sunset while we were only about a mile off shore near Cross Point, and we were feeling pleased about heading down a lead that looked as though it would get us to shore, our luck suddenly ran out.

Slowly the open water lead closed in front of us.   As we looked behind to see if we could turn back we saw that it was also closing there.   We were trapped!   Fortunately we were in a wide spot in the rift.   The two huge masses of ice slowly crunched and ground against one another as it seemed, they moved in opposite directions.   That was indeed an awesome sight.   The noise and the irresistible power of the scene was most impressive as that pressure ridge continued to build up on both sides of us.   What had been an open lead only a few minutes before had suddenly become a growing ridge of tumbling, grinding, noisy ice.   We sat there in that small spot of open water growing smaller and smaller, and wondered what we were going to do.   We watched the unusual and spectacular display of the forces of nature until finally all became quiet.   The shifting ice had come to rest and we still had a few feet of clearance on each side of the canoe.   We were in the only spot of open water for as far as the eye could see.

"Boy-oh-boy, are we lucky!" I heard Clint say.

"That's for sure, but we are not out of this yet.   How are we going to get to shore?"

"I'm not sure.   It will be a little uncomfortable if we have to spend the night out here."

We sat there and discussed our situation as the sun slowly sank out of sight over the distant tree-lined horizon.   As if to assure us that it was all right, we were treated to a most beautiful sunset. It would be hard to describe the strange feelings that went through me, a mixture of apprehension and exhilaration, a feeling of being a part of the whole picture and belonging where I was in the midst of God's wonderful creation. At times like these my instinct was to pray, which I silently did while we waited for an answer to our problems.

Finally the wind must have shifted, for the rift slowly opened a little and we hustled down the narrow, slush and ice choked, lead. We made it to shore at Cross Point. I thanked the Lord!

We set up camp near the point and continued to watch and listen as we prepared supper in the fading light. We were glad that they wouldn't have to put up two more crosses on Cross Point as we had learned that the place was so named because there were at one time eleven crosses erected there from drownings which happened just off the point. "If we can make it into the French River in the morning, this has to be the last of our ice problems," Clint remarked.

"I hope so. We have had enough ice canoeing experience to last us a lifetime."

We had progressed over four hundred miles having many more problems than we had anticipated. It had been a test of body and spirit. But then, the test of self was one of the reasons we made the trip. It had been a day to remember.

The canoe, too, had its test in taking abuse, in ramming rocks and logs and in being used as an ice breaker. Sometimes we forced it through foot-thick, soft, honeycombed ice. At other times we backed up and rammed ice jams that were rock hard, but the canoe still showed no sign of ice damage. I had reinforced the bow to withstand just such punishment. It was gratifying to know that my construction foresight had apparently been adequate.

Nipped by the Ice on Nipissing

DAY 20

We finished breakfast and were ready to break camp by six o'clock. The mercury had dropped quite low overnight under clear skies, and about a quarter inch of new ice had formed. There had been no wind during the night, and as far as we could see the lake was again completely frozen over. After testing it with our paddles we figured that with a little hard work we might be able to paddle through it. It was difficult getting the canoe to run, but once we had all of that weight under motion it wasn't too hard to keep it moving. It sure was noisy though. We would reach out, jab our paddles through the ice and pull. The noise and flying pieces of ice reminded me of breaking window glass. "Who was it that said that our problems with the ice were over?" Clint asked.

We were getting the full treatment. For the next two hours we paddled through the glassy ice before the wind came up and the waves made fast work of breaking up the new ice.

Around noon at the French River Dam, we made our first portage of the day. The chutes were fully open and the water was almost as high on the downstream side as it was in the backwater. There was nearly a half mile of rapids below the dam. In the afternoon we made three additional portages. We probably could have run a couple of them, but with four cameras and other expensive equipment we resisted such temptations. There were also a number of tamer rapids that we did paddle through. French River frequently widened and the current became rather slow.

We kept going later than we intended, as we wanted to make it to the town of French River. Darkness had settled in and we were cold, tired and hungry when we finally arrived in the village of French River, at a little after ten. Every build-

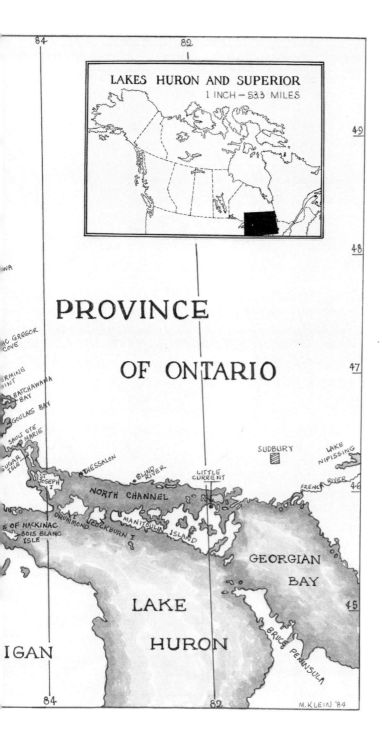

LAKES HURON AND SUPERIOR
1 INCH = 53.3 MILES

PROVINCE

OF ONTARIO

SUDBURY

LAKE NIPISSING

MAC GREGOR COVE

ERMINE POINT

BATCHAWANA BAY

GOULAIS BAY

SAULT STE MARIE

SUGAR ISLE

ST JOSEPH I

THESSALON

BLIND RIVER

LITTLE CURRENT

NORTH CHANNEL

FRENCH RIVER

S OF MACKINAC

BOIS BLANC ISLE

DRUMMOND

COCKBURN I

MANITOULIN ISLAND

GEORGIAN BAY

LAKE

HURON

BRUCE PENINSULA

IGAN

M. KLEIN '84

73

ing was closed, and either it was a smaller settlement than we had expected or possibly we never did find all of the town. In the darkness we found only a few buildings and no people. We pitched camp along the river in the yard of a closed lodge. We couldn't find any wood for a fire, so for the first and only time we used Clint's small gas stove. There is not much comfort or warmth in one of those contraptions when you are cold and hungry.

Friday, 7 May

DAY 21

A strong head wind swept up the river all day, even though the weather was perfect in every other way. We had a tendency to try to keep up the canoe speed in head winds. Consequently, we found ourselves working harder on such days. The French River was an unusual stream with many bays and channels that lead off in nearly every direction. The lower end was relatively low, with terrain very rocky and well wooded.

At noon we stopped on the wind sheltered point of an island where the river divided into multiple channels a few miles before it emptied into Georgian Bay of Lake Huron. It was one of our better noon stops. We had an ideal spot for a cooking fire, which made it handy to whip up a large order of pancakes. I had such a nice fireplace that I made an extra batch to have ready for supper. After a good hot meal, Clint laid down on a patch of soft, dry moss and caught a nap. I wandered about a hundred yards down the shore of the island and found a scenic overlook partially in the shade of a small scrub pine, where I studied the map and caught up on my journal. For some reason, that spot seemed very remote with little sign of man. That is one of the marvels of the Canadian bush country. Sometimes you don't have to travel very far to find yourself in as wild, rugged and un-spoiled a place as could be found anywhere.

From there we held to the north channel, trying to stay on the same route as the voyageurs. With all of the channels and islands, and the sameness of the country, we weren't too sure where we were at times. Mostly by luck we found our-selves heading down the narrow, fast chute of water that so many of the voyageurs called 'LaDalle,' or The Eave Trough. It must have been about one hundred yards long with a rock wall ten to fifteen feet straight up on the left side, and on the right it was nearly as high but more sloping. It gave a short, fast ride with some respectable standing waves at the lower end. In those big "Montreal" canoes, it must have been a snug fit to keep from scraping the sides. Then in a few minutes we made a short portage around 'Petite Faucille,' or The Little Sickle, as the river poured around a sharp bend. Another half hour and we were threading our way through a maze of small, rocky, tree-studded islands and headed out into Lake Huron. Our first look at the lake was a pleasant surprise. We especially noticed the clearness of the water. The country was quite low, with no real hills. I climbed a tree to get a panoramic view and it presented a very nice scene. Looking westward out over Georgian Bay towards Sault Ste. Marie, the calm lake was an inviting prospect to our trip.

"We have about two hundred miles to go along this north shore and we'll arrive in Sault Ste. Marie. How long do you think it's going to take to make that two hundred miles?"

Clint replied, "If we have a good break with the weather, we should average fifty miles per day. That means we could arrive at the Soo late next

Tuesday, if all goes well."

"If the lake stays as calm as it is tonight that might be possible, but it isn't likely that we'll get many days of this kind of weather."

Heading into the setting sun, we took a straight course for Green Island about fifteen miles into the lake. There we made camp for the night. The island was almost like a bird sanctuary. We went to sleep to the sweet music of hundreds of singing birds.

Saturday, 8 May

DAY 22

Georgian Bay stayed mirror calm overnight and it had been so cold that ice again formed over the entire surface to a depth of more than a quarter of an inch. That made for noisy paddling as we again headed west, after an early breakfast.

About an hour later a breeze broke up the ice and gave us a most welcome tailwind. It was one of those beautiful canoeing days of sunshine and light breezes, and we appreciated the rarity of flat water on that big lake.

We went under the bridge that lead from the mainland to Manitoulin Island and we found out why they called the town on the island Little Current. Out there in almost the middle of the huge body of water where it pinched down to the narrows between Georgian Bay and North Channel, there apparently was a little current most of the time. The direction of the current depended on the direction of the wind. The town seemed to be a modernized Indian town. There appeared to be considerable large freight traffic. We could see lake-going freighters at the docks.

It was one-thirty p.m. when we tied up to a small dock. We had purposely delayed lunch with the idea of having steak and ice cream at a restaurant. We settled for roast beef. While enjoying our meal, Clint said, "That's Great Cloche Island over there. I'm happy to be here in Little Current, but it would have been nice to have gone around the other side of Great Cloche. Then we could have stopped at "LaCloche" and rung that famous old rock bell, just as the voyageurs used to do."

"That's right! I forgot all about that today! I must have been anticipating this food as we came by that little channel which would have taken us up along the north side of the island. Why didn't you remind me?"

"I was getting hungry, too," Clint replied with a grin.

"I remember reading about that "cloche" or bell. According to Dr. John J. Bigsby, one of the early voyageurs, 'the place is called Cloche from some of its rocks ringing like a bell upon being struck.' He said the name 'particularly applied to one loose basaltic mass lying on the shore.' It was an object of wonderment to travellers and voyageurs who had to pass within a few paces of it.

According to Eric W. Morse in his **Fur Trade Canoe Routes of Canada: Then and Now:**

> *Anyone looking for this stone should have no trouble. It lies in wild surroundings, away from cottages. The narrow, swampy canoe passage comes in off the lake immediately south of Swift (not Little) Current, where the highway and railway make their first short jump from the mainland toward Manitoulin Island. Looking across the last mile-long stretch of water as one heads south, having rounded the final point from the Swift Current*

bridge, appears what seems to be a flat, low meadow. This little ditch is short, and from its southern end the rocks, LaCloche, lies on an open rocky beach to the east of the reedy swamp, which was once the voyageurs' way through. It lines up at an angle of about 45 degrees to the axis of the "ditch," and at a distance of 100-150 yards from its southern end. Two or three smaller "cloches" are nearby. Seekers should perhaps be warned that the name, "Bell Rock," is locally and mistakenly given to a large block of granite half a mile west, which of course does not ring.

Before leaving Little Current, I phoned Jenny at home to give her the date of our expected arrival at "The Soo," as everyone in Michigan calls Sault Ste. Marie. Several people had expressed a desire to come to see us as we passed through. I always got a funny, exhilarated feeling after talking to her, which lasted for hours and sometimes for days.

A short distance out of Little Current we came up against a heavy ice jam that the wind had blown together. It looked as though the small bay we were in was completely blocked off. I really hadn't expected an ice jam on Lake Huron, but with our luck with ice that spring we shouldn't have been surprised. By going a few miles out of our way, tight to the south shore, we found an opening and continued on.

We stopped for the night and made a late camp under the tower frame of a light beacon, on the north side of Clapperton Island. I noticed that the sun set at exactly seven thirty-five p.m. It had been a good day. We made up for lost time and hoped that Lake Huron would stay like that until we arrived at The Soo.

Nipped by the Ice on Nipissing

DAY 23

It was eight o'clock before we embarked. We were late getting up because there had been a strong wind during the night and as we lay in our sacks we were fooled by the loud crashing and splashing of the waves against our unusual limestone shoreline. The shore there was like a ragged miniature cliff, four to five feet high, and it exaggerated the wave sound effects.

I crawled out of the tent expecting to see big, mean waves, but instead they were only moderate and we had a nice tail wind blowing. I told Clint what I'd discovered and he was in such a hurry to break camp that he hustled around and took down the tent and packed the bags before he even got dressed. "Phil should be here with his movie camera," I said as Clint continued to run around in his long johns. Meanwhile, I hurried to make a fast breakfast of cold pancakes. They were part of the same batch that I'd made three days before. This was our fourth meal of those pancakes. By then it seemed that they had lost most of their personality and appeal.

It was another of those beautiful canoeing days and we moved right along. For several days in a row the wind seemed to have followed a pattern. In the early morning a light breeze came up from the direction of the sun, and it more or less followed the sun around until noon. Then it switched to the west and became stronger.

I especially like paddling among islands. They make a lake more colorful and the day more interesting. This was one of those days. We were surrounded by fascinating islands. Every once in awhile we found some excuse to go ashore and explore.

The water along that part of the lake was so

clear that when it was calm we could see the bottom. During the afternoon as we paddled in about ten feet of calm water, we spotted a large boulder that came to within less than a half inch of the surface of the lake. We stopped and took some interesting pictures as we took turns standing on the water about a mile from shore! Even with that large boulder under me it was an uneasy feeling when Clint paddled away to take my picture. He didn't do anything to help the feeling when he said, "Good-bye Verlen. I'll see you in the Soo!"

We had lunch near the light beacon of John Island. Then by eight o'clock, we stopped for the night at Hennepin Island, which was eight miles beyond Blind River, Ontario. With good weather and mileage we were not feeling any pressure to put in longer days. Our schedule gave us a little more evening campfire living. It was especially enjoyable that evening as we sat around the fire, sipped one last cup of hot tea and enjoyed the full moon rising in the east.

Monday, 10 May

DAY 24

We were out of the sacks at four-thirty. It seemed to require nearly an hour and a half to get a hot breakfast, break camp and load the canoe. We could beat that though, if we really needed to hustle. That morning however, it seemed wiser to set the tune for the day with a comfortable, relaxing start. It was hard on the morale to hurry so much that you broke camp underfed, and then to discover later in the day that you'd left something behind.

That morning the lake had been dead calm and a dense fog made navigation along the shoreline and islands out of the question. We couldn't see a hundred feet in any direction. That was where those compasses I had glassed into the canoe bottom in front of our seats really came in handy. It was surprising how soon a canoe could get off course when you had nothing to aim for! We were able to move along in the fog, which began to lift by mid-forenoon.

A little later we came upon a group of small, nearly barren, rocky islands which had been completely taken over by herring gulls. As we approached an island, the birds would take off and circle overhead in a noisy, threatening cloud. There were thousands and thousands of them. It was truly amazing that so many of them could have been on such a small island. We didn't like the idea of bothering them but we wanted to learn more about them, so we decided to go ashore. "I've never seen this many gulls in my life," Clint kept repeating. "And they look so gullible!"

It must have been at the peak of their egg-laying season. There were nests of eggs all over the place. We had to be careful where we stepped. To say that we were unwelcome would be a gross understatement. They continually made bombing runs at us. We had to wave our paddles to keep them from coming too close. The noise, the smell and the sight were almost unbearable. The island was totally plastered with a "whitewash" which did nothing to enhance or beautify the environment!

Talk about your overpopulation and pollution problems! Taken in much smaller doses I have found sea gulls utterly fascinating and useful birds, but in that extremely high concentration they were repulsive. We were glad to leave, and I'm sure the feeling was mutual. There may be a similarity between bird and people pollution. Then again, perhaps it is more a lack of really understanding the situation.

As we approached the mouth of the bay near Thessalon, there were several more small rocky islands. These islands were fully occupied by a cloud of common terns. The terns put up a terrific fuss as we approached, chattering and diving at us. They acted in much the same way as the gulls which we had encountered earlier in the day, but the terns were a joy to watch and were beautiful in flight.

We paddled into Thessalon at noon and had our lunch in a restaurant. Then during the afternoon, with perfect weather, we moved along to the extreme north end of St. Joseph Island where we made camp.

We averaged more than fifty miles a day on Lake Huron and handled the pace better physically as time went by. We were encouraged because if it had turned out that we couldn't hack the pace, we would have been in danger of not reaching the Bering Sea.

Tuesday, 11 May

D A Y   2 5

"It's time to rise and shine, Clint! This looks like another beautiful canoeing day." Those were my first words that morning. While getting breakfast my thoughts were; it's only about thirty miles to the Soo. We should be there early this afternoon and it will be so good to see Jenny and my six youngest children again! I could hardly wait.

We headed due west through St. Joseph Channel, then into Neebish Channel, along the north side of Neebish Island to the west side of Lake Nicolet. I had not been feeling up to par that morning. The greasy meat balls we'd had in the canned stew the night before were not processing too well in my energy system. By the time we headed north along northern Michigan's eastern shore however, I had recovered and was again feeling normal. On long,

Nipped by the Ice on Nipissing

narrow Lake Nicolet we shared the traffic with large ocean freighters and ore boats. We met several and gave them a wide berth, but we found ourselves racing a couple of them as we neared the Soo.

A few miles out of the Soo we did what the early voyageurs used to do when arriving at a main fort. They would clean up and put on their best clothes. While still in the canoe I got out my washcloth, stripped down and washed up. There were times that one wanted to look his best, but I still haven't learned how to take a bath in a canoe.

The wind began to whip up real strong at about noon. Then just as we were about to paddle past the Sugar Island ferry dock a mile or two east of the Soo, we were met by a small group of people. It included Phil Pemberton and his crew, Ernie Michael of WSOO radio and a number of others. We soon learned that the people of the Soo area had

Cleaning up for a date in the Soo

83

been hearing about our journey. We were given a lengthy interview and Phil did some movie takes.

Jenny and the family hadn't known about the meeting at the ferry docks so they were still looking for me in town. Phil said that he had seen them earlier in the day, so I knew that they were around. Following the interview we paddled on up the St. Marys River to take out at the Coast Guard dock. From there we made the mile and a half portage down Portage Street to Lake Superior, going through town with crowds of people following us. We probably could have lined up the St. Marys Rapids, or we could have taken the easy way through the locks with the big boats. We had learned that they would have put us through without charge.

Most of the early voyageurs' traffic had been on the Canadian side. The North West Company had even built a channel with a locks system to by-pass the rapids. A remnant of these locks is still

Portaging along Portage Street in Sault Ste. Marie

preserved for history. They were just large enough to handle a Montreal canoe.

Jenny and the family caught up with us as we started the portage through the city. It was good! We had made it to the Soo, and none too soon. A heavy wind storm brewing out across Lake Superior took a few heavy shots at us as we carried our loads down Portage Street.

Wednesday and Thursday, 12 and 13 May

DAYS 26 AND 27

Sault Ste. Marie gave us the royal treatment. We were the guests of the Ojibway Hotel for our stay. The people were friendly and we were impressed with the Soo hospitality.

For more than two days the high winds continued. It was cold, with frequent showers of snow and sleet. I couldn't have enjoyed it more. Being wind bound had never been like that, before or since. Those were a wonderful two days with my family. We had actually planned to stay a day or two anyway, but for once I was thankful for a storm.

I have always enjoyed my family, but I especially appreciated them at the Soo. It was very satisfying to be able to share our adventure with Jenny as much as possible. She seemed to understand, or at least sympathize, with what I was doing and why I had to do it.

We saw the sights around town, visited with friends, asked a lot of questions about Lake Superior and tried to plan our strategy for the journey ahead. We were also asked a lot of questions such as: How do you canoe across Lake Superior? What route are you going to take? Do you go straight across? How far is it across? How long will it take? We were able to answer most of the questions but we added that we would know more about it in about two weeks.

"Gitche Gumee" or "The Shining Big Sea Waters" of Hiawatha fame, is the largest fresh water lake in the world. It has a total surface area of thirty-one thousand, seven hundred square miles. In elevation it is six hundred feet above sea level. With a maximum depth of thirteen hundred and thirty-three feet, it is also one of the deepest lakes in the world. It has a total shoreline of twenty nine hundred and eighty miles. One of the early fur trade records gives the total canoe course around the lake as eleven hundred and fifty-five miles, by traversing all the bays. Captain Bayfield, R. N., followed the coast line more closely and gave the distance as seventeen hundred and fifty miles, which probably would more closely approximate a practical canoe route. There wasn't much chance that any two canoe trips across this inland ocean would have travelled the exact same mileage or have followed the exact same canoe path. The shoreline in those sections exposed to violent storms was washed bare of vegetation of any kind for twenty to thirty feet above the normal water line. In all the years of the fur trade history at Grand Portage, no noticeable variance in the water level was ever recorded. A strong wind or a storm created a temporary tide effect of raising the shoreline water by a few feet. Apparently there were extreme instances of a severe storm pushing the water up the shore for unusual distances; some claimed as high as twenty to thirty feet above normal. I found that hard to believe but on the other hand, I didn't know how to explain the sand, gravel and logs which we were to find up to thirty feet above the lake shores. They actually appeared as though they had been placed there by the water. The main body of Lake Superior has never been known to freeze over, although it may freeze solid many miles out from shore. Because of its vast volume and great depth, the water temperature remains constant and very cold the year around. I had read several accounts which gave different figures for the water temperatures, varying from thirty-eight to forty-four degrees Fahrenheit. Superior's waters are among the clearest and purest drinking waters to be found. They test better than some well waters. Always cool, we were to find it tasting like good spring water.

In reading several journals we had learned almost the exact canoe route of the voyageurs in their Montreal canoes, and found them to be fairly consistent in recording their route from the Soo to Grand Portage. The distance was four hundred and fifty miles and their route followed the north shore rather closely.

Clint and I figured that those fur traders knew best, so we followed their route. Even those big Montreal canoes usually tried to stay within a mile or two of shore, except under ideal conditions when sometimes they would traverse bays up to ten miles across. This became our policy. At no time, even under the most favorable conditions, would we get more than an hour from shore.

There were many exciting challenges on our journey, and crossing Lake Superior was one of the most interesting. We weren't able to find out much about what it would be like to canoe across that great inland ocean, even though it had been one of the major topics of our conversations for more than a week. Our biggest concerns were not the hardships or dangers, but how long it would take. People talked about being stormbound out there for a week at a time, but then they hadn't been across it in a two-man canoe. During our stay in the Soo waves up to fifteen feet were reported, and that made it a little tough to be optimistic.

6

STORMY LAKE SUPERIOR

> *Be strong, O paddle! Be brave, canoe!*
> *The reckless waves you must plunge into.*
> *Reel, reel on, your trembling keel,*
> *But never a fear my craft will feel.*
>
> — *E. Pauline Johnson (Tekahionwake),*
> ***The Song of my Paddle***

Friday, 14 May

DAY 28

We were excited by the challenge before us as we put our faithful canoe into a protected harbor of Lake Superior waters off the west end of Portage Street. There was much hustle and confusion as strangers and friends arrived to see us off. Apparently our departure time had been broadcast on the radio. We had to pack and repack our gear to make room for about forty pounds of extra food, to get it to fit under our spray cover. We did not want to depend on picking up supplies enroute. My time and distance schedule allowed fifteen days for us to get across that Great Lake, but there was no way of knowing just how long it would take us.

Once again, it was tough to say goodbye to Jenny, my children and our friends, but we had to move on. As we were about to step into the canoe and head out, Ernie Michael from radio station WSOO showed up to cover our departure. This was how the brief interview went:

Announcer: *Verlen Kruger, forty-eight, of DeWitt, Michigan, and Clinton Waddell, thirty-six, of St. Paul, Minnesota, left the West Pier this morning in their twenty-one foot canoe. Ernie Michael was on hand to talk with the men as they put their canoe in the water.*

Michael: *Well, gentlemen, you have completed your first tenth and have many tenths to go. Verlen Kruger, you have a paddle in your hand. How do you feel this morning?*

Verlen: *Ready to roll.*

Michael: *Clint, ready to paddle?*

Clint: *It's time to get going again. It has been nice at the Soo. Some real nice people.*

Michael: *The water this morning is just like a mirror. How do you feel about that?*

Verlen: *Great!*

ONE INCREDIBLE JOURNEY

Michael: Clint Waddell, you have been held up by bad winds off Lake Superior and have been doing a lot of repairing, and supplies have been picked up. How has that aspect been at the Soo?

Clint: We are loaded down, believe you me. We have eight hundred pounds this morning.

Michael: You have the weather with you. You have all of our hopes here at the Soo. Best of luck. What more can we say and why don't we say, gentlemen, "grab the paddles." Well, they are heading down to their twenty-one foot canoe, walking to the water's edge. You hear some noise in the background. Verlen is kissing his wife, Jenny, goodbye for the time being. The rest of the family is waving from near the large homemade family camper. Now the gentlemen are seated. Say goodbye to the listening audience.

Verlen: Goodbye, Soo. You have been good to us.

Michael: There they go! They're off and upward on their journey to the Bering Sea. The time, by my watch, is seven-thirty a.m. Pictures are being taken. We can tell now why they call them "professionals." Look at those paddles work!

Our introduction to Lake Superior was off to a good start. It was a beautiful, warm canoeing day. As strangers with the usual apprehensions and uncertainties, we paddled out into the lake. Later, in the bigger, unprotected part of Superior, we were treated to long, easy swells that gently lifted and lowered us with a rather pleasant, soothing effect. We pushed along steadily all day to take advantage of the weather conditions. During the afternoon we boldly traversed the entrances to both Goulais and Batchawana Bays.

We didn't talk much that first day out. My mind and heart were still partly back in Sault Ste. Marie. About sundown we pulled ashore off Corbeil Point, prepared a hot supper and filled our thermos jugs with boiling hot tea in preparation for paddling on through the night. While the water was heating Clint caught a few minutes' snooze as he sat by the fire. Everything looked good for paddling right on through the night, and we were all for it. We found it hard to believe that the good weather would last.

When we stopped we had been enjoying a light tailwind, but as we put the canoe back into the water it suddenly changed ninety degrees to a brisk wind out of the southwest. Darkness settled in as we headed across Pancake Bay and the wind and waves got steadily worse. Off Pancake Point it became too rough for comfort. As we bounced around in the dark we made a unanimous decision to head back inside Pancake Bay, where we found a protected shore which enabled us to disembark and make camp. Our sleeping giant had awakened! It was after ten p.m. when we crawled into the tent. We were tired, but satisfied. It had been a good day and we had moved fifty-five miles.

Saturday, 15 May

DAY 29

It rained off and on all night and the wind

continued to blow, but snug and dry in our homemade tent we had a good night. By morning the wind and rain had stopped.

By eight o'clock we were paddling out of Pancake Bay toward a threatening sky and rough waters. As we went around Pancake Point it seemed almost as bad as the night before. By nine o'clock, after making only a couple of miles, we were practically blown off the water into Sawpit Bay. By coming around into a rocky inlet, we found enough protection to beach the canoe. The rain clouds had gone away and we enjoyed a sunny but windy day. We climbed the rocks and hills and scouted the surrounding countryside, and after satisfying ourselves we watched in fascination the force and patterns of wind and waves. There seemed to be some kind of rhythm and design to their actions, but I suspected that the exact science of it shall never be fully understood.

The wind had died down enough by mid-afternoon to encourage us to move on, even though it would mean getting wet again. It was hard, rough paddling all afternoon. By early evening, as we approached Point Aux Mines, the wind became stronger and a particularly mean looking storm cloud formation bore down on us out of the northwest. We hurried ashore on the point, pulled the canoe out high up on the shore and secured it by rope to a large rock. Hastily, we put up the tent on a high ledge, where looking out of the tent door downwind we had an exceptional view over Lake Superior. The tent was so well protected by huge boulders and surrounding trees that we would hardly have known that a storm was going on, except for the loud howling of wind and the roar of the white caps and waves crashing ashore.

We had just settled ourselves in the tent when a deluge broke loose. It was an intriguing sight to sit in the tent opening and watch that fantastic display of wind and waves with sheets of rain pouring down, all to the tune of awesome, cannon-ading thunder and blinding flashes of lightning. For some strange reason, I have always immensely enjoyed a monster storm like that, the wilder and fiercer the better. There was something about it that seemed to vibrate me to the very roots of my being.

The storm quickly passed over and the sun came out. Clint and I crawled out of our tent and climbed to a high rock hill where we could look out over the vast inland ocean towards a magnificent setting sun. The view was breathtaking. Off to the distant west we could make out three more distinct storm formations shaping up. Behind us was the dark, ominous mass of storm that had just passed by. Occasional flashes of lightning played through it and a piece of a rainbow uniquely accen-tuated its backside. The sun before us was partially covered with scattered, dark clouds, some fringed with varying degrees of reds and yellows. Rays of the sun streamed through at all angles and cast intricate patterns of light and dark shadows on a still rolling, whitecapped lake. Neither of us spoke for several minutes. What was there to say? We just stood there, looked and absorbed, our senses intoxicated.

Finally, almost in hushed tones, we got around to discussing the weather forecast. "Notice that red cast to those clouds around the sun?" said Clint. "Those cloud formations look like a storm front will be moving through. Most likely we'll have good weather tomorrow."

"Yes, but the front hasn't passed yet and conditions will probably be unstable for the next several hours. So, let's get a good night's sleep. Then we can hit it early in the morning."

"I think those storm formations in the west will miss us. I vote that we move on now. We could move quite a ways before dark." Clint didn't press his point any farther, or we would have been on our way. I think having had our tent already pitched was the deciding factor. Besides, I'd already been wet to the skin twice that day. In white caps and spray the bow of the canoe, where I sat, was much wetter than the stern. In the bow the big stuff would hit you in the face, whereas in the stern it only splashed into your lap.

We made only about twenty miles but it had been a good and satisfying day.

Long after the sun had set and Clint had gone back down to the tent, I lingered on, reluctant to break the spell. All alone then, I felt very close to God. I lifted up my eyes to a still light sky, prayed and enjoyed my God. I enjoyed all His creation and was glad that I belonged to Him.

Sunday, 16 May

DAY 30

We were up and eager to be underway at three o'clock. By taking a look at the wind and waves, we saw that it promised to be a good canoeing day. The lake was moving around some, but there were no white caps. After a hot breakfast, we broke camp and loaded up. By first light we were in the canoe and paddling on toward the north shore.

It was extremely interesting to watch the shoreline of Superior unfold as we paddled along. There was no dull, drab scenery there. It was always changing, always revealing new and exciting formations, bays, inlets and rivers. They were all begging to be explored, but it was good to leave something for next time. At times during the day we were given trouble by the wind, partly created by some of the high mountainous country that often came down to the shore. Between Point Aux Mines and Cape Gargantua we noticed several stretches of sand beach, particularly along the shore near the

Lizard Islands.

We had moved along very well until we rounded Cape Gargantua, where we were hit by some heavy winds and huge waves. We fought our way around the point and by looking on ahead up the shoreline, we saw that the prospect didn't look any better. So, we struggled around into Indian Harbor and found a spot where we could dock our canoe. By then it was five in the afternoon and much too early for quitting, but again, we were blown off the water. We had made about forty-five miles for the day.

We found a nice spot for our camp which was protected from the wind, and it was so situated that we also had a view of Lake Superior by looking between some of the islands in Indian Harbor. Before crawling into our bags we sat around the campfire, wrote in our journals and meditated. Clint said, "Verlen, I'll bet you miss your family at times like these."

"I would like it if they could all be here tonight to enjoy this scenery and our fire. Perhaps sometime in the future, I can come through here with Jenny and my kids. They would sure like to see this, especially if the weather was good."

"They are such nice children," he continued. "Your Christine is such a likeable young lady. How old is she?"

"She's eighteen. She graduates from DeWitt High School this year. I guess she has a steady boyfriend. His name is Richard Jessop."

"Those boys, Jon and Philip, are sure live wires."

"Yup! They've settled down a lot now. You should have seen them when they were growing up. They used to scrap a lot."

"You and Jenny must have had your hands full. How old are those boys now?"

"Well, let's see. Jon is seventeen and Philip is sixteen. Jenny still has plenty to look after, even though the kids are getting pretty well grown up now."

"Those three youngest girls of yours seem like such nice young ladies, too. And that little Sarah; she is really a doll. How old is she?"

"Let's see. I think she is twelve now. Mary must be fourteen, and that makes Debbie fifteen."

"You missed a year between Sarah and Mary," Clint said with a grin.

Chuckling and shaking my head, I responded, "Yes! I guess by then we were beginning to slow down."

"You have some older children, too. Were they also born a year apart?"

"Well, more or less. Our oldest is Nancy. She's married to Terry Norris who works for me in the plumbing business. I think she's twenty-one. Then there are our two older boys, who also help in my business. David is twenty and his wife is Carol. Daniel is nineteen and single, but he's dating a fine young lady by the name of Kathie McNeilly."

"Your plumbing business must be going well if you have two sons and a son-in-law working for you."

"Yes. It has been good to us. My brother, Lawrence Kruger, is in charge of our business this summer. He is now a Master Plumber."

"Gee! I sure do miss my children," Clint said. "I hardly ever get to see them anymore, since my wife left me."

"That's too bad. How long have you two been separated?"

"Nearly two years!"

"That has to be rough! It must be especially hard on your four children. They're still quite young aren't they?"

"Yes. I wish I could spend more time with them. Carla is ten, Kim is nine, John is seven and little Christopher is five. I know it's not good for children to have to grow up without a father.

I sure hope that they will make out all right.

"I didn't tell you before Verlen, but I seem to be getting serious about a lady I know in Minneapolis. At least, I think about her a lot of the time, if that means anything."

"It sure does! Is that why you're so quiet sometimes? What's her name?"

"Beverly Renko. She's a receptionist for the Dorsey law firm in Minneapolis. I called her from the Soo on Thursday night. She told me that she was lonesome and that she really misses me. I asked her to drive up to International Falls and meet us when we get there. I sure hope she can. I would really like to see her."

"That would be nice. Jenny's planning to meet us there too, providing I can give her enough advance notice of our estimated time of arrival."

"Good! I hope it all works out for both of us."

We crawled into the sleeping bags to the tune of the howling winds and crashing waves.

Monday, 17 May

DAY 31

Some time during the night the wind let up. So, again we were up early and were on the water before five. There was very little wind and the lake had settled down. As we paddled along, heading toward huge Michipicoten Bay, we kept looking across to the far north shore, which looked deceptively close because of its high, mountainous terrain. After about two hours, as we passed Cape Chaillon, we talked about making a traverse instead of going all the way into the bottom of Michipicoten Bay.

We moved past Old Woman Bay and neared Brule Point. The lake was calm and the weather condi-

97

tions appeared stable. We checked our maps and decided that the prominent high point that so attracted us along the north shore and to our left was Bare Summit, just twenty miles away. It would take us four hours of steady, healthy paddling, so we hesitated. It just didn't look that far. We both wanted to make the crossing but neither of us cared to make the decision. In the midst of our discussion, somehow the canoe got pointed towards Bare Summit.

It was a clear and nearly cloudless day. For three hours everything went great and we felt good about cutting off the bay. Then I happened to notice that way out in the distance near the horizon a dark line was appearing. It stretched across the lake and across Michipicoten Island to our southwest. As time went on the line moved closer. From previous experience in watching wind effects on lakes, I knew it was a squall line. In the gentle breeze and mild waves, the water all around us had a shininess to the surface. However, out beyond the squall line the water was rough and dark, with strong winds. As it moved nearer and nearer, the effect became almost weird. We paddled along in a gentle crosswind from the northeast. The squall line approached us from the southwest, but the winds within it were from out of the northwest and in between us and the squall line was a dead calm, made evident by a narrow band of shiny water. Back under the squall itself we could see huge, dancing waves and hear the roar, as of a hundred rapids, from the mean looking white caps and the windblown sprays. As interesting as it was to watch, that was no place for us to be.

We were still several miles from shore. We turned slightly and raced for the nearest land, heading as much as we could away from the squall. It hit us nearly a mile from shore. Surprisingly the waves hit us first, then the winds.

Fortunately, it wasn't as bad as it looked. I

think it was weakened by the high hills we were heading for. As we neared shore we became concerned as to where we could land the canoe. There was too much surf and waves to safely get ashore. Then to our relief, we spotted a small, rocky island that partially protected a lovely sand beach, thus enabling us to put ashore on the beach. It was early afternoon when we pulled our canoe up on dry land about a mile east of the University River. We were wet but grateful. The beach made a splendid place to camp. We were at one end of a one hundred foot wide sandy beach that stretched off in a curve for about a quarter of a mile. Back of the beach, up a six-foot cut bank, was a flat, heavy wooded shelf in which we found a clearing to pitch our tent.

We immediately gathered firewood and built a fire on the beach to dry out and get a hot meal in a wind protected spot. We were windbound for the rest of the day. Late in the afternoon it rained for awhile. Sometime during the night the storm let up. We must have made thirty miles that day, and perhaps we learned a little bit more about canoemanship and Lake Superior.

About fifteen miles to the east of us the Michipicoten River issued into the bottom of Michipicoten Bay. Up that river, by way of the Missinabi River, is the shortest canoe route from Lake Superior to Hudson Bay, a distance of about five hundred miles, with eighty-some rapids, falls and portages. It is not a tourist route, but was frequently used by the fur traders. It was the route which Clint and I had travelled as a final test run for the "Big One" in 1970.

From our campsite, along the shoreline to Marathon nearly one hundred miles away, then inland from forty to fifty miles, is some of the most wild, rugged and inaccessible country of the Lake Superior coast. The area is known as the Ontario High Country, the highest, most mountainous country in all of Ontario. Even the roads and railroads go around it. Several small Indian settlements are located inland just off Highway Seventeen, and a few trapper's shacks can be found along some of its many rivers and lakes. At one time there were a couple of lumber camps on the bigger rivers. These have all but disappeared and only seem to add to the mystery and enchantment of the area. Very wild and remote, there are probably still some high, rocky hills on which no white man has ever set foot. Much of this area has been set aside as the Pukaskwa National Park. The weather and vegetation along this section were more noticeably Arctic than the rest of Lake Superior. I was utterly fascinated. This was my kind of country. I vowed to return, and much to my satisfaction and pleasure I have cruised this section of the coast a couple of times since, once all alone in a homemade one-man canoe, but that would make another story.

Just west of where we were camped the University River makes a spectacular fast drop into the lake. About a mile and a half upstream is Denison Falls, one of the most beautiful falls in Canada. On the map, four fifty-foot contour lines crossed here, making a total drop of around two hundred feet as it cascaded through a long "S" turn in two major falls. One mile west of the University River is lovely Dog Harbor with a fine sand beach, all very neatly protected by a narrow, rocky mouth.

Tuesday, 18 May

DAY 32

The tent flapped and rattled all night from the wind gusts. It was still rough and stormy as we broke camp and paddled out at about seven-thirty. We headed west, tight along the shore, and the coastline got higher, more rugged and closer to the water. The wind and waves whipped up more and more. Not far from Point Isacor we pulled ashore in a small rocky cove nestled in huge rock hills that went almost straight up from the shore. It got a little too rough. Ahead for miles was nothing but a sheer cliff and the waves looked even worse than before. It could be a trap. The wind seemed to be undecided, for it continuously shifted around. We built a fire to dry out while we bolstered our courage, hoping that the wind would change for the better. We were windbound until early afternoon. Following our usual exploration of the area, we made use of the time to fix an early dinner of pancakes.

The wind had now changed to a strong tailwind, but it was debatable whether the waves were less dangerous. Still, it was all the encouragement we needed. We hopped into our canoe and enjoyed a fast, wet ride as we held tight to the cliffs and dodged occasional boulders. Once around Point Isacor, the hills broke the wind except for unusual down draft crosswinds that came roaring down the ravines and valleys out of the mountains and into the lake. They created an agitated path of white caps and spray.

In some cases the off-shore wind would be sufficient to make white caps within fifty feet of the shore. Sometimes those crosswinds would blow waves right across our canoe, and of course, they got us wet.

One time, as we rounded a point and headed shoreward to get inside of a little bay, we headed directly into one of the strong down draft winds. Right at that moment a particularly violent gust hit us. It picked up spray and blew it into our faces like a heavy horizontal downpour of rain and slowly filled our canoe with water. The hood of my nylon windbreaker snapped in the gale force wind like the crack of a bull whip. We paddled hard, but to my surprise I noticed that we were being blown backward past the point that we had just rounded. We leaned into the paddles with all our might, and inch by inch slowly gained the calmer water. We continued on to shore, where we landed, dumped the water out of the canoe and in the shelter of woods, built a fire to dry out. Apparently these exceptional winds were caused by the high mountainous terrain close to the lakeshore. Most likely a cold, Arctic air mass was moving into the area at the same time.

"Wow! It's a good thing we had the power to make it into here," said Clint.

"That's for sure! This shoreline seems to have a surprising number of exceptionally nice little harbors, bays and coves."

Towards evening we found ourselves paddling into another rain storm. Before ten o'clock we decided that we'd had enough, so we pulled into a small cove to make camp. That was one of the poorest spots we had ever camped in. The protected shoreline was nothing but a huge bank of rocks varying between the size of a small egg and the size of a softball, interspersed with a little gravel, but in the darkness we couldn't find any other place to pitch our tent. We were cold, wet and weary. On ahead around the point, the pile up of waves appeared vicious so we would have to make that place do. The tent pegs wouldn't hold, so we found large rocks to hold the tent corners and guy ropes. In the darkness we had to feel around and try to throw out the larger rocks and to rearrange the smaller ones to make a sleeping spot. In strong gusts of wind and driving rain, we somehow managed to get it all together and crawled inside the tent for a well earned night's rest.

That four-inch foam pad of mine was worth its weight in gold that night as I slept very comfortably on the lumpy pile of rocks. I have never been more pleased with a piece of equipment. That pad was pure luxury in the wilderness, contributing immensely to my overall morale, and giving vital comfort at times when I needed it the most.

Gusts of wind continued to flap and rattle our tent throughout the night, interspersed with pelting rain. It only served to make our sleep all the sweeter. We were then about five miles from Otterhead and must have moved about forty miles that day.

Wednesday, 19 May

DAY 33

About seven o'clock the rain stopped; then, just as we crawled out of our tent, the wind blew it down. The wind velocity dropped as we ate a cold breakfast of canned peaches and leftover pancakes. Then we loaded everything into the canoe, still wet, and by the time we started paddling a fog had rolled in. It was tricky to identify islands from points or to tell where we were. We stayed about a canoe length off shore and zigged and zagged with every crook and turn of the shoreline. We had to stay alert for boulders or abrupt changes in direction. Sometimes sudden, violent maneuvers were necessary to avoid collisions with those boulders.

By the time we arrived at Otterhead the fog had lifted, but visibility was still limited. Later in the day we were plagued by mean crosswinds. It was one of those days not meant for canoeing. Otterhead was considered the halfway point from the Soo to Thunder Bay. On the northwest end of Otter Island was a well manned, meticulously kept lighthouse.

On a channel between Otter Island and another small island to the north was an old commercial fishing camp which was being used by four men. Later, we learned that all four of them drowned a few miles south of there in a big storm a couple of years after we had passed through.

Shortly after lunch we passed Simons Harbor, a designated shelter for big freighters in time of storm. Even the big ones get off the lake when it really acts up!

By mid-afternoon huge swells came in off Superior and the wind was kicking up white caps and spray. It made the going wet and tough. A chain of islands gave some protection until just past White Gravel River. There, the heavy swells crashed up against the high, rocky shoreline in a fearsome manner. We were in that awkward situation of wanting to get off the water very badly, but not daring to get even close to land. Finally we came around a small, rocky point and spotted a cove that offered protection by the way it wrapped back around the point. We were practically blown off the water and into the shelter. We made a tricky landing, as the only piece of shore available that would accommodate our canoe was covered with several feet of ice-hard snow.

It was not a likely campsite. We were in a narrow, rocky gulley at the foot of a cliff. There was no flat spot for a tent. Clint made a tent base out of pulpwood logs that had washed ashore. He built it over the hard snow and rocks. Under the center of the tent base, a little rivulet flowed, from the melting ice and snow higher up the gulley. We had an early, hot supper. Then, taking my personal bag, Clint and I climbed the nearest high rock hill. On top of the hill we found a wind sheltered rock ledge where we had an exceptional view of the surrounding country, including a breathtaking panorama of the coastline for many miles up and down the shore. It was a soul-stirring interlude as we took time for church services. We read a few chapters from the Bible, prayed, worshipped the Lord and enjoyed our own private vesper services, just as the setting sun disappeared behind the distant, jagged mountain peaks.

Another day was done, and we felt good about it all. We had made twenty-five miles that day. The setting sun, however, did not promise anything better for the morrow. Once again, that four-inch foam pad proved its worth, as I spent a comfortable night sleeping on Clint's corrugation of pulp logs.

Thursday, 20 May

DAY 34

We were on the water by four and got off to a good, early start. The big wave action had died down to let us move on, but we still had a pretty frisky wind. We hoped that with an early start we could get in some mileage before the wind picked up again, but by six it whipped up so badly that we turned into Oiseau Bay for shelter. We landed at the southeast end of a beautiful, one-half-mile-long sand beach. We didn't make camp, as we hoped that the wind would let up and allow us to move on. Instead, the velocity picked up more and more.

Hundreds of eight-foot long pulpwood logs were scattered about the beach, most of them fifty to one hundred feet from the water's edge. The farther north we advanced along the lakeshore, the more logs we found. We used some for cooking and drying fires. Clint made a lean-to shelter with the logs. Then he stretched out his pad behind them and caught a siesta in preparation for paddling all night, providing the wind velocity dropped.

I found an old trail that led inland and back to a couple of small lakes. Later I followed a wolf's tracks along the shore until I lost them in the heavy forest. I also found plenty of bear and moose signs. Windbound days were always busy days. It was a time to reorganize our packs, do cleaning, mending, fixing and of course, to do my "office" work. That consisted of checking maps, catching up in the journal, writing letters home and doing the bi-monthly newsletter. Sometimes it got to be a chore, but I felt it was a necessary one.

"With all of this lousy weather, we are not going to establish any records for crossing this big lake," Clint said as he walked over to see what progress I was making.

"That's for sure," I replied. "The records show that back in July of 1793 a fur trader by the name of John McDonald, with fourteen paddlers in a Montreal canoe, raced from the Soo to Grand Portage in only seven and a half days. They carried less than a half load of freight and were wind bound only one day. That was really moving a canoe."

"It sure was! We've already been at it for seven days and we're only about half way to Grand Portage."

As the sun went down, there was no let up in the wind and no sign that we would be able to paddle that night. Reluctantly, we pitched our tent and turned in to be prepared for an early start the next morning. As we crawled into our sacks, we talked about being prepared for two days of non-stop paddling if wind and weather conditions became favorable, rather than fight for mileage on those nasty days. We had only made about eight miles that day.

Friday, 21 May

D A Y   3 5

We finally crawled out of our warm bags at five-thirty and found a cold morning. The water in the tea pot was frozen solid and the spray covers were frozen stiff. Earlier in the morning the sound of the surf seemed quite loud, so I was slow to get up. The wind had died down to a reasonable breeze, but the waves were slow in letting up. It didn't look like the best day for paddling, but we had been windbound for twenty-four hours so it was time to move on.

Within the hour we launched the canoe. There was still a respectable surf that rolled onto the beach and gave us the problem of how to break through without getting wet. After much consideration we engineered some pulpwood logs to be used as rollers on the beach, then put the canoe on top of them with the bow heading into the surf. We then loaded the canoe, buttoned the spray cover down tight, put on full rain gear, timed the waves to catch the smallest ones and made a mad rush to get off the beach and out beyond the breakers without swamping. As the canoe rumbled down our log roller ramp I jumped into the bow and pulled the spray skirt up around my waist, while Clint continued to push from the stern. When the canoe dropped off the last log, he jumped in and we paddled furiously. It worked, and we were on our way.

It was thirty-eight miles nearly straight north up the coast to the pulp mill town of Marathon. We planned to make this our only settlement stop on Lake Superior, providing we passed by during business hours. Otherwise we would keep on moving, as stopping was not essential to our plans or to our supplies. After paddling for about an hour that cloudy morning, the wind picked up and the waves began to whitecap and big swells developed as the day wore on. It became a hard, roller coaster day of paddling into a heavy headwind. On those kind of days, we leaned into it and pulled just a little harder on the paddles to keep up the mileage. The shoreline was still rugged and mountainous, and it kept the day interesting.

The sun came out late in the afternoon. The wind was from the north and we could smell the sulfur from the pulp mills of Marathon from thirty miles out. From almost that far away, we could see the high, round mountain that jutted out into the lake. The town was located at its base. That mountain became the landmark that told us exactly where the town was, long before we could see it.

It had been slow going for several days with the kind of hard work that took a lot of energy for us to make headway. As we neared Marathon, the paddling improved for the wind and waves began to calm down. It was about four-thirty that afternoon when we paddled up to the shore of the settlement. We were thankful to be there.

Below a thirty-foot cutbank, we pulled the canoe out on a pebble beach and got wet during the process. On top of the cutbank we found ourselves on the edge of town. We learned from some kids that the laundromat was not open. We had hoped to dry out a few of our wet things, so then we spread our damp clothing on the beach to dry. We walked the mile and a half to the business section. There we found a restaurant, ate a big meal, bought a little grub and made a phone call back home to set a date for arrival at International Falls.

Shortly after eight that same evening, we pushed off the pebble beach. While sliding through the surf, we managed to get everything wet that we had just dried out. It was that old, familiar, eternal struggle of trying to keep dry in a canoe! At Marathon the Lake Superior shoreline made a ninety degree turn to the west. We paddled off into the setting sun, with no thought of stopping. I don't recall that we even discussed the subject that day. Wind and weather permitting, we would paddle all night. The weather signs prophesied bad weather for the next day. The wind at that time was only a gentle crosswind out of the north. We got some protection from being close to the north shore. The big swells continued to roll as darkness settled in. That gave us an uneasy feeling, for we couldn't see the waves coming that lifted the canoe up and down.

After a couple of hours, as we moved through Thompson Channel and passed Pic Island, the swells disappeared. From there it was very good paddling on a clear, starlit night, and we found it enjoyable to keep right on going. There was no moon, and when occasional patches of fog blanked out the shoreline, we switched to navigating by the stars. It was an awesome feeling as we gazed up at the universe and began to feel ourselves a part of it all. We were just two people, two specks on the planet Earth, paddling on and on through the seemingly vast and immeasurable distance of endless time. Added to that was the amazing wonder that I felt, because I knew the Maker of it all and I knew that He knew me! Some people might have called it a religious experience; I called it worship.

Saturday, 22 May

DAY 36

Time had little meaning way out there, and even less so at night. Sometime after midnight it began to get cold. The splash on the spray covers froze.

At about two o'clock in the morning we pulled ashore on a flat, gravelled beach of an island, to get a good, hot meal. We built a large fire, and we made a kettle of stew and a pot of hot tea. We felt warm and comfortable, and we cat-napped, first while sitting on a log, then while lying on a tarp on the gravel beside the fire. We toasted on one side and froze on the other! We didn't oversleep that way. Fifteen to twenty minutes of it and we found that we'd rather be paddling.

We resumed our journey at four. Once again, we were treated to the incomparable magic of watching the first rays of dawn. It slowly got brighter and brighter, until the red ball of the sun came up above the distant horizon to herald the beginning of the new day.

We stopped for a hot breakfast on a rocky point near the town of Terrace Bay. By the time we re-embarked, the wind had started up again. At first it was a welcomed tailwind, but it soon switched to a strong crosswind out of the southeast. Coming from that angle, it meant that before long it probably would chase us off the lake. The waves grew higher and higher. When we came to Schreiber Channel we decided to take the passage inside of Nipigon Bay where a long chain of islands would give us protection from the wind. It was about fifteen miles farther that way, but it turned out to be a wiser decision than we knew at first. We were able to keep going all day in the midst of the developing storm.

The vegetation on the bay side of those islands grew right down to the water, in contrast to the Lake Superior side where no vegetation grew for twenty to thirty feet above the water level because of the fierce storms. The mouth of Nipigon Bay is almost blocked off by islands which were separated by fairly long channels. As we crossed the channels between Copper, Wilson, Salter, Simpson and St. Ignace Islands, we were blasted by heavy crosswinds which funneled in off the lake. Each crossing got us a little more wet. The last and longest of these islands was St. Ignace, which is about fifteen miles long.

In the late afternoon, as we paddled tight along the north shore of St. Ignace, we were surprised to find ourselves blessed with a brisk tailwind from the east. With the good came the bad. The rain that had threatened all afternoon began to fall. After a few miles, the waves picked up into a pretty good roll which travelled just a little faster than we did. Those big swells came up under the stern, lifted it up and started us surfing as the wave moved on under us. We played the game too, and paddled harder to hold the surf as long as possible. The next thing we knew, we were racing full speed to see if we could keep up with it. For nearly a half hour we really had that canoe moving. Sometimes, on a big wave, we could almost keep up with it. We got a long, fast ride before it slipped under us and let us down into the trough. It was crazy, for we had paddled thirty-eight hours and had moved one hundred and fifteen miles since our last camp. We had been cold, wet, miserable and very tired only a few minutes before. Then, we raced the wind and the waves, and enjoyed it. We no longer felt tired. It was just the thing we needed to make our hearts pump harder and faster, to force the circulation of blood through tired muscles, and to stimulate our bodies. We both remarked how good it made us feel. To sprint like that to make the heart beat faster was part of a long distance, marathon canoe racer's strategy. It pumped some life back into a dead tired body.

We were better than halfway around St. Ignace Island and had only a few more miles before we would head out into the full force of the storm, so we started to look for a good campsite. As we rounded Burnt Point we found an ideal spot, well sheltered from the wind. It was a good, sand beach with some flat, level ground back in the trees to pitch a tent on. We pulled ashore at six p.m. and prepared an appreciated, hot meal just before the deluge of rain set in.

It was with great satisfaction that we crawled into our sacks early that evening for a well-deserved rest. We went to sleep to the soothing lullaby of the wind in the trees, the rain on the tent and the surf lapping on the shore only a few feet away.

7

NO PLACE
FOR GREENHORNS

> *Dark behind it rose the forest*
> *Rose the black and gloomy pine-trees,*
> *Rose the firs with cones upon them;*
> *Bright before it beat the water,*
> *Beat the clear and sunny water,*
> *Beat the shining Big-Sea-Water.*
>
> — *Henry Wadsworth Longfellow,*
> **The Song of Hiawatha**

Sunday, 23 May

DAY 37

My built-in alarm clock went off as usual at four in the morning. The sound of heavy wind howling through the trees and a steady, driving rain beating on the tent kept me from waking my partner. The storm had continued throughout the night without let up.

Finally, a little before nine we decided to get up and face the facts of life. We had a cold breakfast inside the tent consisting of orange

juice, a can of peaches and bread and peanut butter. Soon we were ready to go. We embarked and
paddled on along the northwest shore of St. Ignace
Island with the wind coming at us from the south-
southeast.

Clint and I both had trouble with our hands
swelling and the circulation being cut off so that
we had to take aspirin in the middle of the night.
One hundred and fifteen miles straight through,
with some of it very difficult paddling, seemed to
be too much for our hands, especially when we had
already been pushing it. This was a price we were
willing to pay to make extra mileage when conditions allowed. We never did let our hand problems
slow us down for they always improved when we got
back to a normal sixteen-hour day.

While lying in our bags that morning and analyzing the situation, we were sure from the direction of the wind that we would not be able to
travel outside the protection of the islands. We
hadn't been too anxious to break camp in the rain
and paddle off into that storm. But after nearly
twelve hours, a cold, wet tent is no great comfort
either! The day was made interesting by an unusual
display of unpredictable, weird winds, sometimes
mean and violent and sometimes coming from every
direction, but by paddling close to shore we usually were able to avoid the worst of them. It was
almost unbelievable the way the wind could come so
strongly from two different directions in so short
a distance. At one point as we were paddling in a
strong tailwind, with whitecaps and spray blowing
ahead of us, we crossed a narrow channel between
islands where a fierce headwind howled through. It
blew wicked whitecaps and spray right in front of
us. The place where these two strong currents of
wind and the paths of waves and whitecaps converged
out in Nipigon Bay is hard to describe. They
created a kind of "no man's land" of crazy water,
dancing waves and swirling sprays.

ONE INCREDIBLE JOURNEY

With our spray covers buttoned down, we gritted our teeth and paddled on through, as we didn't want to be stuck there. Fortunately, it was only a short distance or we would have swamped. As it was, we took on a lot of water and got pretty wet. We came to the end of our chain of islands then headed southerly down the east side of Nipigon Straits, right into a strong, wet headwind. In those vicious gusts, the wind-driven rain and spray hit me in the face so hard that I would have to close my eyes, as I pulled even harder on the paddle to keep from being blown backwards. The next few miles were difficult, heavy paddling.

A few miles from the open lake where Nipigon Channel forks, we crossed the channel for about one mile to get to the mainland shore. The wind really howled up Blind Channel and big rollers from Lake Superior made themselves felt. It was a rough, wet, violent crossing. About midway, I would have liked to have changed my mind, but it was too late for that.

After crossing Blind Channel, we headed southwest down Nipigon Strait, and to our amazement we suddenly were in a strong tailwind. We continued down the shore close to the mainland and when we entered the narrow channel between Moss Island and the shore, the high, wooded banks made it quite calm. We paddled on through to take a look out into open Lake Superior, and it was awesome!

By then it was five p.m. and we had moved twenty-two miles on another supposedly windbound day, so we didn't feel too bad about turning around and paddling back a mile or so to a spot in Moss Channel called Moss Harbor, where three commercial fishing boats were anchored, also waiting out the storm. This was our first real hint of how huge that storm really was. We never carried a radio, so we had no contact with news or information about the outside world. In fact, we didn't really want any.

We pulled ashore on the mainland near an old, abandoned trapper's shack, with broken down floor and hardly any roof. It was of no use to us. We pitched our tent nearby and made a wet, soggy camp. Neither wind nor rain had let up all day long, not for a minute.

We'd take time later to visit our neighbors anchored nearby. Our first concern was to make camp and get a fire going, and to get a hot meal before the inevitable chill hit us. Now that we had stopped paddling and were soaked to the skin, we would soon feel the cold. It was difficult to start a fire. All the best wood had been used in that area, and what we could find was thoroughly wet. Under the circumstances, it gave me a brief moment's satisfaction to accomplish my usual "one match fire." Supper was a pot of Lipton's beef vegetable soup, with a can of ham and rice and hot tea. Cooking over a camp fire in a rain storm is not likely to be habit-forming.

Darkness was settling in, and in spite of the fire we were becoming increasingly miserable in our wet clothes. It felt great to crawl into our warm dry sleeping bags, snug and secure, with not a care in the world that couldn't wait until morning. The patter of rain and the wind howling through the treetops were all the tranquilizer I needed. Those were the kind of nights when I slept best.

Monday, 24 May

DAY 38

The storm was still raging when we finally crawled out of the tent around nine-thirty. There had been no let-up in either wind or rain. There were puddles of water standing inside the tent and everything was wet. When we walked on the tent floor the ground underneath was soft, and the floor fabric sank nearly to our ankles with each step. "This sure isn't one of our better days for paddling," I quipped.

"I'm afraid we're stranded here for the day," Clint replied. "How in the world are we going to get a fire started in this rain?"

"We'll make it, some way. Let's get out there and see what we can do."

As we stood in front of the tent in our rain suits and damp clothes, trying to decide how to get a fire going so that we could prepare a hot meal, a short, stocky, middle-aged man walked down the trail along the shore.

"I'm Charlie McDonald," he said. "I'm the lighthouse keeper at Lamb Island."

We introduced ourselves and he invited us to his houseboat that was tied up to a couple of large trees two hundred yards away.

We made only feeble, polite protests at imposing on his hospitality, as we hurriedly threw together some grub along with the cook gear and griddle. We followed him back through the dripping trees along the high banked shore to his steel hulled, converted ex-tugboat, with its nice, warm, dry cabin.

We immediately liked Charlie! On his very small, cast iron wood burning cooking stove, we soon produced a combination breakfast-dinner of pancakes and more pancakes.

"How far is Lamb Island from here?" Clint asked.

"Only a couple of miles, but it's out in the mouth of Nipigon Straits. I was stranded here by this storm and I can't get back out there until it blows itself out."

While we wolfed down our meal, Charlie brought us up to date on the storm. The winds were up to fifty miles per hour, and four inches of rain had fallen so far, washing out roads in the Nipigon area. Someone in Ft. William reported ducks swimming in their back yard! Charlie's latest radio report said it was one of the worst rain storms ever recorded for that area, closing schools, vacating homes and closing roads. Looking out the cabin window after dinner, we saw the rain had increased and was blowing across the channel in sheets. Many trees had fallen along the shore. Their roots had been loosened by the rain, and they were toppled by the wind.

We told Charlie about our trip. He seemed interested, but we also noticed that he frequently shook his head as we talked about it. Later in the afternoon we visited with the other stranded fishermen.

Still later we went ashore and helped Charlie cut up a supply of spruce firewood for his small stove. Then we hiked down the shore about a quarter mile, with a gaff hook, to a small creek where Charlie had spotted some suckers spawning a couple of days before. They weren't there, but Charlie promised us he'd pull one of his nets in the harbor the next day to give us all the fish we could eat. He was also a part-time commercial fisherman.

There was no let-up in the steady wind-driven rain during the day. Towards evening we were dreading going back to our cold, wet, soggy tent for the night, when Charlie insisted that we go get our sleeping bags and hole up in the cabin with him. It was only a small, one man cabin with one bunk, but we gladly accepted.

Clint was able to fix up a place on a foot locker and some boxes. I placed my foam pad on the narrow aisle floor and slept there. All of us had to go to bed at the same time and get up at the same time or somebody would get stepped on, but it was pure luxury for Clint and me at a time like that.

DAY   39

The storm continued without let-up of rain or wind. Charlie untied the boat from the shore and took us for a boat ride out beyond the protection of the islands, to see if he could get back to his lighthouse on Lamb Island. That gave us a taste of Lake Superior in a storm. Huge swells were cresting with the wind blowing spray off the top. We unanimously agreed it was not canoeing weather, but we also thought that the wind was not quite as strong as it had been. It was still too rough to get into the lighthouse dock, so Charlie took us back to one of his gill nets and pulled in just enough net to take ten big whitefish.

We ate fish all the rest of the day and we really stuffed ourselves. Charlie showed us an easy, simple way to prepare the fish. "You just gut them out, cut off their heads and throw them in a pot of boiling water with plenty of salt," he said. That didn't sound too good, but they sure tasted great. We fried up more fish than we knew what to do with.

Charlie was a pretty good storyteller. He'd been around quite a lot, and it was interesting to hear some of his experiences. Mostly as a sailor, he had done a lot of commercial fishing. He'd been all over Lake Superior, Alaska, most of Canada and the United States. It was interesting to learn that all of those lighthouses had microwave telephones.

Towards evening, the wind seemed to be letting up or changing directions. It was hard to tell, back in that channel-harbor. Also, the rain showed signs of lessening, as it was becoming more intermittent. That was all the encouragement we needed to make plans for an early morning take-off. Three days of heavy rain and wind ought to be about all there could be in one storm.

Shortly after dark the rain stopped, and some time near midnight it cleared up and the stars came out. Charlie kept advising us to wait another day, saying it takes the lake a while to calm down and there were some treacherous bays to traverse. But two days of inactivity had made us restless and anxious to be moving on. I set my mental alarm for three in the morning.

Wednesday, 26 May

DAY 40

It was still dark when we rolled out at three. After a hurried breakfast, we packed our food and gear down the muddy, slippery trail to our canoe, in the semi-darkness of pre-dawn. We couldn't thank our good friend Charlie McDonald enough for his exceptional hospitality to a couple of bedraggled, cold, wet, hungry paddlers who were much in need of a friend. Shaking the water out of our tent, we packed up the canoe and were under way before five.

It was good to be back on the water, although we were somewhat apprehensive about what Lake Superior might be like. The morning was clear and cool, and the wind had lost some of its velocity and shifted to the west. As we paddled out into the lake, some pretty big swells were still crashing into the ragged, rocky shore, but it really wasn't too bad. During the first part of the day in traversing some deep bays, the heavy offshore crosswind came funnelling out into the lake and gave us a hard time. We were concerned about traversing Black Bay, but the wind continued to die down as the day wore on, and the ten mile crossing of that bay went fairly well.

It was about one hundred and ten miles to Grand Portage, and the good Lord willing, that would be our next stop. We pushed steadily on but still took time to enjoy things of interest, such as scouting out an old, abandoned shack on an unnamed island. At about that time, I was beginning to be bothered by a sore throat and head cold, and wondered if I might have picked up a flu bug back at Marathon.

In the afternoon, off in the distance and ahead of us, we had a good, long view of the "Sleeping Giant" that the early voyageurs always watched for. It is a formation of high hills that did look remarkably like their name. We made it to Thunder Bay just before sundown and stopped to have supper on Thunder Cape Point. About fifteen miles straight across the bay we could make out lights and high points of the city of Thunder Bay, Ontario. The waters had calmed considerably, with only an occasional gentle swell coming in off the lake.

At about ten p.m., we pushed off on the six-mile traverse of Thunder Bay to Pie Island. What does it feel like to have a big freighter bearing down on you out of the night, miles from shore? We were soon to know. About midway in the traverse we suddenly noticed a brightly lit ore boat coming in off the lake. In the darkness it looked as though we were in the dead center of its route. It was difficult to judge how fast it was traveling or to be sure just which way w should go to get out of its path. We had a few uneasy moments till we saw that by keeping on our course, it would miss us. As it crossed our stern we stopped paddling and watched it for nearly ten minutes. It was heading for the city of Thunder Bay. We wondered if they even knew we existed or if their radar had picked us up. What kind of frantic moments they might have had trying to locate such a small blip in the darkness. It was a beautiful but cold, starlit night, and it was rather enjoyable just paddling on and on.

DAY 41

Around two a.m. we pulled ashore on the southwest end of Pie Island, built a large fire and prepared a hot meal. We stretched out our foam pads and sleeping bags on the gravel beach beside the fire and slept for about an hour. We had to use our jackets and gloves to keep warm, as it was one of the coldest nights we had on the journey. Ice formed along the shore. It took a little self-discipline from both of us to get out of those warm sleeping bags and get going again after only one hour's sleep. But we were psyched up by an impossible goal and we were willing to do whatever had to be done to accomplish it. Strangely, we were getting immense satisfaction out of even the hardest parts.

At four-thirty we were paddling along on mirror-flat water, when we were surprised to find ourselves paddling noisily through fresh frozen skim ice. This part of Lake Superior was freezing over! For nearly an hour we paddled through patches of ice, until the rising sun and a gentle breeze broke it up.

There is something special about paddling along in a canoe and watching the first rays of dawn and the first peek of the red fireball of the sun coming up over the lake. It kind of grabs you in the gut and makes you feel a part of something much greater than yourself.

We were now less than forty miles from Grand Portage. That last day turned out to be the best day we had on Lake Superior, a sunny day with gentle breezes, and it was ideal for canoeing.

At two-thirty in the afternoon we pulled into the dock at the reconstructed fort of Grand Portage. It certainly was a most welcome sight.

"Hooray!" Clint yelled, waving his cap over his head.

"We've made it!" I responded.

I am sure that's how hundreds of fur traders and travelers must have felt in years gone by as they rounded Hat Point for their first glimpse of the fur trading post a few miles across the bay. It was nice to leave Lake Superior on friendly terms.

Phil Pemberton was supposed to meet us there, as it was a key point for his movie, but he didn't show up that afternoon. We made inquiries and found that he'd been there that morning. We decided we would stay overnight and if he didn't show up by the following morning we'd proceed on our way and let him catch us wherever he could. We pitched a nice, comfortable camp inside the fort, on the first green grass we'd had on the entire trip. Strangely, the climate seemed to be warmer there. Other vegetation also showed much more advanced greenery than any we had seen all spring.

Personally, I welcomed the chance to rest before starting up the nine-mile-long Grand Portage trail, as I was feeling a little weak from the flu bug. Being there was a good feeling. In the last thirty-three hours since leaving Moss Harbor we had paddled the final one hundred and ten miles to Grand Portage. Crossing Lake Superior in a two-man, homemade canoe was much more than just a canoe trip. It was a magnificent, unforgettable experience that shall be forever indelibly stamped upon my memory by the depth of impression and intensity of feeling that it stirred within me. We had crossed it, but we did not conquer it! It was not changed by us, but we were changed by it! We were the ones who had to adapt to its various moods and make the best of what each day had to offer. I am sure that within a year after we had come and gone, not the slightest sign remained that we had ever been there; not so much as a footprint! Likewise, except where forts had been built, there remains almost no sign of the vast traffic of the fur trade days. Most of the north shore fur trade route shows even less signs of man today than it did two hundred years ago!

Every day was exciting and different, with the weather and the scenery continually changing. Our plans were so at the mercy of the elements that never in my life was I so aware, or so frequently did I say, "If the good Lord is willing, today we will do this or that." In terms of miles, crossing Lake Superior was a mere segment of the Cross Continent Canoe Safari, but the far-reaching impressions it made upon us were immeasurable. It was a valuable contribution to our total canoe experience and I wouldn't want to have missed it.

Coming into Grand Portage must have been a great moment for the early voyageurs as it was for us. The fort at Grand Portage was a key rendezvous point in fur trade history. This was as far as the big thirty-eight foot "Montreal" freight canoes, loaded with trade goods, would go. Here they met the smaller twenty-six foot "north" canoes coming in out of the bush, loaded with furs. After a week or so of transacting business, socializing and swapping stories, each crew would go back to where it came from. The round trip sometimes covered as much as thirty-five hundred miles in one season. This is where the North West Company became a fact during the summer of 1779, while the partners from Montreal met with their wintering partners from the interior, in the great hall. Some of those present that summer were Simon McTavish, William McGillivray, Isaac Todd, James McGill, Alexander Henry, Benjamin and Joseph Frobisher, George McBeath and

ONE INCREDIBLE JOURNEY

Peter Pond.

This fort was a busy place for more than a month each summer, as up to twelve hundred voyageurs came in from Montreal to meet the traders arriving from the north. As the Montrealers entered the main gate, they temporarily left behind the distracting confusion of clerks shouting orders, voyageurs cursing as they shouldered packs and the quiet voices of the Chippewa girls talking in their strange, melodious tongue.

Inside the fort, trade goods were sorted for the various districts, and incoming pelts were examined and checked. In the little countinghouse each newly arrived northman was paid his wages. He scarcely paused long enough to check the amount against his expenses before hurrying off for the treat of rum due each man by tradition, and for the first bread and butter he had tasted since leaving Grand Portage the previous summer.

According to Marjorie Wilkins Campbell, in her book, **The North West Company**, the organization of that concern in 1779—

... was a momentous occasion for the partners concerned. To celebrate, they issued a general invitation to a ball, to be preceded by a dinner for the gentlemen at the post, their former partners and the independent traders with whom they were on friendly terms.

Before the festivities the usual precautions were taken; watches were posted along the gallery to guard against fire, one of the constant hazards in the settlement built entirely of wood. In the early evening the various gentlemen and their young clerks gathered in the great hall, each dressed for the event in his best fawn or grey coat and breeches and bright-hued silk vest. After a pleasant interval of drinking they sat down to a great spread of beef, salt pork, hams, venison and fish, Indian corn, bread and butter and cheese, tea, wine and spirits. A couple of hours later, while they were drinking their final toasts to the "Mother of all the Saints" and to the fur trade, the piper tuned up for the dance while the fiddler plucked at his strings. Soon the great hall was cleared of tables and the chairs moved to one end for the gentlemen. Candles, already placed in the massive candelabra, were lit to complete the festive atmosphere.

Though "the people" had been gathering outside for some time, they filed into the hall slowly and a little shyly at first, awed by the presence of the gentlemen and the bright lights from so many candles. But gradually the large room filled. Older Indians and squaws slip-slapped to places along the walls where they squatted on the floor amid sleeping black-haired papooses propped up in cradles. And then, having at last overcome their diffidence, pork-eaters and northmen poured in, the former in clean shirts and bright hand-woven sashes, the latter in new buckskin shirts and leggings and breechcloths. Indian chiefs sported the red or blue coats provided by the traders as marks of honour, and their tawdry medals. Braves had daubed their chests and faces, and every Chippewa girl wore her finest beaded white tunic, for tonight she would dance with the white men.

The piper and the fiddler struck up the first tune. Each pork-eater and northman pranced to the centre of the crowded room with his graceful partner, there to await the customary signal for the ball to open.

Each year it was the same at balls at the depot. The senior gentleman, probably Simon

McTavish, rose to lead the opening reel. With a gallant bow to the prettiest girl present, a chief's daughter, the proprietor nodded to the fiddler as he led her to the front of the room. The fiddler nodded to the piper. Soon everyone who could, danced reels and squares till the floor was filled with prancing feet.

In our crossing of Lake Superior we found that most maps do not begin to reveal the details and information so vital to a canoeist, nor do they show the wondrous beauty and rugged intricacies of the actual shoreline. Nearly one hundred miles of the coast is lined with imposing, irregular, jagged rock cliffs or mountainous shores. This could be a very treacherous place to be caught in a storm. However, the danger is modified by the numerous harbors, coves and small inlets. There are a few charted harbors for the big boats, but it is profuse in small, beautiful sanctuaries which seem to have been designed just for the protection and delight of small craft such as ours. There is probably not a ten mile stretch along the entire canoe route that a canoe couldn't find refuge.

Where the high country comes up close to the shore, it does fantastic things with the wind! It can come at you from every direction within a few miles. Offshore winds come whistling down the canyons and valleys with hurricane force, foraging a path of their own of foaming white water and spray out into the lake. Nearly one hundred miles of this shoreline has a variety of islands offering a screen of protection for island hopping, and adding immensely to the interest and scenic panorama.

Tip Top Mountain, the highest point in Ontario, twenty-one hundred and twenty feet above sea level, is located in Pukaskwa National Park. About fifteen miles north of Otter Head Island, Tip Top is very close to the lake shore. It is just seven miles inland as the crow flies, or eleven miles by foot, straight east from Simons Harbor. There is no trail. To get there you would have to really want to go. The terrain is one continuous mountain after another. The only signs of traffic on top of Tip Top are a lot of bear signs and a brass survey marker embedded in the rock. There should also be a pint plastic jar tied to a nearby tree with the names and addresses of Steve Landick, of Lansing, Michigan, and myself, if the bears haven't destroyed it. That was the high point of another challenging canoe journey through the Ontario high country and along the coast.

It was on Lake Superior that, motivated by instincts for survival, we became most adept at reading weather signs. Having no other source of information, we were our own self-appointed amateur weather forecasters! Our batting average was as good, or better, than the average professional meteorologist. The experts seem to agree that even during the calmest months of July and August a small craft could expect to be windbound one day out of three. In the more unstable month of May, we managed to do as well, being windbound four and one half days out of thirteen and one half, in spite of getting caught in one of the heaviest rain storms ever recorded in the Nipigon Bay area.

Our strategy for crossing the lake had been to paddle every hour that wind and weather conditions permitted, up to twenty-four hours a day! Only once did we voluntarily quit paddling without having been blown off the water.

The Lake Superior segment of our route was one of the most outstanding and challenging highlights of our journey. It was the type of thing that needs to be experienced in order to be fully understood. It was wild, beautiful, rugged and exhilarating. It continually entertained our senses with a complete gamut of exciting moods and temperaments and with its soothing, tranquil heaving of calm swells on warm, sunny days. It offered a wondrous display of intriguing islands of all sizes and shapes, sometimes somberly clad in misty fog, which artfully adorned a coastline fringed with a fantastic variety of sandy, rocky or cliff-lined mountainous shores.

In contrast, Lake Superior could be frightening in its more violent moods; in howling winds, thunder, lightning and raging storms or cold, drenching rains; in wild, wind-whipped, crashing, rolling seas and towering waves; in steady, pounding, roaring surf upon rocky reefs and sandy beaches; and in awesome crashing and splashing of great waves against huge cliffs and gigantic rock promontories. One careless moment could exact a terrible price. It seemed to say, "The laws of nature have not been repealed. Violators will be prosecuted!" Lake Superior is no respecter of persons. The careless and the foolish are efficiently reduced by the natural process of elimination. Lake Superior is terrific canoe country, but it definitely is **not** a place for the greenhorn, the careless or the daredevil. In its extremely cold waters, an upset a half mile from shore would mean certain death, with or without a life jacket.

We had entered the lake as strangers, apprehensive, cautious and not too sure what kind of reception we would receive. We had found no one who could introduce us or give us any first hand information, but in those two weeks we became well acquainted and we left as respected friends!

8

BOUNDARY WATERS CANOE AREA

> *A light broke in upon my brain,*
> *It was the carol of a bird;*
> *It ceased, and then it came again,*
> *The sweetest song ear ever heard.*
>
> — *George Gordon, Lord Byron,*
> ***The Prisoner of Chillon***

Friday, 28 May

DAY 4 2

It was with a consciousness of history that we slept where the voyageurs slept two hundred years before. It turned out to be a beautiful, warm sunny day but we slept in, waiting for cameraman Phil to show up.

Coming in off Lake Superior was like turning the calendar up about two weeks! Suddenly it was spring! Along with it came the mosquitoes and black flies in swarms, the first we'd seen to that point.

A crew of Indian laborers was building a main building inside the stockade to replace the one that had burned in 1970. The early voyageurs seldom had to pack their canoes over the nine mile Grand Portage trail for in those days there was a fort at each end of the portage where they would leave their canoes. The fort at the Pigeon River end was called Fort Charlotte. Today there is only a monument marker and a nice camp site.

This quote from **The North West Company** explains the manner in which both trade goods and furs were transported over the Grand Portage Trail:

> *For a month during the hottest days of summer, a stream of men trudged the nine-mile track in another of the trade's essential shuttles. Both pork-eaters and northmen carried eight ninety-pound packs according to contract, with a Spanish dollar for each extra pack. Looking like apes, their arms swinging free as they bent under two, and sometimes three, packs held by tump lines across their foreheads, they shuttled up and down; shouldering trade goods up, pelts down, cursing, singing, challenging one another to see who could carry the heaviest loads for the longest distances without a stop.*

A new stockade had recently been reconstructed at old Grand Portage. The surrounding area is Indian reservation land. The main highway bypasses the fort and it seldom gets heavy traffic.

The "official" mileage from Grand Portage to International Falls is given as 243 miles, although I never did find out the exact points measured from, nor the exact route. This could vary considerably. I have carefully measured it many times using various map systems. From the Lake Superior shore to the city dock at International Falls I come up with at least 260 miles.

More recently, using a full set of highly accurate Geological Survey topographical maps at a scale of 1:50,000 and measuring with an expensive surveyor's map measuring wheel, I followed a logical canoe path parallel to the border but much shorter than the exact border, by cutting off the corners. It measured out at 262 miles.

Phil showed up at about eight o'clock and Bob McKee was with him. We spent the entire morning making false runs out into the bay and portage starts, as Phil took pictures. I also called home and made a date with a beautiful, sexy woman for 5 June at International Falls, and I think Clint also called Beverly. We would be passing through fantastic canoe country, but now our minds would be on other things.

At 12:15 p.m. we finally got started down the Grand Portage Trail. The circumstances were unfavorable. I had been fighting a flu bug for several days, in the form of a sore throat and bronchitis, and I was feeling weak and listless.

We started without eating lunch and I went for the rest of the day on two jelly rolls, two candy bars, two cans of pop, and one quart of water from the canteen. Clint had something similar. The Grand Portage Trail itself is a big, open and well maintained path that you could drive a jeep down. It appeared to be used frequently by backpackers or hikers, but seldom does any one carry a canoe down it. There is a back woods car trail leading to just above Partridge Falls and that eases the problem for most canoeists.

In settling the exact boundary between the United States and Canada, it was agreed to follow the voyageurs' highway through the area. A splendid example of good will on the part of two friendly nations was displayed in agreeing to make the route an International Boundary, free and open to the use of citizens and subjects of both countries. This extends from the Lake Superior shore

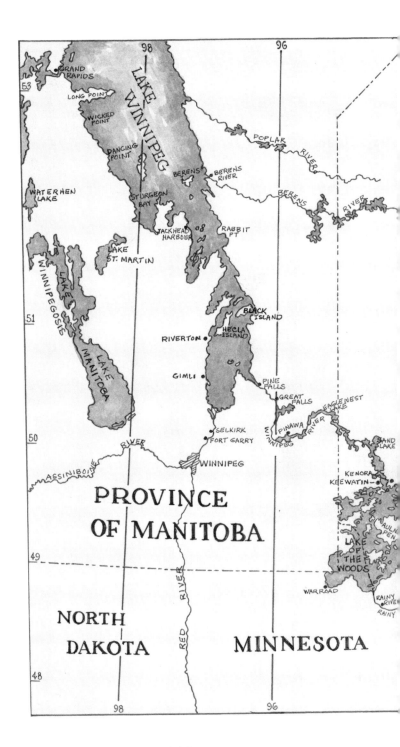

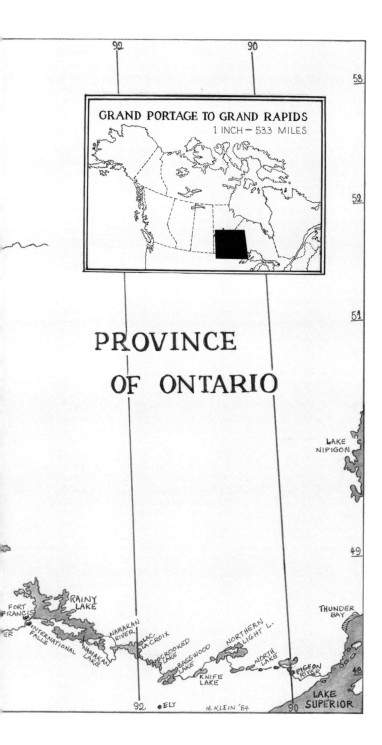

GRAND PORTAGE TO GRAND RAPIDS
1 INCH — 53.3 MILES

PROVINCE

OF ONTARIO

LAKE
NIPIGON

RAINY
LAKE

FORT
FRANCIS

THUNDER
BAY

INTERNATIONAL
FALLS

NAMAKAN
RIVER

NAMAKAN
LAKE

LAC
LA CROIX

CROOKED
LAKE

BASSWOOD
LAKE

NORTHERN
LIGHT L.

NORTH
LAKE

PIGEON
RIVER

KNIFE
LAKE

ELY

M. KLEIN '84

LAKE
SUPERIOR

to the west side of the Lake of the Woods. Furthermore, both countries have set aside vast chunks of bordering land restricted to wilderness use.

The trail after three days of heavy rain was one long, wet, slick mud puddle, with a goodly number of swampy pot holes thrown in. Even on level ground, it seemed that with nearly every step in the slick mud my feet would squish and slide a few inches every which way. Going down hills or crossing gullies it became almost impossible to stay upright. Four times that afternoon my feet went out from under me. The canoe seemed to weigh a ton as it slammed my butt down into the mud. I'd have to squirm out from under it and try to wrestle it back on my shoulders. Sometimes I'd only get it part way up before my feet once again zipped out from under me, and once more I'd be crumpled under the canoe. Altogether I had to pick that monster up off the ground nine times, before the afternoon was over. Once would have been enough. The first time was back at the stockade where I was showing off! Several of us were standing around our gear. We were getting ready to take off on the portage and discussing the joy that was to be ours before reaching the other end. Some one asked how much the canoe weighed. When I said one hundred and forty-four pounds with the stuff that was in it, there was a discussion on the proper techniques for picking it up, all of which were interesting. But when I challenged any one present to do it, there were no takers. I couldn't resist the temptation to demonstrate! My feet slipped and that was number one.

The nine miles of Grand Portage were all we needed that day. We continued on up the Pigeon River, however, as we had agreed to meet Phil and Bob at Partridge Falls. Darkness had settled in before we arrived around eleven that evening. Using our flashlight, we found the portage and soon discovered that Phil and Bob had their camp set up just above the falls. They had a fire going, which we used to prepare a fast supper before crawling into our bags. We were so tired from our struggle over the Grand Portage that we didn't even wash all the mud off until the next morning.

Saturday, 29 May

DAY 43

We slept in as Phil needed full daylight before taking camp movies. While waiting, Clint and I both cleaned up, put on a fresh set of clothing and washed the mud out of our dirty garments. Phil and Bob prepared to follow us along in their canoe at about eleven to do still more filming. The black flies were giving us such a bad time that we didn't wait long. When Clint said "I don't see any sense of sitting around here just to feed the black flies," we decided to move on.

We paddled slowly on up the Pigeon through a rapids to the next portage, slowly crossed that and our camera crew were still nowhere in sight. Back on the river again for about a half mile and we had to portage once more. There we decided to wait.

We had a few snacks for lunch and tried to relax a little. Clint soon muttered, "Those movie makers are costing us a lot of precious time!"

"I agree. I wish they could keep up, but it will be worth the wait. That movie will make us famous!"

"They must have stopped for lunch before this. It's two o'clock. This would be past their feeding time and knowing Phil, he wouldn't ever miss a meal." So the tension began to build. Personally, I was hoping they would show up immediately and then we could forget about it.

There are forty or more portages depending on how many rapids are run and various route options along the way. Without a doubt the Boundary waters contain some of the best and most popular canoe country in the world. Ely, Minnesota, is its main access and a source for outfitters and supplies. It could well be considered the canoe tripping capital of the world. The closer we got to the Ely area the heavier the canoe traffic became.

I have traveled the full length of this route several times and never cease to be pleasantly amazed at the lack of pollution and trash. The only occasion of misuse that I ever came across was where power boats and tourists had a ready access by road, to a small segment of the area. In every case beer cans and liquor bottles were the most common culprits. Who pollutes the wilderness? By simple observation it goes hand in hand with alcohol and gasoline.

We waited an additional three hours that afternoon before Clint convinced me that we had waited long enough. "Maybe our camera crew have lost the trail. At least they must have had trouble of some kind," I told Clint. It was going on six o'clock when we finally left them a note on the trail and headed over the mile and a half Pigeon River portage. The trail was drying out and not nearly as wet and muddy as we had found on the Grand Portage. We were enjoying a streak of warm and sunny weather with a nice breeze. The portage was a gradual slope uphill and then downhill. Then a little steeper uphill and a steep downhill. Just before Fowl Lake there was a nasty hill, very steep and rocky down to the lake. Fortunately, Clint came back to help me over that one.

Fowl Lake was beautiful. We began to see quite a few early fishermen along the way. We made Moose Portage and camped for the night after sundown. That's about the right time as the black flies quit for the day when it begins to get dark. We found a nice campsite on a high rock with a great view overlooking Moose Lake.

DAY 44

Ten minutes after six found us paddling west on Moose Lake in continuing good weather. Then we made the three portages which are close together and soon entered Mountain Lake which is the highest lake on the Pigeon River. Speeding down that lake, ahead of a light tail wind, I said, "We're making good time on these portages. Let's check our time at Watape Portage as we leave this lake."

"That sounds like a winner," Clint replied.

From the time our canoe touched the shore at the west end of Mountain Lake, we had completed the portage and paddled across Watape Lake in sixteen minutes.

"Not bad!" said Clint. "Maybe we can make up for a little lost time today. Especially if we don't meet up with that camera crew."

We continued to the west along a little creek which flows into Rose Lake. West of Rose, a two-mile portage was necessary before we entered South Lake. That long portage through a swamp for the first mile was difficult. Clint was ahead of me with his heavy load. When I caught up with him, I found that he was stuck in the mud. He had gone down, knee keep in the muck, wedging his foot between some roots and was trapped until I came along. We had quite a struggle. Before he came loose, I had to anchor myself to a tree and it was all we could do to work him out sideways for we had been unable to get him out pulling forward. Some fun!

It was six o'clock when we completed the portage, over the Height of Land, between South and North Lakes. At the north end of that trail we again met our lost camera crew. Phil and Bob were waiting for us with a motor boat which they had rented in Ely, Minnesota. They wanted us to go back and come over the trail again so they could shoot some movie footage of us coming over the Height of Land.

We also performed the cedar bough ceremony which was a ritual of the voyageurs at this location. It was done as an initiation to all newcomers to the fur trade as they made their first trip over this portage. Following is a quote from the book, **The North West Company,** in which Marjorie Wilkins Campbell describes the initiation of William McGillivray as that young voyageur made his first crossing of this spot, nearly two hundred years before us.

A few days and some fifty miles beyond Grand Portage the northwest route crossed the **Hauteur de Terre.** This Height of Land was no more than a few acres of scrub trees and rock where all the streams behind the westbound canoes flowed to the Great Lakes and all those ahead to the vague, remote north. For the streams flowing into Lake Superior flowed homeward for each white man. No matter how he had longed for adventure, at the Height of Land he felt a swift, overwhelming panic, part homesickness and part apprehension.

Perhaps it was because the Height of Land was more than geography—it was a Rubicon. A ceremony marked each man's first crossing, as it is marked at the equator. From boyhood each voyageur had heard of this ceremony until it became a legend. Back on his father's farm along the St. Lawrence, or more likely in his mother's warm kitchen, old hands had pictured their own moments of excitement and panic during this unforgettable moment of their first trip to the interior. In a sense they were prepared for it. Young McGillivray had had no such background.

Even before the canoes left Lachine the

voyageurs as well as the bourgeois had made a point of preparing Mr. McTavish's nephew for the ordeal. They had hoped he would be able to measure up to the initiation. "Some men . . . " they commenced to tell him of this man or that——but always they broke off before they divulged the frailties of his predecessors. By the time his own fateful day arrived, William McGillivray was steadying himself for an ordeal equal to that of a young Indian facing the rites of manhood.

The east-flowing streams had dwindled. Canoes and packs and kegs had been carried to the first west-flowing water when the brigage paused at the far edge of the rocky little plateau, covered with sparse clumps of bush. The stream where they would refloat the canoes was little more than a creek of fast water, riffled as much by wind as by current, and here and there shaded by a few scrub cedar.

McGillivray had become accustomed to the noise of a fur-brigade party; the continual profane banter and singing of voyageurs at the carrying-places, and the quieter talk of clerks and bourgeois. The sudden, dramatic silence was in itself a shock. About him stood the men of the entire brigade, doing nothing in broad daylight. As if it had all been rehearsed many times, the guide who had made the most trips to the northwest, a man not over thirty, stepped forward, unsheathing his huntingknife from his belt. A few paces from the tyro, and beside a clump of cedar, he paused to examine the blade of the knife. Not satisfied, he sharpened the blade slowly and carefully, testing it on the hairs of his weathered wrist. McGillivray watched the steel cut through one of the stiff hairs as though it were butter. Still with the air of detachment, the guide, now very much master of ceremonies, looked about him at the scrub cedar, selected and cut off a bough with a single slash of the knife. Only then did he address the initiate, McGillivray, ordering him to a low spot beside the stream. In a voice that rang out across the little plateau he commanded: "Kneel!"

McGillivray had doffed his cap. Now he dropped to his knees. Suddenly his head and shoulders were drenched with cold water, dipped from the stream with the cedar bough. The guide commanded him to repeat the ancient two-fold promise. Keeping his voice as firm as he could, McGillivray swore in French never to permit a new-comer to pass the Height of Land without a similar ceremony—and never to kiss a voyageur's wife without her permission.

Someone fired a shot into the air as he scrambled to his feet. Every man present shook his hand, thumped him on the back, cried out congratulations and called for a drink to toast the newly initiated northman.

The toast was the real reason for the ceremony, some said. But even then William McGillivray sensed that there was much more to it. Already he realized that only a few hundred men made the long, dangerous trip each year. He felt something of the deep emotion behind each northman's proud boast: "Je suis un homme du nord!"

Now he, too, was a northman.

Once more we were in waters flowing in the direction we were traveling. It was a good feeling as we crossed North Lake and shot the rapids below Little Gunflint Lake where we found a smooth sand beach at the east end of the lake. Even though it was an hour before sunset, we encamped beside some other campers as Phil and Bob wanted to shoot camp-site scenes.

We met and chatted for a while with Doug Green who lived on Belair Avenue in Duluth. Doug was only seventeen years of age but we found him to be very knowledgeable on the subject of canoeing. He was planning a canoe trip down the Thlewiaza River through Nueltin Lake. I talked with him about building canoes and he wanted to hear about our crossing of Lake Superior. Then I took him paddling to show him the racer's power stroke. He thought that was great.

Monday, 31 May

DAY 45

We were up early and at sunrise we were moving west on Gunflint Lake. One hour and twenty minutes later and we were waiting once more for the camera crew at the first rapids in the Granite River. We found a good portage trail on the right side of the river.

When Phil and Bob finally arrived, we shot the rapids while they shot their movies. They had returned the motor boat and picked up a thirteen foot canvas covered Old Town canoe from an outfitter at the end of Gunflint Trail that morning. Thus they could follow us down the Granite River as they wanted to shoot some pictures at each set of rapids and at Saganaga Falls.

Clint was having an uneasy day. Each time we would arrive at a rapids, while we waited, he seemed grumpy. This was not like him, so finally as we paddled across Clove Lake I asked what the problem was.

"It's that darn camera crew! This is such a nice day and we continually have to waste time waiting for those fellows. It irks me, because we have so far to go!"

"You're right. They are costing us a lot of

time and miles, but we'll be able to make it up on the days that we can travel by ourselves." I didn't know of anything else I might be able to add to break the tension. Then about mid-afternoon, after crossing Swamp Portage, I accidentally hit on something that eased the pressure when I said, "I wonder how many trips Sigurd Olson has canoed up and down this river?"

"Oh boy! That's right! These are the waters he canoes so much. That had almost slipped my mind. Sig Olson only lives a few miles from here, doesn't he?"

"Yes. In Ely, Minnesota."

"Do you suppose he's out here somewhere now? It certainly would be a thrill to meet him! Verlen, I've read every one of his books and they are wonderful!"

"Yes. I've read most of them too." With that, Clint's bad day disappeared. From then on, he was in his usual good mood as we continued to discuss the writings and travels of Sig Olson.

At about six in the evening we made the short portage on the right passing Saganaga Falls with the camera grinding away. After entering Saganaga Lake, all four of us stopped on the first island out from the river mouth and prepared supper.

"We should have a lot of good pictures from today's trip," said Phil.

"Yes. This is interesting country through here," Bob McKee said. "But on one of those short bends, we were swept into the bushes and I lost my glasses. The current is so fast!"

"We've decided to camp here tonight," Phil spoke as we were eating. "Then in the morning we'll paddle around this peninsula and back to the west branch of Gunflint Trail. We'll see you fellows next in International Falls."

All was quiet as we paddled away. Then five minutes later, Clint said, "Boy o' Boy. That was good news! No more movies until International

Falls!"

The waters of Saganaga Lake were calm so we paddled on for the next three hours. We encamped for the night at Spam Island, just before entering the outlet of the lake.

Tuesday, 1 June

DAY 46

We were underway, after devouring a big stack of pancakes, before six. It was another beautiful morning and we were happy as we realized that this could be a day which in all probability we would not be detained by the filming crew.

First came Swamp Portage and we paddled right past it. Then Monument Portage was well marked and not very long. Shortly we made another portage into Little Knife Lake. As we reloaded the canoe, Clint said, "I can't help but think of the thousands of voyageurs who crossed these portages in the past. These trails looked the same then as now."

"Yes," I replied. "And these same trails were used by the Indians for uncounted centuries before that. This has been canoe country for a long, long time."

Below Knife Lake, our map called for five portages in quick succession into Birch Lake. They were short, well marked and well traveled. We shot two of the five portages.

Lunch time found us in Birch Lake, where we stopped on an island to escape some of the insects which pestered us. There was very little wind to blow them away so we took only about ten minutes before we were back on the water. We also began to see quite a bit of canoe traffic but most of them were not paddling. They were using motors. "That certainly is not for me," I remarked, as the third one appeared from behind an island.

Inasmuch as we were traveling the border route which is open to both countries, we didn't stop at the Canadian Customs office near Prairie Portage. We would enter Canada when we crossed Lake of the Woods. We talked a lot that afternoon about getting to International Falls as soon as possible where we were looking forward to seeing our ladies. Our plan called for meeting them by the following Saturday.

During the afternoon we crossed Basswood Lake and made the portage of more than a mile on the left, passing Basswood Falls and several sets of rapids. Then we shot a rapids which was a little hairy and portaged on the right, past Wheelbarrow Falls. Just as the sun was setting we carried over the portage at Lower Basswood Falls.

Encamping on a high rocky bank overlooking the falls and river, we prepared a good hot supper and relaxed around the campfire. We found ourselves again discussing Sig Olson and his travels through the area. I probably started it when I casually remarked, "We didn't bump into Sig Olson today, did we?"

"No. I didn't see anyone who even resembled him. Sure wish we could run into him."

"Maybe he's up on his Listening Point," I quipped.

"You know, Verlen, something's been going through my mind this afternoon that I memorized from his book, **The Lonely Land,** several years ago. It's Mr. Olson's description of what canoeing means to him."

"I think I have read that book too, but if you memorized it, can you refresh my memory?"

"I think so. It goes something like this. He wrote,

The movement of a canoe is like a reed in the wind. Silence is part of it, and the sounds of lapping water, bird songs, and wind in the trees. It is part of the medium through which it floats, the sky, the water, and the shores. A man is part of his canoe and therefore part of all it knows. The instant he dips his paddle, he flows as it flows, the canoe yielding to his slightest touch and responsive to his every thought and whim .... There is magic in the feel of a paddle and the movement of a canoe, a magic compounded of distance, a feeling of a nearness to God, adventure, solitude and peace. The way of a canoe is the way of the wilderness and of a freedom almost forgotten, the open door to waterways of ages past and a way of life with profound and abiding satisfactions.

That was the way we ended what had been a very satisfying day. We had progressed nearly fifty miles, making nine portages. Things had gone right and we were ready for a good night's sleep.

Wednesday, 2 June

D A Y 4 7

"Verlen. Wake up! Your built-in alarm must have failed us! It's after six o'clock."

That was the first thing I heard. Jumping out of the sack, I muttered, "Wow! I was really sleeping! I don't know what happened to me. It looks like another beautiful morning, but it sure is cold."

"There's frost all over everything out here."

We were off to a late start. The river moves right along above Crooked Lake. As we crossed Thursday Bay we saw a moose swimming across Crooked Lake at a narrows ahead of us. We raced him for

We race with a moose in Crooked Lake

shore and won! We were able to cut between him and the shore, so he circled back toward the south shore. We paddled alongside and took pictures. He had a nice rack in the velvet. He was tiring, so we let him go to shore. We tailed him and took one last picture. That was an interesting episode.

Then, just before entering the main part of Crooked Lake, two bald eagles appeared. One landed at a nest in a tall red pine, close to the narrows of the canoe route. We had seen several bald eagles along the way.

We knocked off twenty-mile-long Crooked Lake before lunch. Then came Curtain Falls with the portage on the left and on across Iron Lake and Bottle Lake. Next came a portage on the right, passing two sets of falls. Now we had arrived in Lac La Croix.

There had been no wind and for the first time the mosquitoes were becoming a problem, especially on the portages or wherever we went ashore.

There are three routes between Lac La Croix and Namakan Lake. The international border route follows the Loon River to the south and is the longest of the three. The shortest is the four-mile Dawson Portage. We chose the northern route down the Namakan River, which flows through the Neguaguon Lake Indian Reservation.

The Namakan is a sizeable river with lots of water going down it in early June. We shot some fast water before making a short portage past Snake Falls. We chose to go to the right, around Douglas Island, and were soon carrying across another portage, Ivy Falls, where we decided to spend the night.

We fished below the falls, hoping to catch something for our supper, but to no avail. Fortunately, we had plenty of other food in our packs so we didn't go hungry.

"The Namakan River seems more remote and wild than anything we've found," said Clint as we were preparing our meal.

"Yes, and there's a lot less traffic. I haven't seen a single canoe since we left La Croix. Running down this river has been fun."

"Sure was! We've knocked off a lot of mileage in the last couple of days. If we can have a couple more days of this perfect weather, we should be almost to International Falls by Friday night."

Thursday, 3 June

DAY 48

We stowed away a big breakfast of pancakes and syrup, mixed stewed fruit and cocoa and were underway by seven. The Namakan was turning out to be an exciting river to run. We shot Quetico Rapids along the right side, getting a little wet as a powerful side current pushed us into a standing wave.

"That was a good run!" Clint said as we pulled into the eddy just below the chute.

"Sure was! I enjoyed that one. Now, let's get this water bailed out of here." Once that job was done, we found that, had we made a short portage along the right, we could have avoided all of that fun.

Approaching Little Eva Island, we chose the north channel. Then came High Falls where the river drops twenty feet. That was a beautiful spot. The trail is on the left and it was only a short haul.

Twenty minutes later we arrived at Hay Rapids where the river is broken up by several small islands as it flows around three bends. We were unable to scout it properly so we made the half mile portage along the left shore. Part way across we overtook and passed four men with two square stern aluminum canoes with motors. They had tried going up the Namakan River along the south side of Little Eva Island. They had lost control and swamped one of their canoes. Inasmuch as they had lost considerable equipment in the upset, they had decided to give it up and were heading back downstream.

Other people had also cautioned us of the dangers of canoeing the Namakan. There had even been several drownings but I suspect that those were caused by attempting to ascend the river with motors, which can be a very dangerous thing to do, with a canoe.

The final obstruction on the river was Lady Rapids. We had been told that it should not be run. After carefully looking it over, we ran it tight along the right shore. That took a little maneuvering and coordination. It was fast and fun. Best of all, we made it without taking a drop of water!

Before noon we were down on Namakan Lake. For the next twenty miles to the west we enjoyed navigating among the many scenic islands. The winds were light out of the southwest and it was one gorgeous day. In late afternoon we stopped at Meadwood Lodge along the south side of the narrows for Cokes and a couple of cheeseburgers for each of us.

The newly created Voyageurs National Park spreads along and to the south of the Canadian border. When the park is fully developed it will contain all of the facilities and supply the same activities of any national park in the United States.

During the evening we continued to the west, down the length of Kabetogama Lake. We encamped on little and rocky Sheep Island which is only about five miles short of the channel leading into Back Bay of Rainy Lake.

Some of the sounds we had enjoyed during the day were the chatter of the ducks which we had startled at the rapids on the Namakan, the clean whistle of the white-throated sparrow and the steady dip, dip, dip of our paddles. Eagles had screamed as they circled overhead. As we settled into camp the sounds changed to the steady hum of the thousands of mosquitoes which descended on us, and the haunting and melodious cry of the loons which echoed from shore to shore.

"We sure knocked off the miles today," Clint remarked.

"It was a good day. If this fine weather holds, we will easily make it to International Falls tomorrow. We've been just six days on these Boundary Waters and that includes a day of lost time for moviemaking. We're almost making it in record time."

"I've been thinking about International Falls most of the time since we left Grand Portage. As you know, Verlen, I haven't seen Beverly in almost two months. I can hardly wait!"

"That's been quite a while. Jenny's flying up on Saturday and should be in by early afternoon. I'm getting a little anxious to see her again too. When do you expect Bev to arrive?"

"I'm not sure. She said that if she didn't have to work on Friday, she would start driving up after work on Thursday. That's today! She may be part way up here right now."

It was with great anticipation for the upcoming weekend that we crawled into our sacks shortly after the sun had settled behind the northwestern horizon.

Friday, 4 June

DAY 49

Sleepily, crawling out of the tent, Clint said, "Boy, oh boy! Was I ever sleeping! The natural silence of this wilderness really makes me rest well."

While we fortified ourselves with pancakes, the first rays of the sun warmed our campsite and dissipated a thin layer of fog. We broke camp in record time. Clint appeared to be in a terrific rush to get underway. He wouldn't admit it, but I could understand his attitude. He was so anxious to get into International Falls that our canoe fairly streaked across those remaining miles of Kabetogama Lake.

Arriving at the channel known as Gold Portage before eight, we found that because of the high water level we were able to scoot right on through it. There is an eleven-foot drop in that mile and a half channel leading down into Back Bay and most of the drop occurs in one short two hundred yard stretch. It certainly did make a fast and joyful ride down through the brush, over sunken logs and then through the swamp below.

The channel is really an overflow course for the waters of Loon and Namakan Rivers as they spill down into Rainy Lake. The main course for these waters flows out of Namakan Lake over Kettle Falls. Not many canoeists seem to realize that the channel west of Kabetogama Lake is so good in periods of high water.

The hot sun bore down on us as we sped across Back Bay and around Rainy Lake Point. Heading west toward the outlet, Clint remarked, "Isn't this weather unbelievable?"

"Sure is. We've had perfect weather since that big storm back on Lake Superior more than a week ago."

"It must be up in the eighties today. This has to be the hottest day of the summer."

"Clint, you're going to need an air conditioned room tonight. I hope you can find one."

At noon we arrived at the entrance to Rainy River and shot the rapids under the railroad bridge. That was a fast slide with some wicked whirlpools at the bottom. After about two miles we passed some log booms and arrived at the city landing.

After walking two blocks into town, we were surprised to bump into Phil and Bob outside the Rex Hotel. While lunching together we learned that Phil had already alerted the newspaper, radio and television people of our impending arrival. Returning to the city landing, we found the word had spread for a number of media people were waiting for us there. They interviewed us and took pictures as we made our way through the city until we were below the paper mills and dam.

Then it was back to the Rex Hotel where Phil introduced us to the hotel owner, Ernie Rosseau, who was also the president of the Chamber of Commerce. We found him to be an accommodating and generous person.

ONE INCREDIBLE JOURNEY

"I want to welcome you men to International Falls and to the Rex Hotel," Ernie said. "The cost of your rooms and meals will be on us for the length of your stay."

We thanked him and soon checked into our rooms, where we took hot showers and washed off the buildup of dirt which had accumulated since leaving the Soo. We did up our laundry at a nearby laundromat. Then at suppertime, it was my pleasure to meet Clint's girlfriend, Beverly Renko, and her daughter, Becky, who had arrived from Minneapolis, late in the afternoon.

Saturday, 5 June

DAY 50

It was a hot night in the noisy city and I didn't sleep very well. During the forenoon, I caught up on some of my book work, sending a report to our newsletter editor, Darwin Gilbert. Then I went over our gear and shopped for a few of the supplies we would be needing for the next leg of our journey.

In going over our planned itinerary, I found that we were scheduled to arrive in International Falls on 5 June so we had again caught up to our original plan. Since leaving Montreal we had canoed nearly fourteen hundred miles and that was encouraging.

Along our route through the Boundary Waters, we had seen many bald eagles, probably more than two dozen of them. Clint had marked on his map, the locations of the nests we had located and before noon he, Phil and Frank Bowman took off in a floatplane to find some of them. They spent several hours in the Namakan Lake area, where they photographed some of the adult eagles as well as young eaglets in their nests.

Bob McKee drove me to the airport in time to meet the North Central plane which arrived at one. Jenny was aboard and it was a real joy to see her again. She soon brought me up to date on family happenings and other news from home. She had been carrying quite a load, being both mother and father in a busy time of life. Our son Jon had just graduated from high school. Jenny had attended his graduation exercises on Friday, the day before coming to meet me. Our son, Daniel, was planning to marry a fine Christian girl Kathie McNeilly in a few days. There was also the usual amount of hectic activities of our other children.

I felt better, being able to share, even in a distant way, some of those things. I'm sure Jenny felt better too after releasing some of her burdens.

That evening, following a fine supper in the Rex Hotel, the four of us, Clint and Bev, Jenny and I went bowling while Becky came along to watch the fun. In a way it seemed rather unreal, like part of another world, to be out on the town in the midst of our long journey.

I could tell that my bristly beard was going to get in the way, so before we went bowling, off came the whiskers. That was my first shave in more than seven weeks. Phil Pemberton was unhappy and really chewed me out about that. He wanted the beard to grow for effect in the movie, but Jenny was overjoyed! To make up to Phil, I promised not to shave again until the end of our journey.

Sunday, 6 June

DAY 51

The four of us went to church. It was very satisfying to the spiritual nature after having missed so many Sundays. Obviously man is much more

153

than just a physical being.

Clint wasn't feeling too well. We thought he might have a touch of the flu bug. Probably the same one that almost had me down at Grand Portage. We were hoping he would be fully recovered by Monday as that was our day to head on down the Rainy River.

The weather had turned bad for canoeing, but we didn't mind the rain showers or the strong gusty winds as long as we could be in a comfortable hotel with our ladies. It turned out to be a fantastic weekend of enjoying the city life, as we talked, rested and walked around the business district taking in the sights and window shopping.

Late in the afternoon Phil and I held a business meeting about the movie. He was enthused about the footage that he had been getting and was brimming over with confidence. He had big ideas about future market plans. We discussed points of interest and the filming sequences he still needed.

9

NATURE'S DELICATE BALANCE

> *Like winds and sunsets, wild things*
> *were taken for granted until progress*
> *began to do away with them. Now we face*
> *the question of whether a still-higher*
> *standard of living is worth its costs*
> *in things natural, wild and free.*
>
> — *Aldo Leopold*

DAY 52

Right after breakfast, Beverly and Becky said their goodbyes and headed back toward Minneapolis.

Clint wasn't feeling any better so we decided it would be wise to take the time to see a doctor while we were in town, even if it meant losing most of the day. There are not many doctors out on the rivers. The villages ahead are getting smaller and smaller and we would be less likely to find a good doctor. Clint thought he might have a parasite of some kind, but the doctor didn't think so, more or less dismissing it lightly with no real diagnosis.

While Clint was waiting in the doctor's office, I saw my beloved Jenny off on the plane for Lansing. I appreciated the time we'd had together. I certainly have a real conflict of interests.

We still had a few supplies to buy and some repacking to do. We put in down a steep high bank just below the dam, on the west edge of town. The two paper mills just above were causing a lot of foam and pollution, making the water unfit for drinking. On rare occasions such as that, we tried to plan ahead and carry canteens of drinking water, along with cans of fruit juices and pop to get us through to good water.

It was four in the afternoon when we finally paddled off down the Rainy River. The weather was fine and it felt good to be pulling hard on our paddles again. It would take more than a few hours of pollution and stench to spoil our enjoyment. We had been told by local people in International Falls that it was 40 miles to Manitou Rapids. We hoped to make that our stop for the night.

We arrived at Manitou Falls at nine thirty and were pleasantly surprised at the speed we had made. We pulled the canoe out on a grassy spot on the right and looked over the rapids. There was a lot of heavy water and big stacks, but we figured that a couple of 'hot shot' canoeists who could put the canoe right where they wanted it, could run that rapids. It was after sundown but there was still plenty of light to make a good supper before darkness settled in and to pitch our tent right there in the Manitou Rapids Indian Reservation.

Tuesday, 8 June

DAY 53

Clint was feeling better so we were underway by a little after six. We put in above the rapids and went through on the right, as we had planned.

It was a short, fast run, and we narrowly missed some pretty big stacks out in the middle of the river.

About an hour on downstream we came to Long Sault Rapids, not much more than a long, fast riffle. That one didn't require scouting, but we kept a wary eye up ahead in case of a sneaky drop-off. The rapids looked as though it could be run on either side, or down the middle.

The river seemed to slow down and build up just before each set of rapids. We were enjoying this section, through farm lands and downstream travel. At noon we stopped at the town of Baudette, where we found a hamburger joint, and had two large hamburgers and two large milk shakes apiece for lunch. Forty-five minutes later we were back in the canoe and paddling on. It had been quicker than making a camp fire meal.

As we neared Lake of the Woods, the river widened out and slowed down. We arrived at that big lake at three p.m., less than 24 hours from the time we had left International Falls. Up until then we had no wind at all, but all the rest of the afternoon we fought a heavy, gusty head wind with choppy waves. Even with our spray covers snapped down, we still got wet.

When we entered the lake, we began to see a lot of fishing boat traffic, especially out around the opening and inside of the long, narrow reef that blocked off the south end of the lake. Lake of the Woods is a pretty impressive piece of water, nearly eighty miles across, and we weren't sure which course we would navigate across it. The wind decided that question for us. We headed northeast along the shore where we had wind protection from the reef for the first seven or eight miles.

The water there was shallow and murky. When we got out beyond the reef, we hit some exceptionally strong wind squalls that forced us into the protection of some small islands. At one time we were wind bound for nearly an hour. Then by island hopping, we managed to get to a small island off the east side of Bigsby Island where we were faced with a traverse into the fierce, unprotected headwind.

It was then eight in the evening, so we decided to call it a day and besides, Clint still was not feeling well. We had knocked off nearly seventy miles during the day and that wasn't bad with a sick man in the stern.

Supper consisted of making use of our perishables such as cold meat, cheese, rye bread, pineapple juice, oranges, and hot tea. Clint turned in early while I put things away and secured the camp for the night.

We were in pelican country. We saw many flocks of them that afternoon, mostly standing around in shallow waters off the small islands. Pelicans are interesting and fascinating birds to watch. With the wind blowing, there was no mosquito problem so I sat and watched as more white pelicans entertained me. A flock of fourteen came flying past our island in a single line. When the lead bird would flap its wings to gain altitude, all of the others flapped their wings in unison. Then when the lead bird held its wings outspread, to ride the air currents, all of the others did likewise.

I have heard that sometimes they even catch fish by working together as a team. They will form a long line, beating their wings and driving a school of fish into shallow water where they scoop up the fish in their large pouched beaks. Then holding their bills vertically, they let the water which was also scooped up, drain out before proceeding to swallow their catch.

Bigsby Island, just to the west of our camp, was named for Dr. John Bigsby who traveled through Lake of the Woods and the Boundary Waters with explorer David Thompson in 1823. Dr. Bigsby was neither fur trader nor explorer. He was David Thompson's physician as well as an artist. He wrote of the country through which they traveled.

DAY 54

I awoke at five to make what Clint called 'A Scientific Sleeping Bag Analysis' of the weather. The howling wind and crashing waves sounded as bad as ever, so I went back to sleep for a couple hours. Finally I got up and cooked us a hot breakfast. By walking around the island and looking out over the route we'd have to take, I confirmed that we were indeed windbound. A heavy wind from the northeast was whipping up a mean mass of white caps.

Clint was not feeling too well either. He lay back down for while after breakfast, then got up to vomit. He didn't seem to get real bad, just that nagging lingering sickness that caused us worry. He seemed to eat pretty well. I had been watching that very closely, figuring that if it got so bad he wouldn't eat, then it was really serious.

By noon, the wind had died down a little, but the waves didn't show it much. Looking at my maps, I figured, if we could get a few more miles around Bigsby Island and behind Dawson Island, we'd be protected somewhat from the wind and possibly could keep moving on. I asked, "Do you feel up to it, Clint?"

"Yes," he replied. "Let's have a go at it."

It was a beautiful sunny day with puff ball clouds, but still strong gusty winds. On the west side of Dawson Island we were still being blasted by the winds but they were of less velocity than earlier in the day. We stopped for a late lunch on a small rocky island where we devoured more of the perishables. I was happy to see that Clint seemed to eat his share.

While he stretched out to rest on a flat rock in the sunshine out of the wind, I went down on the shore for about a hundred yards and sat in the shade of a lone pine, where I had an exciting view of the wind and white caps, as I wrote in my diary. In the peace and quiet, and loneliness of the moment, I thought how fortunate and how wonderful it was to be here enjoying all this. I get absolutely charmed by the wind and waves. Spring was in full bloom, and our expedition after nearly two months was still moving on.

I got to thinking, too, about International Falls. Here is a quote from the diary:

> *I am still glowing from one of the most wonderful weekends of my life. Happiness was International Falls! Happiness is being with the one you love! Happiness is being in love, being together, praying together, enjoying together. Living and loving in oneness with nature. As the sap flows, flowers are blooming, bees are buzzing, all things are growing and greening in full cycle of life. And here am I in the midst of it all.*

An hour later we decided to have another go at it. We made it across Basil Channel, then to North Island, past McPherson Island and into the protection of The Two Channels where it was easier going. We had to work hard most of the afternoon, but it was satisfying to make headway on such a marginal day.

We were surprised to see a few abandoned cars on some of the islands along the way. They must have been driven across the ice in the wintertime. We were also surprised to find so many Indian houses and a small village with a church in the middle of Lake of the Woods. The settlement is called French Portage.

Just beyond the Indian settlement along French Portage Narrows, we made camp for the day. For supper we heated a can of Big John Beans and a can of sweet potatoes. We also had rye bread, chipped beef, cheese and onion sandwiches, with hot tea. Clint was able to eat a good meal.

We observed more bald eagles and enjoyed the antics of many more white pelicans along the way. There were numerous water fowl of many varieties as well as the usual spring birds such as robins, common grackles and red wing blackbirds.

We went to sleep to the soothing natural music of the many birds.

Thursday, 10 June

DAY 55

We awoke to a wind-blown, drizzling rain coming at us from the northeast, so we were not too anxious to get an early start.

"How are you feeling this morning?" I asked.

"Not much better. I'm not sure how much help I'll be today."

"Would you like to lay over here for the day? That might be just what you need to shake that bug."

"No! We'd better be moving on. Let's have a go at it."

So we decided that we would poke along and try to make it into Keewatin on the north shore and get Clint to another doctor. It was an uneasy feeling, being out in the wilderness with a sick man, especially when we couldn't figure out the cause of his problems.

I had told Clint to paddle only as much as he felt like, or none at all, as I didn't mind paddling alone. It still wouldn't take all day to make the thirty miles into Keewatin.

The weather continued nasty with rough waters and occasional gusty, wind-driven rain. Most of the time we were able to get some kind of shelter from the wind with the hundreds of islands along the way. In the northern part of the lake, the islands are more numerous. I kept close check on the maps and compass as it would be very easy to get confused in such a place on a rainy day. Some of the islands were almost impossible to identify unless I kept myself pinpointed on the map at all times.

When it began to look like we might make it into Keewatin in time for a late lunch, we put off stopping to eat in the rain, and kept right on moving.

At two p.m. we tied our canoe to a dock only about a block from a hotel in downtown Keewatin. By then we were really hungry, so the first thing we did was get a good solid meal at a nearby restaurant. Then while Clint headed for the doctor's office, I picked up a few groceries and got a haircut. The doctor here was considered one of the best in that section of Ontario.

Clint reported that the doctor didn't think he had any parasites, or anything serious, only a little virus, gave him some Lomotil, and said he saw no harm in continuing our journey. When the doctor found out what kind of adventure we were on, he wouldn't take any pay for his services. He was a good doctor! I don't think Clint was ever really convinced that his only problem was a little virus. Neither was I, but then we didn't have any other answer.

It had settled down to one of those dull, dreary, rainy days, so after discussing the situation, we decided to get a room for the night and see how Clint felt in the morning. We found a room in an old multi-story wood frame building. From our second story room we had a view of our canoe, securely tied to the dock.

There seemed to be no activity of any kind going on. We saw very few people around town. To brighten up my day, I telephoned home to talk with Jenny, just to hear her voice and to fill her in on our situation. I love to hear her talk. She has about the sweetest, kindest voice a man ever heard. That night I suffered another attack of home sickness.

We had a brief flurry of excitement about midnight when we were jolted out of a sound sleep by loud noises, hollering and thumping in the hallway outside our room. I was glad we had locked our door.

Friday, June 11

DAY 56

We were slow to start the day. I had looked out of the window shortly after daybreak to see that we were socked in with a heavy fog.

When we stepped out into the hallway, leading down to the lobby, we saw patches of fresh bloodstains all over the hardwood floor.

"Maybe this isn't such a dead town after all," Clint remarked. In talking to the hotel manager, we found that some drunk had tried to commit suicide by slashing his wrists. Each to his own thing, I guess. I think I'll stick to my own way of getting kicks.

Clint was still not feeling too hot. I urged him to go to the doctor one more time, to see if he wouldn't reconsider his earlier diagnosis. We would soon be heading out into Lake Winnipeg, and I didn't think much of the idea of going out there with a sick man. The doctor reaffirmed his first opinion and insisted that Clint had no serious problem.

By noon, the clouds were breaking up and the weather was improving. We decided that we might just as well move on, taking our time to suit Clint's pace. Across the bay from the hotel was a short easy portage under the highway bridge and down a long, grassy slope to the start of the Winnipeg River. We had a slow leisurely afternoon of paddling. In the narrows we often found a pretty good current. We were pleased to make nearly thirty miles during the afternoon. We set up camp early near the town of Minaki, Ontario.

Saturday, 12 June

DAY 57

It was a dull, grey morning and we were off to another slow start. We had camped on a solid rock shore which gently sloped down to the water's edge. We were sitting around the camp fire silently eating our hot oatmeal with raisins breakfast, when a rabbit slowly hopped up to less than a canoe length away to nibble at a few scraps of leftover noodles. We carefully watched the rabbit while it continued to feed and we continued to eat. Needless to say, we enjoyed that animal's company.

At White Dog Dam we portaged around the first of many dams that have changed the Winnipeg River from what the voyageurs were familiar with. "The river must have really been something before these power dams were put in," I remarked.

"Yes. There must have been some beautiful sets of rapids and waterfalls along here," Clint replied. "This river drops about three hundred and fifty feet between Lake of the Woods and Lake Winnipeg and the voyageurs had to make as many as thirty-eight portages in this stretch."

Nature's Delicate Balance

There are few people who love the wilderness, who enjoy it and appreciate it more than I do. I wish it were as it was two hundred years ago. I find something in me that regrets such inventions as the internal combustion engine and electricity, but I still think it's a great, wonderful world. It seems like nearly every publication one looks at today takes the extreme ecological view. There are some who would have us believe that every dam is wrong, every mine is a rape of the earth, every river should be untouched, and every species should be preserved. I am not certain that this is true. What kind of energy crunch would we be in today, if we listened totally to such voices? Whatever happened to the impartial theory that there are two sides to every story?

The "delicate" balance of nature isn't going to be destroyed by the lack of a few species. This "delicate" balance has survived some pretty violent changes in the ages past, and who's to say we're any better or worse off? I, for one, don't mourn the passing of the dinosaur.

Fortunately, not all those involved in ecology are extremists. I am strongly in favor with sensible ecological measures, and even the preservation of all species, but not at any price. We need to exercise reasonable conservation practices that would maintain a balance between the needs of man and preservation of nature. Much good has come of this environmental kick that we are on, for it has made us more aware of how we are handling our earth. The ultimate product of earth is mankind. It is far more essential that we handle each other with all due love, respect and consideration, than to let issues come between us.

Clint was feeling better and we moved along steadily, enjoying the day. We traveled nearly fifty miles before we encamped for the night on an island near the north end of Eaglesnest Lake as a dense fog closed in.

DAY 58

It was still foggy and misty in the early morning. Shortly after leaving camp we saw another bald eagle proudly silhouetted on a small dead tree overhanging the water.

We shot Lamphrey Falls which was only a fast chute because of the dam at Point du Bois. Then in the hydrotown of Pointe du Bois, we found that everything was closed, including all stores, and even the gasoline station. So without wasting much time there, we portaged on the right, putting in close below the dam at a small foot bridge.

At Slave Falls Dam, we again portaged on the right, over the end of the dike. Then in a short distance, we met an officer of the Ontario Provincial Parks, in a patrol boat. We chatted for several minutes and picked up a lot of information about the area.

He told us of two people, a man and wife, who had drowned only a couple days before while trying to come up Barrier Rapids in a canoe with an outboard motor. This made the third set of drownings we had heard about on our journey, all involving outboard motors on a canoe. Motors seem to make a canoe doubly tricky, especially going up a rapids. A quick movement of the steering lever, and you've flipped the canoe.

We shot Sturgeon Falls, taking the upper part tight right, and pulling hard right into an eddy to stay out of the "hay stacks" below. Then we lined up to go on through the lower section of the rapids. It was a good ride. It's always a feeling of satisfaction to be able to put the canoe right where you want it, and come through dry.

Next, we shot Barrier Rapids. Here we were cautious remembering the drowning, but it was rather tame as rapids go. I think we could have even paddled up it. Which supports my theory that most canoe mishaps are the result of foolish mistakes, and not because canoes are dangerous.

We paddled through a couple of small rapids between the islands at Pinawa, where we took the center channel.

We had talked about taking the Pinawa River, as an optional route for getting into Lac Du Bonnet, but decided against it, for lack of reliable information.

We arrived at Seven Sisters Dam at nine. The dam was so named because it drowned out seven rapids and falls with its backwaters. It is one of the larger dams on the Winnipeg River. It was built in 1931, and added to in 1949. The fur traders had to make seven portages where we were making one. With all the dams on the river, it has to be considerably different now than it was in the early days.

We pitched our tent on top of the dike on the right of the dam, where a nice breeze kept the mosquitoes at bay.

Monday, 14 June

DAY 59

From our camp on top of the dam we portaged down a steep trail to a channel that had been blasted out of solid rock. There we found a fast chute of water for nearly a half mile leading right into Lac Du Bonnet which was mirror calm as we crossed it. Another portage on the right over the dam at the outlet of Du Bonnet and we headed north to Great Falls dam. Just below the dam we stopped for lunch. We lucked out by finding a good supply of cold pop in a dispenser at a nearby building.

It went well with our lunch.

"Do you think we will make it out to Lake Winnipeg today?" Clint asked.

"We really should," I replied. "That's going to be different."

"It sure will! It will seem good to be able to paddle all day and not have to make a portage."

"Once we hit the lake, we can paddle at least three hundred and thirty miles before we come to the next portage and that's at Grand Rapids on the Saskatchewan River."

Thirty minutes later we arrived at the next rapids where another boat channel had been blasted out along the left, creating a forceful chute of water. While we watched, a motor boat roared up through the chute. We believed it could be shot, but as we were already ashore to look it over, we portaged right down what had once been the middle of the rapids, but was now only dry rock, washed clean and smooth by its years and years as part of the river bed.

Winnipeg River had been steadily growing bigger and wider. Silver Falls and Pine Falls are now only fast water, drowned out by another dam just above the settlement of Pine Falls, Manitoba. There we shot Manitou Rapids before paddling ashore at the lower end of the fast water. It was six o'clock.

Pine Falls was to be our final stop before crossing Lake Winnipeg so we walked into town to take care of a few necessities. The only place open was the hotel which fortunately had a restaurant. Our most pressing need was a large supper. Once that was taken care of, we talked with the hotel manager. When he learned about our journey, he went out of his way to help us. The man soon telephoned the manager of the grocery store and that gentleman kindly opened his store for us. Then he insisted that we use his auto to get some laundry done up and to deliver our supplies to the canoe.

Our supplies purchased there consisted mostly of canned goods. With no more portages for a while the extra weight would be no problem. The canned goods would add variety to our diet and allow us to prepare speedier meals on the good traveling days. We also picked up some onions and potatoes. For the anticipated hot, sunny days on the open lake we each bought a straw hat and a short sleeved white shirt.

Then I called home to talk with Jenny and asked her if there was any way that she could meet us at Flin Flon, Manitoba, in about two weeks. She said that she would try to work it out. She filled me in on the news around DeWitt. Most important was the wedding of our son Daniel to Kathie McNeilly a couple of days before.

"That makes three of our children married," Jenny said. "That leaves only the six younger ones at home."

Those were only a small part of the hectic responsibilities that she was facing without me. We talked on and on. I couldn't seem to hang up but finally, with Clint pacing back and forth, I made it.

"Wow!" he said. "I sure wouldn't want to have to pay your phone bill."

"I'm sorry! Talking with Jenny always makes my day. I still get that funny lovesick feeling, the same as I did some thirty years ago, when we first met. I even asked her to meet us in Flin Flon."

"That's a good idea. I'm going to call Bev, and see if she will meet us up there too!"

It was ten in the evening before we shoved off on the river. At about eleven thirty we passed Fort Alexander and soon entered Traverse Bay of Lake Winnipeg. A half hour more and we set up our tent on Provost Point, completing another interesting and action-filled day.

DAY 60

We were underway before six. A light breeze from the south made the paddling easier. Three hours later, a sudden squall hit us but in about five minutes, the storm was passed and it became hot and sunny.

Cumulus-type clouds hung above the shoreline of the lake as we moved from point to point along the east shore. We hugged the shoreline as close as the shallow water would permit, traversing many small bays. We had been advised to be extremely careful on Lake Winnipeg because of the way the wind could whip up the water. They say that it is probably the most treacherous lake in Canada for small craft.

In Alexander Henry's journal, **Travels and Adventures in Canada,** he tells about his experience in traveling across the lake in August, 1775. He was joined by Peter Pond and his crew. They were only a couple days out into the lake when they were hit by a severe gale from which they escaped by making it to what was then called Buffalo's Head Island. "But not without the loss of a canoe and four men." About three weeks later they were over-taken by Joseph and Thomas Frobisher and crew, and at that time all together they composed "a fleet of thirty canoes and 130 men." It must have been an interesting sight. So unpredictable can the weather be that it took Alexander Henry thirty days to cross the lake, but only six days to cross on the return voyage.

The lake is shallow. The entire west side of the lake is low and flat, offering no protection from the winds coming across the vast prairies which can whip up huge rolling waves very rapidly.

We lunched on a bare rocky island near the mouth of Sandy River. While eating, we took advantage of the ideal conditions, drying out some wet clothing, aired our sleeping bags and then went for a fast swim with a bar of soap. We didn't stay in the water long. The water was still very cold, but it was certainly refreshing.

We were appreciating our new straw hats and white shirts. However, we did paddle for several hours with our shirts off, getting more sun tan.

Late in the afternoon as we neared Gray Point of Black Island we thought we were looking at a smaller island to our right, so we kept to the Black Island shore. When we arrived at the place where the channel between the two islands should have been, we discovered that there was no channel, but a low narrow sand bar. It was an excellent sand beach, and inasmuch as Clint had still not completely recovered from his sickness, we set up camp.

I never ceased to marvel at the skill and daring of the terns who entertained us during the evening. They'd fly twenty to fifty feet above the lake and suddenly fold their wings and like an arrow, dive head-long into the water, with a loud noise and a splash, and come up with a fish! Sometimes they'd get one a little too big and there would be a furious flapping of wings and flopping of the fish.

This must have given Clint ideas. It didn't take him long to catch a couple of northern pike. But he did use a more conventional method.

I walked the beach for an hour with note book and pen in hand, lonesomely thinking and writing to my lover back home. A guy has lots of time to think on a trip like this, and has time to re-evaluate and appreciate some things taken for granted.

The mosquitoes swooped down on us as soon as the breeze died down. We carried no Raid with us, so out of necessity we had to get clever at entering the tent without letting them in.

171

Total progress during the day was about fifty miles.

DAY 61

We were slow to start due to rain showers which continued until nearly six. A breakfast of cold cinnamon rolls with butter and jam with a large can of orange juice and we were on our way by seven thirty. By then the clouds had cleared away and we were enjoying a light breeze from the southwest.

A couple of hours later while paddling past a small island, we got a whiff of the sweet smell of wild roses. We stopped and investigated. It was a regular rose garden, with lots of bumble bees hard at work doing their thing. There seemed to be an unusual lot of birds singing also. It made an enchanting combination. Under the spell, we were a little slow in moving on. It seemed to be one of those days that had a lazy kind of spell about it. We must have lost track of time and purpose. It was a day to enjoy, and be glad that we were there and doing just what we were doing. It all seemed so right.

A little later we found ourselves threading our way through dozens and dozens of low, marshy islands. We were in the midst of a busy bird sanctuary. This area seemed to be alive with birds and fish. There were flocks and flocks of huge white pelicans. They are utterly fascinating birds to watch in the air, so graceful in flocks with their synchronized flight.

No matter where we went, we seemed to be intruding in an excited red wing blackbird's territory and almost came to blows when we got too close to their nests a couple times!

172

Herons were all over the place, and lots of Black Brant and Canada geese. As we rounded a point of an island, we surprised a mother goose on shore with a bunch of fuzzy little goslings. Dozens of varieties of ducks were hurtling through the air or exploding off the surface. One wood duck paid us a pleasant compliment by mistaking us for a part of the sanctuary. The bird almost landed on our canoe. Just as its feet were about to touch down, it discovered its mistake and hastily took off in horrified disgrace.

Several small, barren, rocky islands had been taken over by noisy colonies of common terns. Some other islands were controlled by herring gulls. We saw several bald eagles including one on a big nest in a tree top.

Fish were popping up everywhere. The huge carp were especially noisy, rooting around clumps of marsh grass and cattails. Apparently they were spawning. We tried to blend in with the environment as we stopped often to learn, listen and enjoy. After all, a canoe is right at home in places like that.

We were a little sorry to leave that ten mile stretch of enchanting islands but the magnetism of the Bering Sea kept drawing us irresistibly onward.

We stopped at a nice sand beach beyond these islands for a fresh fish dinner with bread and butter, pickles and hot cocoa. Then in the afternoon we had a long stretch of shallow sandy shore line with a heavy crosswind blowing on to it. That made for tricky and wet paddling, especially around Sand Bar Point. In some places the waves would start to break a long way out from shore.

It was a hot, sunny afternoon. We were beginning to get that half baked feeling as cumulus puff ball clouds were again ringing the lakeshore. Nearing Loon Straits, the wind picked up and by the time we had crossed Loon Bay to the east shore, a wicked-looking storm was brewing off to the west.

It was heading our way.

We found a protected sandy beach inside a small harbor. We hurriedly made camp among the trees. The spot had a lovely view looking out over the lake.

Clint went fishing while I tried to fix supper. He caught a couple northern pike, but because of the storm, I didn't have time to fry them.

In the meantime, I had prepared baked potatoes with butter, Lipton vegetable beef soup with macaroni and half a pound of cheese, hot tea, onions and pickles. I just made it, getting everything ready, when we had to race inside the tent to eat, as the storm broke. We enjoyed a comfortable, satisfying meal to the exhilarating music of pounding waves and wind howling through the tree tops. What more could a man ask for! What better way to end a special day!

Occasions like that proved the wisdom of not having a tent any smaller than our three-man size. We were very pleased with it. Even though we only made thirty three miles, it was a good day! I was getting a good sun tan but Clint was having a little problem of burning, especially on his nose.

Thursday, 17 June

DAY 62

I crawled out of the tent at four-forty to find very little wind but the lake's surface was still rough from another storm that had hit us during the night.

"How does the weather look out there?" Clint asked.

"Not bad, but there is a suspicious formation of clouds in the west."

By the time I had a fire going and the fish on the griddle, another storm was rapidly heading our way. It was like a re-run of the night before. For the second meal in a row I was racing a storm in preparation of our breakfast. I just barely made it inside the tent to sit in the doorway, and comfortably eat breakfast, while looking out across the lake, as the full fury of the storm hit. I've always enjoyed storms, but never more so than when there's a little feeling of victory at having won the race! We took our time, eating all of the fresh fish we could handle, along with bread, butter, jam and tea.

"Verlen, you're getting quite adept at timing and beating these storms."

"That's just luck. Now I wish I could figure how to outwit the mosquitoes. They are heartless, hungry tormentors when I'm preparing a meal."

"They bother me a lot too! We probably should have brought headnets and some repellent. Then the problem wouldn't be so great."

"Never! I wouldn't be bothered with that stuff. We just have to find a way to outsmart them."

Violent waves continued to pound the shore on our side of the cove until after seven. Then the wind quickly died down and made a complete change to a helpful tailwind.

As we were paddling along we found ourselves in another unusual wind and wave condition. We were at the moment enjoying a tailwind from the south, but we were being hit by heavy waves and whitecaps from the west. At the same time the large swells that had made up during the night were coming at us from the south. Several times during the day we had 180-degree wind changes. That was the kind of day in which we had to be especially cautious. We proceeded along the east shore to The Narrows where we made the traverse to the west side. Lake Winnipeg is only two miles wide at that point. Then it was across to the north tip of Matheson Island and on to Cub Island for a lunch break. The lake was so calm that we ventured the seven miles from Cub Island to Little Tamarack Island. From there we kept heading northwest and traversed another five miles to Jack Head Island.

As we neared Jack Head, a heavy wind out of the south whipped up heavy seas and pinned us down. It was six or seven miles to the next point of land. We started across, but changed our minds as it seemed to be still building up more and more. We had learned to be a little suspicious of the lake. It could get treacherous amazingly fast! We came back to the protected side of Jack Head Island and into a nice little harbor where there was an abandoned fish factory.

We had paddled forty-five miles since morning. If the wind would let up, we would have another go at it, but that didn't happen. I was worried about Clint who was still not feeling very well with frequent discomfort and weakness. He suspected that he had picked up an intestinal parasite from some bad drinking water, probably on Lake Superior. I wondered what his problem really was. In a two-person canoe, what concerns one, concerns the other and all the more so in such a remote place.

We set up the tent on the old dock of the abandoned fish factory, about four feet above the water. Then I went exploring the island. I watched the waves from the cliffs off the far west end, watched the frogs in a marsh, checked out all the flowers and butterflies and examined every one of those old buildings. Some were still in good shape. Apparently it was quite an operation in its day but everything had been thoroughly looted.

Clint had rested while I explored. When I returned he was feeling somewhat improved. He had a nice camp fire going and wanted to know all about the island so we sat and talked until after sundown. In spite of the smoke from our fire, the mosquitoes finally drove us into the tent.

10

FOUR MILES
PER PANCAKE

> *I will praise Thee for I am*
> *fearfully and wonderfully made.*
>
> — *Psalms 139:14*

Friday, 18 June

DAY 63

Windbound!

From inside our sleeping bags we could hear
the wind getting stronger and stronger. There was
no need to rush around. Clint's health still was
not what it should be. His pulse and temperature
appeared to be normal, but at times he was listless
and had no appetite.

I tried to make things easier for him, doing as many of the camp chores as I could without being too obvious. When there was work to be done, he always wanted to do his share, and kept plugging away. On many occasions since we crossed Lake of the Woods, I told him that if he didn't feel like paddling, to just take it easy, or even lie down in the canoe as I didn't mind paddling alone, but he hung in there doing his full share.

Following a late breakfast, we did our laundry. Then while Clint lay on his pad in the tent, I re-explored Jack Head Island, taking some pictures and going through the ten old buildings of the fish factory. I tried to enjoy the day but I kept thinking and worrying about Clint. It had been more than two weeks since he first went to the doctor in International Falls. Two doctors had said there wasn't anything seriously wrong -- that it was only a light virus. Out in the middle of Lake Winnipeg was not a convenient place for a sick man and especially when we didn't know what the problem was.

I even found myself wondering just what was wrong. Maybe he was having too much of me! Maybe he was sick of my company! Maybe he had a case of 'tent fever,' or maybe he was homesick, or maybe he was lonesome for Beverly? I just didn't know, so I worried on and on.

When I returned to our tent about five hours later, Clint still lay on his pad. I stuck my head inside the tent and asked, "How are you feeling now?"

"Oh! I don't know. I guess I'm all right."

"Are you getting hungry? You should be! You had very little breakfast!"

"No! I don't think I'm up to much food."

"I'm going to fix us something. How does soup sound?"

"That will be O. K."

By the time I had a fire lighted, Clint was

out and ready to do his share of the work.

The wind howled on steadily all day, until finally at about six we noticed that the velocity was dropping and it soon shifted to the east. We were soon underway, heading to the northwest toward Stony Point, a few miles north of Jackhead Harbour. Huge swells made the going somewhat difficult at first but the lake gradually calmed down. From Wicked Point we made a traverse of Kinwow Bay to McBeth Point.

Clint was paddling with power as we scooted past Cat Head and Lynx Point at about midnight. I had noticed that sunset occurred right at ten and there was still some light as we headed across Lynx Bay.

Saturday, 19 June

DAY 64

We made camp on a rocky beach, in the dark, at Turnagain Point. The time was one-thirty and we had progressed thirty-seven miles. That wasn't bad considering that my partner was a sick man.

Three hours later, my built-in alarm clock had us out of the sacks and we were underway by five-thirty. We were most anxious to make the twenty-two-mile crossing of Sturgeon Bay under favorable conditions. The north wind began to blow when we were about halfway across. By the time we neared the southernmost of the St. Martin Islands, we were forced ashore. The wind had again beaten us.

We prepared a good hot meal. It was pancakes for the first time in about a week as we had been eating mostly canned goods since leaving the Winnipeg River. We were surprised to find that in the

179

dark of the night, we had set up the tent right beside a gull's nest. One had just hatched and was a fuzzy little ball of fluff. We fed it some small pieces of pancakes and it seemed as though the little fellow adopted us as it tried to follow us around.

A pair of Canada geese followed by an awkward young gosling popped out of the bush and headed for the water, only missing us by a canoe length. The island gave the appearance of another bird sanctuary. There were birds of many kinds, chattering, quacking, and squawking constantly. It was a real bird island.

The high wind continued to blow from the north all day long, bringing colder temperatures. We soon had put on our wool shirts and windbreakers in an attempt to keep warm. I explored the island with my camera and found it was alive with birds and their nests were everywhere. I had to watch my step to keep from stepping on some of them. There were even birds nesting in the bushes and trees.

When I returned to our camp, Clint seemed to be feeling better. He had also been fascinated by the birds. "How many species of bird life do you think are on this island?" I asked.

"A lot of them! That's for sure! I've seen at least a half dozen different kinds of ducks. I've seen pintails, wigeons, mergansers, scoters, blue-winged teal, mallards, goldeneyes, and even some northern shovelers. Then there are both franklins and herring gulls. I've seen both black and common terns fly by, as well as those flocks of white pelicans."

"The island is loaded with spring flowers, too. Clint, I even found several clumps of lovely little violets back a ways from the shore."

"By the way, Verlen, what are we going to have for supper? I'm getting hungry!"

That was the best news I'd heard in several days! Clint was feeling better. I soon was building a little fireplace with some of the limestone slabs which we found nearby. Then we stewed some mixed dried fruit, baked some potatoes and made up a triple batch of pancakes, some of which would be for future use. We wanted to be ready to roll as soon as weather permitted.

We turned in early that evening as the wind howled on.

Sunday, 20 June

DAY 65

Up and paddling before five-thirty following a breakfast of stewed fruit, cold pancakes and syrup. The wind had slackened and we were anxious to complete our traverse of Sturgeon Bay. When arriving at Carscallen Point we followed the west shoreline closely. The wind once more picked up out of the east-southeast. The lake became pretty rough at times but we kept digging away.

The west shore of Lake Winnipeg was very low land. The water was shallow and muddy, but then the word 'winnipeg' in the Indian language means 'turbid or muddy waters.' The land was covered with willow, spruce bogs and marshes. The shoreline consisted of a tangle of washed-out trees and willow roots, interspersed with rocks. It would be a difficult place to land a canoe in a storm.

The seas were running so high by mid-forenoon that we found ourselves in an absurd situation. We had to stay out beyond where the surf was breaking as there was no possible way to paddle in it. We seemed to be trapped out there beyond the surf. It was too rough to stay out and it was too rough to go ashore.

Empty eagle's nest near shore of Lake Winnipeg

We kept riding those huge swells in that situation until we finally rounded Dancing Point, where we were able to put ashore. What a relief that was!

There we found a tombstone at the water's edge that had been uprooted in a tangle of downed trees and roots. The stone was still partly upright and was dated 3 February 1933. The name on it was John Turnan. He was nineteen years old and died while fighting a fire on a fish freighter.

On the point, we also found a large eagle's nest in a Balm of Gilead tree. We had seen several bald eagles during the morning. I climbed a taller tree, which was about eight feet away from the one with the nest in it, taking my camera up with me. Looking the nest over from above, I shot a picture.

The wind and sea conditions were unchanged when we decided to have another go at it. Needless to say, it took courage as well as a little fool-hardiness to get back out there. Fortunately, we lucked out, making it to a gravel beach only a couple of miles south of Wicked Point by nine forty-five. We made camp and prepared hot soup, macaroni and cheese and tea. A downpour of rain chased us into the tent just as supper was ready to eat.

"These mosquitoes around here are beastly!" said Clint, as he was zipping up the tent.

"They are really terrible! It was a good day even though it was a lot of work. We've progressed another sixty-five miles."

Monday, 21 June

DAY 66

On the first day of summer and the longest day of the year we were underway by six. The wind had switched to the southwest at a moderate speed. The Indian village at Sand Point appeared to be a partly abandoned fishing enterprise. At Sand Island where the shoreline swings to the east for twenty-five miles toward Long Point, we made a short shore break. There we found another abandoned fish factory. "Apparently, Lake Winnipeg is pretty well fished out," I quipped.

"That may be so, but I've also heard that the environmental people of Canada have banned commercial fishing here because of suspected mercury poisoning."

"That sounds like something our Environmental

Protection Agency in the States would do. I thought these Canadians had more common sense than that."

"They're just using good judgment, Verlen. A buildup of mercury in a person's system could be deadly."

"What about those fish that you caught the other day? We did eat a lot of them, you know. Do you think they may have poisoned us?"

"Don't be silly! Those were excellent fish! We could eat the fish from this lake every day all summer and we would have no harmful effects. The mercury pollution that's in this lake was here long before man ever came along."

"If that's the case, the Canadian consumer protection people have apparently ruined the fishing industry in this lake. They must have put a lot of people out of work. Why would they want to do that?"

"I don't know. Maybe the lake was being over-fished. But it sure isn't now!"

"It reminds me of the time in the States when our Environmental Protection Agency banned the sale of cranberries. They said that cranberries contained high levels of arsenic and that had been known to cause cancer in rats."

"Yah! I remember. All cranberries were destroyed that year. We couldn't even buy cranberries. The news media played it up so much that it ruined the cranberry market for years and a lot of cranberry growers were forced out of business."

"The part of that story that was kept secret by the media was the fact that a person would have to consume more than two thousand pounds of cranberries within a year, in order to take in enough poison to do any possible harm."

"That is a fact. It's probably the same with the fish from this lake. I don't understand why the masses believe everything they see or hear on television or radio."

Four Miles Per Pancake

"It's our education system! Clint, we are living in an over-educated society! Now they're making a big fuss about acid rain. There are lakes in the north that have been barren since time immemorial and now our 'over educated' people are telling us and the news media that those barren lakes were caused by acid rain from our factories. I think that the eruption of volcanoes does more damage to the environment than man is doing. At any rate, I would like to know more unbiased facts, before I swallow everything I hear."

We kept moving, even though the winds and waves were giving us a bad time. For several miles we followed along between a sand reef and the shore. Later we stopped on a beach for an early lunch. It's quite a trick to beach a canoe without getting wet when there is a heavy surf rolling in. We weren't too successful that time either. Several thunderstorms moved across the lake during the day. One of them caught us dead center with sheets of blowing rain and hail. We couldn't find a place to get in through the surf so we kept on paddling.

Just before five we rounded the tip of Long Point and an hour later were on a gravelly point preparing supper. I made up fresh, hot pancakes to go with stewed apricots. We also had hot Tang, which is a good drink on a cold day.

Three hours later we were blown off the lake again by a strong north wind as huge waves were building up rapidly. We pulled onto a sand and gravel beach at the mouth of a small stream draining a marsh. After exploring we found we were in a real animal haven. Lots of bear sign. A mother and cub had been hanging around, with fresh tracks all over the place. We were then only about thirty miles out of Grand Rapids, Manitoba. We had made fifty miles that day, and were pleased with the progress. We probably would have paddled on into town that evening if wind and water had been more favorable.

185

ONE INCREDIBLE JOURNEY

DAY 67

The wind had died down. The lake was still rough but acceptable so we embarked at five minutes after five following a cold breakfast. Later that morning the wind became strong out of the northeast. Then it became even stronger. We were so anxious to put Lake Winnipeg behind us that we kept on going through some huge waves for the next three hours. Even though we had the spray cover tightly buttoned down, we both became soaked to the skin, and the water ran out of our britches when we stood up. At one fifteen we slid into the mouth of the Saskatchewan River going under the new highway bridge.

It had taken us seven and a half days to cover the three hundred and thirty mile canoe route from the Winnipeg River to the Saskatchewan River. We didn't try to follow the exact route of any particular voyageur but used our own judgment, based on the direction of the winds. In crossing Lake Winnipeg our strategy had been the same as it had been for Superior. That was, to be ready to go at any hour of the day or night when the weather was favorable.

Grand Rapids is a settlement of about six hundred people, consisting mostly of Indians. There were a couple stores and two restaurants which were combined with filling stations along the highway to the west of the bridge.

We celebrated our crossing of Lake Winnipeg with a big dinner in one of the restaurants, each having two cheeseburgers with french fry plates, Cokes and chocolate milk shakes. With that taken care of, I called home, talking with Jenny for a half hour. Wow! That sure made my day! She and the family were planning to come up and meet us in Flin Flon.

Four Miles Per Pancake

Then after restocking a few food supplies, Clint telephoned Beverly and we shoved off and paddled up to the huge power dam. We made our portage on the right up and over the high and rocky dike. It was treacherous going, but we made it. The water level behind the dam was one hundred and twenty-nine feet above the river below.

Two men from the Manitoba Hydro came out to see what was going on, as we portaged the canoe over the dam. We learned that they were also canoeists and had made some sizeable trips. They seemed impressed with our journey. We chatted for several minutes. They said that the dam was built in 1965. They gave us some topographical maps of the area and were helpful in sharing information on Cross Bay and Cedar Lake.

Here is what Alexander Mackenzie had to say about the river:

On entering the Saskatchiwine, in the course of a few miles, the great rapid interrupts the passage. It is about three miles long. Through the greatest part of it the canoe is towed, half or full laden, according to the state of the waters: the canoe and its contents are then carried one thousand one hundred paces. The channel here is near a mile wide, the waters tumbling over ridges of rocks that traverse the river. The south bank is very high, rising upwards of fifty feet, of the same rock as seen on the south side of the Lake Winipic, and the north is not more than a third of that height. There is an excellent sturgeon-fishery at the foot of this cascade, and vast numbers of pelicans, cormorants, &c., frequent it, where they watch to seize the fish that may be killed or disabled by the force of the waters.

187

DAY 68

The wind flapped and rattled our tent during the night, which made it difficult to sleep. Part of my problem was that I again had Jenny on my mind. She had told me that she and the family could stay in Flin Flon for about ten days. She would be there for the canoe race which Clint and I had entered, which would be a part of the Flin Flon Trout Festival during the first week of July. I could hardly wait!

We were off to a late start. Once out into Cross Bay the crazy winds gave us more problems. The weather had turned sunny and warm but the wind continually changed directions and speed. Sometimes it would be very strong. Then it would die down to a calm and a few minutes later it would hit us from a different direction, which caused some weird wave action.

We saw another bald eagle and a nest in the top of an old tree stub but this time I didn't take time to climb a nearby tree to peek into the nest. We both had Flin Flon on our minds!

Before noon we met six large canoes loaded with thirty-five boys. We pulled in among them and talked. One young man said, "We're on a camping trip and headed for Grand Rapids."

"Yes," said another. "We've canoed all the way from Easterville, Manitoba. This is our third day out."

They continued to talk about their great camping trip. Then finally the first young man asked where we had started our trip.

Clint replied, "In the St. Lawrence River, near Montreal, Quebec."

They didn't seem to comprehend. I guess they thought we were 'pulling their legs.' There were a few seconds of silence. Then another young man shyly asked, "How long did it take you to get here?"

"We started on 17 April. More than two months ago."

"Wow!" three or four of them uttered in unison.

"How much farther are you going?" he asked.

I replied, "We hope to make it to the Bering Sea, west of Alaska, before the Yukon River freezes up next fall."

"Wow!" several of them exclaimed in unison.

The water level of Cedar Lake was raised twelve feet by the Grand Rapids dam. No trees were cut, so consequently we found a messy lake with lots of half-submerged dead trees behind where the shorelines used to be. At camping time, we found a spot on one of the higher islands just off Oleson Point.

We talked about how the lake must have changed since the Grand Rapids dam flooded everything. Once more, I checked to see what Alexander Mackenzie had written about the area.

The Mud Lake must have formerly been a part of the Cedar Lake, but the immense quantity of earth and sand, brought down by the Saskatchiwine, has filled up this part of it for a circumference whose diameter is at least fifteen or twenty miles: part of which space is still covered with a few feet of water, but the greatest proportion is shaded with large trees, such as the liard, the swamp-ash, and the willow. This land consists of many islands, which consequently form various channels, several of which are occasionally dry, and bearing young wood. It is, indeed, more than probable that this river will, in the course of time, convert the whole of the Cedar Lake into a forest. To the north-west the cedar is not to be found.

From this lake the Saskatchiwine may be considered as navigable to near its source in the rocky mountains, for canoes, and without a carrying-place, making a great bend to Cumberland House, on Sturgeon Lake. From the confluence of its North and South branches its course is westerly; spreading itself, it receives several tributary streams, and encompasses a large tract of country, which is level, particularly along the south branch, but is little known. -- Beaver, and other animals, whose furs are valuable, are amongst the inhabitants of the north-west branch, and the plains are covered with buffaloes, wolves, and small foxes; particularly about the south branch, which, however, has of late claimed some attention, as it is now understood, that where the plains terminate towards the rocky mountain, there is a space of hilly country clothed with wood, and inhabited also by animals of the fur kind.

Thursday, 24 June

D A Y 6 9

It was still very windy and overcast as we embarked at nine. We were off to a late start because it just didn't look like a canoeing day, but we needed to keep moving. Once we were out in the full sweep of the wind, there were times when we thought that we should have stayed in camp. It was a rough crossing. We had a real roller coaster ride over and through the biggest waves either of us had ever canoed in.

The Grand Rapids dam had more than doubled the size of the original Cedar Lake. Once west of the shoreline that the voyageurs had known, we began to hit islands of submerged trees which were partly under water. The farther we went, the thicker the dead trees and obstructions became. Finally we decided to follow one of the numerous old channels that were evident by the tree tops sticking out, which formerly lined the river banks. Progress was slow as we followed a small and crooked channel, until finally we were in the old Saskatchewan River. There we worked our way up a good current even though still many miles out in the new lake.

Late in the evening, we left Cedar Lake behind and headed up the river toward The Pas. There we started seeing all kinds of trash and garbage. There was a fresh moose skeleton near the shore which was being picked clean by the ravens and gulls. Then we saw a dead cow and a pig floating and rotting in the water. The gulls were feeding on the flotsam. "By Jove! I don't like such a messy river. And to think we have been drinking out of that!" Clint moaned.

"For sure, we better boil any drinking water we take out of the Saskatchewan from now on."

We kept on fighting the stiff river current as darkness settled in, and were still hard at it at midnight.

Friday, 25 June

DAY 70

"This is a dark night," said Clint. "We may have a problem finding a good campsite."

"Yes. Unless we keep going until daylight. Personally, though, I'm getting tired. I'm ready to stop whenever you are."

"I'm ready anytime. Let's see what we can find."

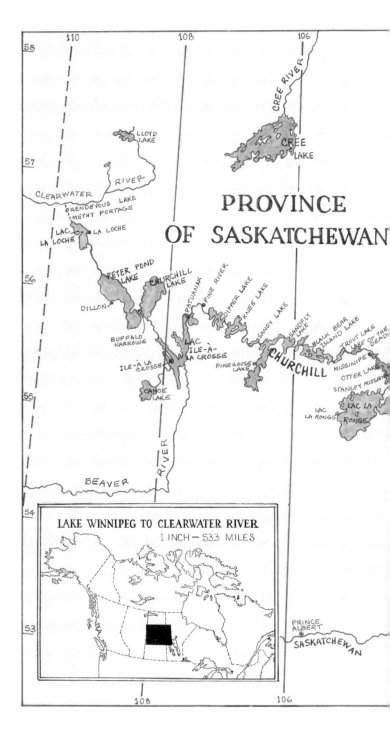

PROVINCE

OF SASKATCHEWAN

LAKE WINNIPEG TO CLEARWATER RIVER
1 INCH — 53.3 MILES

192

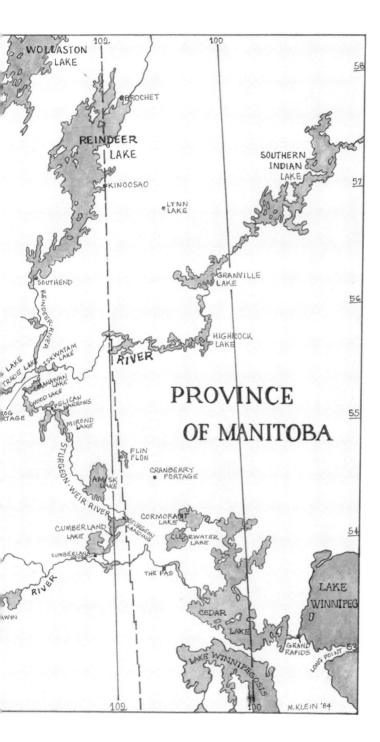

We tried to find a place to put ashore but tag elders and willows hung out into the river all along the swampy shoreline. We crossed to the opposite side of the river and found more of the same. We searched for a break in the brushy vegetation which might lead to solid ground. Finally, at one thirty in the morning, we put ashore. It was difficult to find a place to set up the tent in all of that brush. The only level spot turned out to be in a muddy moose trail. The mosquitoes came at us by the thousands as we pitched the tent and tried to crawl inside without letting any of them in with us.

We had just dropped off in a deep sleep when I was startled awake by the threatening sound of the sloshing and suction of a couple of moose coming down the trail. They were heading right for our tent. In the black darkness, I hoped they wouldn't walk right over us. Fortunately they sensed our presence and passed us by.

Three hours later we woke up to the tune of the swarms of mosquitoes and the song of the happy birds. At about the same time, there came the sounds of a couple of noisy moose walking through the muddy swamp hole nearby. With that, we were out of the sacks with our heads peering out of the tent door.

Wide awake, we decided to get back on the river and try to make it to The Pas. We embarked at five thirty on that cloudy morning. There was some wind blowing, just enough to hold the mosquitoes at bay.

The Saskatchewan River flows with a brisk current below Cumberland House. In places it is very fast. We had to stick tight along the shore to make any upstream progress. The wind picked up more velocity and it looked like rain as we stopped and prepared a hot meal at mid-day.

By eight that evening we had completed the forty-two miles and arrived at The Pas, Manitoba, in the rain. We walked into town and secured a hotel room and were soon luxuriating in a hot shower, washing off the buildup of sweat, dirt and grime of many days of toil. That was followed by a big supper in a nearby restaurant before we turned in for a good night's rest.

Saturday, 26 June

DAY 7 1

We slept late as we needed supplies. We did our laundry and when the stores finally opened, we bought more food. I also bought a Timex wristwatch to replace one which had given out as we crossed Lake Winnipeg. There, I had also left on an island my pocket knife, so I purchased a new one. A good jackknife certainly comes in handy on a camping trip.

The rain continued to fall but by the time we were back on the river, shortly after noon, it had slackened to a light drizzle. The Saskatchewan flows with a brisk and steady current. It is of uniform width of about one-eighth mile below Cumberland Lake and we also noticed much less pollution of the water above The Pas. We pushed steadily along upstream during the afternoon. By playing the currents and the bends of the river, we progressed thirty-five miles before camping time.

One of the highlights of most days was the delightful occasion of selecting just the right campsite. Sometimes it had the proportions of house shopping in which we had hundreds of sites to choose from. Then it was just a question of which one struck our fancy. The decision would usually start in the late afternoon, by consulting our maps for possible likely spots up ahead, to coordinate with our expected quitting time. Islands were always preferred, as we were less likely to have food snitched by hungry little animals, or be threatened by molesting bears. Somehow on islands we could always feel as though it was ours, that we were the sole owners. On the mainland, it was harder to feel that way. Selecting the campsite gets to be a very important project. We always wanted a good place to land the canoe to unload and reload, and to secure it for the night. We wanted a high and dry, bug-free spot, open to the breeze, a level spot for the tent, a sheltered convenient cooking site, a safe place for a fire, stones for a fireplace and lots of available wood. I also wanted a fantastic scenic view, a high hill or mountain to climb or a place to explore -- and Clint would like good fishing, right off shore! Many times we had all that and more. But there were times to the other extreme when we would settle for just anything we could get, such as on a dark night in the middle of a storm, even if it meant hacking a wet, lumpy, miserable spot out of the brush.

It didn't seem like a campsite until the tent was up and a campfire going. Then, as if by magic, even the most unlikely spot was transformed into our "home." As a wolf sniffs out his territory and marks it with scent and sign, I always had to scout the area, look it over, get a feel of it, before I felt completely comfortable and in possession of a spot. Sometimes it was no more than a wood-gathering ramble, or a climb to a high point to look around.

We did select a fine campsite that night. The banks of the river had gradually been getting higher as we moved upstream. Everything west of Cedar Lake had been flat, silt-type country. There been a lot of bank erosion at the bends of the river, with frequent overhangs of brush and sod. Except for an occasional island and the game trails down to the water, it had been the type of paddling that could soon get monotonous, if we hadn't been so psyched up by the excitement of realizing our dreams.

Those game trails were the only places to put ashore due to the twelve-foot-high, steep banks. Around ten o'clock we ascended a game trail and found a great spot overlooking a bend in the river. Just after sundown we listened as a pack of coyotes sang a chorus in the distance. The skies had cleared, and at midnight we could still see some daylight in the far northwest.

Sunday, 27 June

DAY 72

While in The Pas, we decided that we should try to get eight hours of sleep each night, as part of our training for the coming canoe race in Flin Flon. We also really needed to get in some running and other exercises as there would be several portages in the race.

We were heading on upstream by nine under sunny skies. There were numerous broods of baby ducks following their mothers along the shores. Most broods consisted of ten to twelve ducklings. However, at times there would be only one or two. Perhaps some predator had been at work. There were also Canada geese with small goslings along the way. It was a pleasure to watch those broods of birds and their reaction to us. The mother would always try to lead the little ones into a place of safety, somewhere out of the path of our canoe, talking to them all the while.

It was a steady upstream pull all day. At times we faced strong headwinds which changed to crosswinds at the bends of the river. We entered the Province of Saskatchewan and by late afternoon arrived at the junction where we kept to the right, entering the Tearing River, which in reality is only a side channel of the Saskatchewan River as it flows out of Cumberland Lake.

The Tearing River was shallow with many gravel bars and at least a dozen sets of rapids and riffles. Several of those were pretty fast, but we did manage to paddle up every one of them, even though it was hard on both canoe and paddles. "Maybe this is why they call it the Tearing River," Clint remarked. "If you're going to paddle up through here, many a person would want to just sit right down and cry. There's probably been many a tear shed by those who couldn't make it."

"Or, to be successful in paddling up through here, you sure have to tear into it," I added.

It was nine thirty when we located a good camp site at the south end of an island and we had knocked off another thirty-five miles. That evening our talk was again of the voyageurs. We also talked about the former great herds of buffalo that used to roam the plains to the south of us and of Peter Pond, who began the practice of trading with the Indians for pemmican. The meat of the buffalo was the main ingredient used in the production of pemmican. It was a high-energy food and could be carried on long journeys without spoilage.

During our evening discussion, Clint mentioned that the Indians used horses in their buffalo hunts. I again pulled from my personal bag my excerpts from Sir Alexander Mackenzie's **A History of the Fur Trade.** I located the place where he had written about the Indians of the area and then he continued:

> *They have great numbers of horses throughout their plains, which are brought, as has been observed, from the Spanish settlements in Mexico; and many of them have been*

Charlie Laberge works on a birch bark canoe.

We cross Chats Falls Dam.

A grinding ridge of tumbling ice.

We pause in Campion Provincial Park.

Clint snoozes for a few minutes.

Sunrise on Talon Lake.

Pancakes on the griddle.

Andy Green in the stern and Charlie Laberge in the bow of Montreal canoe on Lake Superior.

Thousands of Herring Gulls.

Verlen in 1971.

Stormy Lake Superior.

Reconstruction of the fort at Grand Portage.

Camp scene on Lake Superior.

Sled dog puppies on an island in the Churchill River.

Anglican church at Stanley Mission.

The Sturgeon-Weir River.

Juvenile Bald Eagles along the Churchill River.

We move along.

The trail along the Methy Portage.

The Clearwater River.

Phil Pemberton and Northern Pike.

Bill Flett joins us for lunch along Slave River.

Barges of freight along the Mackenzie River.

Fish on drying rack above Fort Good Hope.

Phil and Tony search for our trail in Mackenzie delta.

Suddenly it's autumn.

Our first camp on the Rat River.

The Richardson Mountains from lower Rat River.

Packing to leave Summit Lake.

The lower Rat River.

We leave Summit Lake.

We say goodbye to Tony Mercredi below Fort Yukon.

CROSS CONTINENT CANOE SAFARI
MONTREAL, QUEBEC TO THE BERING SEA ALASKA 1971

Winter closes in.

Photo by: Carroll Ramsay

Verlen and Jenny Kruger and family.
Left to right: back row – Philip, Jon, Daniel
middle row – Christine, David, Mary
front row – Jenny, Deborah, Sarah, Nancy, Verlen.

seen even in the back parts of this country, branded with the initials of their original owners' names. These horses are distinctly employed as beasts of burden, and to chase the buffalo. The former are not considered as being of much value, as they may be purchased for a gun, which costs no more than twenty-one shillings in Great Britain.

Of these useful animals no care whatever is taken, as when they are no longer employed, they are turned loose winter and summer to provide for themselves. Here it is to be observed, that the country, in general, on the west and north side of this great river, is broken by the lakes and rivers with small intervening plains, where the soil is good, and the grass grows to some length. To these the male buffaloes resort for the winter, and if it be very severe, the females also are obliged to leave the plains.

"That is interesting, Verlen. I had no idea that horses were used way up here nearly two hundred years ago."

Monday, 28 June

DAY 73

It rained during the night, but the skies had cleared by morning. The mosquitoes were merciless, descending on us by the thousands as we prepared breakfast and broke camp. On the river a breeze picked up from the north by mid-forenoon and blew the pests away.

Arriving in Cumberland Lake, we decided to paddle the extra eight miles to Cumberland House as we did want to visit the post because of its historic interest. There, a Hudson's Bay post was established and built by the famous explorer Samuel Hearne in 1774, making it the oldest continuous settlement in all of Saskatchewan. Cumberland Lake was very shallow with a flat, marshy, weed-choked shoreline. The water of the lake was muddy and murky as we worked our way across to the Indian settlement.

Cumberland House is located on Pine Island and the post was difficult for us to find, even though our maps showed its exact location. Finding that settlement was like a Chinese puzzle as we worked our way through the swampy, shallow, grass-filled water until we found a channel on the far shore which cuts the island in two.

The following is a quote from **The Beaver** in articles published on Cumberland House:

Samuel Hearne and nine men left York Factory on Hudson Bay in five canoes on 23 June 1774 to erect a new fort inland. Their food consisted of 12 lb. of Bisquett' as Hearne planned on living off the land. It was not until September 3rd that they found a suitable location. This was a fine bay on Pine Island in the Saskatchewan River, near the present Saskatchewan-Manitoba border, and the men started to clear a level area on which to build a log tent.

The winter was spent trading a few furs, setting nets in the lake, and shooting game. In April work was begun on the new fort -- to be called Cumberland House -- and on 30 May Hearne left with the furs for York Factory.

Cumberland House was the first western inland trading post of the Company, and it was built to meet the competition of traders who came chiefly from Montreal. Five years later these traders would form the beginning of the

North West Company.

The first winter the men lived in a log tent and kept their supplies in a warehouse at the east end of the shelter. Fresh moss was stuffed between the tent logs for insulation; the storeroom was plastered with clay and thatched with long grass. As winter approached, Hearne was soon concerned for the morale of his men. Transportation was dependent on the Indians, some 150 rival traders surrounded them and food was in short supply. Hearne wrote: 'it is with the greatest difficualty I can Preswade them from thinking that Entire famine must Ensew.'

Few furs were traded the first winter, but in the post's third season Matthew Cocking, then in charge, traded 6,162 Made Beaver, up from the initial return of 1,647.

During the years 1789 to 1792 Cumberland House was moved about one and a quarter miles along the lake to its present location.

The North West Company maintained a post nearby and when Captain John Franklin R.N. visited the area in January, 1820 he noted that the 'houses of the two Companies, at this post are situated close to each other . . . They are log-houses, built without much attention to comfort, surrounded by lofty stockades, and flanked with wooden bastions.'

On the union of the Companies in 1821 the English fort, being 'large and tolerably well built' with glass windows and gallery in front, was the one to be occupied.

Strategically located at the junction of several water routes, Cumberland House remained an important distribution depot until it was overshadowed by Norway House. From about 1830 it declined in importance, although it continued to be a pemmican depot and provided supplies for passing brigades.

ONE INCREDIBLE JOURNEY

> *Today there is still trapping in the*
> *muskrat marshes and fishing in the lake that*
> *was once known as Sturgeon. In 1967 an all-*
> *weather road was completed and a ferry was put*
> *into operation to link Cumberland House with*
> *'road's end.' Four years later telephones*
> *were installed. The years of isolation which*
> *followed the abandoning of the Saskatchewan as*
> *a river highway had ended.*

We explored the town finding the business places closed as the day was Monday. Apparently they are closed on both Sundays and Mondays. A lodge, however, was open and we had a good roast beef dinner in their restaurant.

The north wind was strong as we headed back to the east and then north, crossing Cross Lake, then through the Whitey Narrows and into Namew Lake. As we entered the Narrows, we suddenly were back in good clear water again. That was the first really clear water we had dipped our paddles in since leaving the Winnipeg River.

The wind and waves were so rough that just after entering the main part of Namew Lake we made camp on a low, flat rocky area. The only fuel we could find for firewood were a few dry willows but they served us nicely for cooking. Then late in the evening we used green willows for smoke to drive away the mosquitoes.

Tuesday, 29 June

DAY 74

We embarked at eight-thirty on a beautiful, sunny morning with a light tail wind to assist us in crossing the ten miles of Namew Lake to the settlement of Sturgeon Landing. By mid-forenoon we were looking up over boulders and rapids, into the mouth of the Sturgeon-Wier River, which flows out of the Indian reservation of the same name.

Long ago, Alexander Mackenzie had written: "In latitude 54. 16. North, the Sturgeon-Weir River discharges itself into this lake, and its bed appears to be of the same kind of rock, and is almost a continual rapid. Its direct course is about west by north, and with its windings is about thirty miles." That thirty miles, when ascended, would put us into Amisk Lake, which is nearly ninety feet higher than we were in Namew.

The rapids were almost continuous for the first three miles to the junction of the inflowing Goose River. Then came another rapid which we lined up on the right. An hour later we stopped at a scenic spot on the river bank for lunch and a short siesta.

Back on the river we moved along upstream. At times we did some lining, wading, brush pulling and we even tried poling. The poling, however, didn't work out very well. The inconvenience of cutting poles, carrying them, getting them out and putting them away, all consumed more time than we gained by using them.

There were flocks of ducks with young at nearly every set of rapids along the Sturgeon-Wier. Once we counted fifteen of them racing for dear life, scooting across the river like water bugs. Then as we got too close, they popped under the surface to escape.

In an expansion in the river we raced another bull moose who had been feeding some distance offshore. We could have easily caught him if the shore hadn't been so close. That time we didn't have a chance.

The only portage we made during the day was the one past Crooked Rapids. All of the other rapids were negotiated from the river. After fifteen hours we still had enough ambition and energy left to paddle fast and furiously up through the top set of rapids just below Amisk Lake. It was a satisfying feeling to make that one and suddenly find ourselves paddling across the calm surface of Amisk. We soon encamped and were pleased and somewhat surprised with our forty-one miles of progress, of which thirty were up the Sturgeon-Wier with its dozens of rapids and fast water.

Wednesday, 30 June

DAY 75

"Clint, it would be nice if we could make it all the way up to the Hanson Lake Road today. That's forty-six miles. I have an idea that Jenny and my kids will make it to Flin Flon today, as this is our wedding anniversary."

"That's right, it is! Happy birthday, Verlen! That reminded me. Your birthday and wedding anniversary are on the same day."

"They sure are! This is the forty-ninth birthday of a soon-to-be famous canoeist. Famous, that is, if we can complete our journey before the Yukon River freezes up."

That set the tone for the day. Everything was beautiful. We had a warm, sunny morning with a few fleecy, cumulus-type clouds and a light wind. For breakfast I made a triple batch of my special pancakes. "We really are getting good mileage on these pancakes," I said. "I've checked it out and we're averaging about four miles per pancake."

"I'll bet we didn't average four miles per pancake coming up that thirty-mile stretch of rapids yesterday!"

"No, we probably didn't get more than three miles per pancake, up through there."

We soon headed across Amisk Lake. It was an

enjoyable crossing as we passed many small islands, loaded with birds, along the way. By noon we were once more working our way up the Sturgeon-Wier, along the southwest edge of the Amisk Lake Indian Reservation. It was different from the lower section. There are only four sets of rapids in the thirty-five mile stretch below the Hanson Lake Road and they were right where the map shows them to be. The portages were well marked, and with good trails.

We portaged Spruce Rapids, then lined and waded the three drops of Snake Rapids, as we had missed the portage trail which was on the left, well below the rapids. There we found an aluminum canoe that had really been busted up. It was twisted into a U-shape and looked like it had been wrapped around a rock with its gunwale facing upstream into the full fury of the rapids. We pressed right along through Attree Lake and by eight-thirty, were portaging past Scoop Rapids. Then came the portage at Leaf Rapids and by eleven that evening, looking ahead and to our left, I viewed an utterly delightful scene. It was our camper, at the roadside campsite just below Maligne Lake.

I let out a Whoop! Before we could make it to shore, Jenny, Jon, Christine, Philip, Debbie, Mary and little Sarah, all were standing there to welcome us ashore. An instant "Happy Birthday, Dad" were the first words I heard from each of them as they came running down to meet us. That was one happy reunion!

They had arrived there at five that same afternoon. We soon loaded everyone and everything either into or onto the camper and drove the forty-one miles into town where we found rooms at the Flin Flon Hotel.

11

FLIN FLON
INTERLUDE

> *The woods are lovely, dark and deep*
> *But I have promises to keep,*
> *And miles to go before I sleep*
> *And miles to go before I sleep.*
>
> — *Robert Frost,*
> ***Stopping by Woods on a Snowy Evening***

DAY 76

We looked up our old friend, Mrs. Stuart Crerar, to let her know that we were in Flin Flon. We also wanted to pick up route maps and rules for the Twenty-First Annual Gold Rush Canoe Derby, which Clint and I had entered during the previous winter. Mrs. Crerar told us the race, along with the entire Flin Flon Trout Festival and Rodeo, which was scheduled to start on 2 July, had been postponed for one full week. What a blow! We had planned all along to arrive just in time for the race, then following a five-day break be on our way again. This meant that we were going to have to lay over for a full week before the race would even begin.

"Do you think we should cancel our entry in this race, Verlen?"

"No. We are all set to run it. We can use those extra days to scout out the routes and do some additional training."

"But what if it costs us so much time that we fail to make the Bering Sea before freeze up?"

"We'll make it! Once we get on the Mackenzie and the Yukon, we'll really roll. We should be able to knock off seventy or eighty miles most every day."

"You're probably right. I'd like to participate in this race. Let's do it."

So it was settled. With those extra days, we would do some proper training and familiarize ourselves with each of the three separate routes that were to be run on the three days of the race. We knew that we would be up against some pretty tough competition as the Flin Flon Gold Rush Canoe Derby was considered to be one of the most important Marathon Canoe Races on the North American continent.

Friday, 2 July

DAY 77

Jenny had brought along our eighteen and a half foot special marathon racing canoe and we were anxious to get the feel of it. Right after breakfast, we drove east of town and put the canoe into Manistikwan Lake. Jenny waited the seventy-five minutes that it took us to paddle around Big Island. Then we ran down the road for a mile, carrying the canoe and paddles with us. From there Clint and I jogged the three miles back to the Flin Flon Hotel.

During the afternoon, we took the family and visited the giant statue of the fabulous Flintabbatey Flonatin, which stands on the east edge of town near the tourist bureau's Visitor Reception Centre. The real Flintabbatey Flonatin was a character in a dimestore novel, and it was from him that Flin Flon, Manitoba gets its name.

In the evening we spent some time with Norm Crerar and Gib McEachern, who were the Canadian Professional Canoe Champs. They reside in Flin Flon and Norm is a son of the Stuart Crerars. Clint and I had also met up with them in our earlier canoe racing careers.

Saturday, 3 July

DAY 78

We were up early to practice and get in another day of training. We explored and followed the course of the first day of the race on Schist Lake and were back in town in time for lunch with our family. During the hot afternoon we drove into Saskatchewan and the kids went swimming at Denare Beach on Amisk Lake. When we returned to our hotel in the early evening, we had another pleasant surprise. Our son Daniel and his new wife, the former Kathleen McNeilly, were waiting to see us.

"Dad, you didn't have time to come to our wedding so we decided to come up to visit you on our honeymoon," Danny said.

"Wonderful!" I replied, giving them both a big hug and a kiss. "This is really great!"

Verlen and Clint with Bill and Roger Carriere

"How's the canoe race going?" Kathie asked.

"The race has been postponed until next Friday but we're going to wait for it. We're getting in a lot of training. We want to win this one."

We chatted on and on that evening. I learned all about the wedding and what was going on at home. It was good to again spend some time with my family.

209

ONE INCREDIBLE JOURNEY

Sunday, 4 July through Thursday, 8 July

DAYS 79, 80, 81, 82, 83

Each of these days was somewhat similar. Clint and I would do a practice run of one of the three courses each morning, except on Thursday, the day before the race. We also trained for speed on the portages and jogged at least three miles per day.

On Sunday, Clint's friend Beverly Renko arrived. She had driven up from Minneapolis with her daughter, Becky, and son, Chris, in a motor home.

Monday afternoon, we all took the guided tour of the smelting plant at Hudson Bay Mining Company on the west edge of town. That was also the day that our honeymooners, Daniel and Kathie, headed back toward Michigan.

On Tuesday and Wednesday we met some of the other teams who were arriving in Flin Flon for the race. We met Ken Hardy and his brother Bob, who were the racing champs from the Province of Alberta and we met Manitoba's King Trapper, Roger Carriere, and his nephew, Bill Carriere. Roger was one of the oldest men to enter the race.

Thursday was the day it seemed just about everyone in central Canada arrived in Flin Flon. The Trout Festival was in full swing. The rodeo people and the midway people moved in and set up for business. Around noon our camera crew Phil and Bob again put in an appearance. Late in the afternoon we met Luc Robillard and his partner, M. Theberge, from Three Rivers, Quebec, as well as Versteeg and McDougall from Michigan.

Marathon canoe racing came into its own as the pleasure of being able to move a canoe with maximum efficiency, to move it faster and easier and to be in complete control. Of particular interest to me has been the marathon racer's power stroke. As all racers know, it's a short, fast stroke that once developed lets you paddle on and on, efficiently and tirelessly. It's the only power stroke I have ever used. It's the only stroke my wife Jenny and my kids will ever use. It's the only power stroke Clint and I used on our journey. We cruised along at fifty to fifty-five strokes per minute, hour after hour. In racing, of course, our stroke picks up to fifty-five to sixty-five or more per minute.

None of the canoe books I had read even mentioned this stroke. It would seem those writing on the subject would have consulted the real experts, the racers, who spend considerable time and effort testing and perfecting the technique to peak performance. It was this stroke that gave us the efficiency to keep going and cover so many miles without feeling dog tired near the end of the day.

There are still vast sections of this continent where the canoe is the only practical vehicle. In some areas there are even less traffic and fewer people living today than there were two or three hundred years ago. We are now seeing a revival of interest in that kind of canoe country and that kind of canoe adventuring. Year by year more and more hardy souls with the same adventurous blood as the early explorers are beginning to rediscover the land of the canoe. Once again, for a brief moment, for a week or a month in the summer, the canoe is king. Long live the King!

Friday, 9 July through Sunday, 11 July

DAYS 84, 85, 86

A total of fifteen teams were on the starting line, consisting of many of the best paddlers from across Canada and the United States. Even though Clint and I were there to win it, things just didn't work out too well for us. We found that we could pass any other team on the portages, but when it came to paddling, we just didn't seem to have enough speed. Clint had not been feeling well much of the time since we left Lake Superior, and he didn't seem to be in very good spirits. On Saturday he was feeling especially bad and at about the halfway point in Athapapuskow Lake, near Baker Narrows, he said, "What's the use! Let's quit! We can't win this thing anyway!"

I was shocked! I didn't expect to hear Clint say anything like that and I told him so. I continued to talk to him and he continued to paddle, but I could tell his heart wasn't in it. On Sunday, the final day of the race, things went pretty well. We could still gain on the competition on the portages but just couldn't pick up much time while paddling.

After three grueling days we finally crossed the finish line. We were one of the twelve teams who finished, but we just didn't live up to our potential. That was a real disappointment. When the winners were announced, we learned that we had finished in fifth place.

Here is the official list of the first six finishers with their total time:

Team	Hours	Minutes	Seconds
1. Jean-Guy Beaumier and Claude Corbin	10	3	24
2. Joe Michelle and Irwin Constant	10	11	40
3. Luc Robillard and M. Theberge	10	15	54
4. Ken Hardy and Bob Hardy	10	20	31
5. Verlen Kruger and Clint Waddell	10	24	13
6. Roger Carriere and Bill Carriere	10	25	51

Flin Flon Interlude

Marathon canoe racing is still relatively unknown in most sections of the continent. Thanks to a few places like Flin Flon, Manitoba, racing is finally becoming a fast growing sport.

Monday, 12 July

DAY 87

We were planning to leave Flin Flon right after breakfast to continue on our Cross Continent Canoe Safari, but Phil Pemberton said that he would like to have a short meeting. I met with Phil and Bob McKee in their hotel room on the movie. They were making big plans for a theatrical production with an early 1972 release throughout Canada and the United States. Phil's enthusiasm for its success was again expressed.

To that point I had financed the operation myself, investing heavily in the project with almost everything I owned, but now there was a real problem. Phil was nearly out of money.

"We just can't let this project die," Phil said. "We have to complete the film or we will have nothing to show for our efforts."

"Wow! It sure is costing a lot more than I expected," I replied. "And a lot more than you projected. You were supposed to have ample funds to complete the film. How could you have spent so much more than we planned?"

"Travel expenses are costing more. We're using more film but getting some excellent sequences, so I'm sure it will be worth it. Verlen, could you get me some more money?"

"Well, I don't know. I suppose I could call my banker and get another loan, but I don't know what Jenny will think! I would want to talk with her first. How much more money will we need?"

213

When I obtained an answer to my question, our meeting soon broke up and I went back and talked with Jenny about our problem. We discussed it in detail. I knew she didn't like it any better than I did, but she said, "Do whatever you think you have to do." So after much thought and further discussion, I called my banker friend, Jim Herrick, at American Bank and Trust Company in Lansing, Michigan. I told him about our problem. Then I requested another big loan. The only thing I could offer as collateral was our family home in DeWitt, which is a suburb of Lansing. He said that he would see what they could do. Their loan board was meeting that afternoon and he would call me back on the following morning at the Flin Flon Hotel.

Consequently, we would have to hold up another day. When I told Clint about what had developed, I'm sure that he was also unhappy as we had planned for an early start on 12 July. "I'm sorry for this delay, but I guess it can't be helped."

"That's O.K.," he replied. "When we finally do get started, we'll have to put in a lot of extra hours to make up for lost time."

Earlier that morning, Beverly, Becky and Chris Renko headed back toward Minneapolis in their motor home.

Tuesday, 13 July

DAY 88

Everyone was up for an eight o'clock breakfast in the hotel as we waited for the call from Jim Herrick. Later, while I remained near the telephone, Clint, Jenny, Christine and Jon walked to the grocery store for a few last minute supplies. During the previous afternoon we had gone to the laundromat, bought $36 worth of groceries, and repacked all of our bags.

We were ready as we waited with great anticipation for word on our loan. If the bank turned us down, our camera crew would pack out for Michigan that very afternoon. If they approved the loan, the crew would follow us for a couple of days in a motorized freight canoe, with its owner Jim Pieke and our son Philip going along to help them over the the portages, up along the Sturgeon-Weir River.

Finally at a little before noon, a telephone call came from Jim Herrick. He said that our loan had been approved and that in my absence, both Jenny and my brother, Lawrence Kruger, would need to come in and sign the necessary documents. I assured him that they would.

We left Flin Flon almost immediately, driving out on the Hanson Lake Road with our camper to the exact spot where we had met my family on the evening of my birthday. It was two-thirty by the time we had said our tearful goodbyes, and again started paddling up the river. My family were off for home that afternoon and with the exception of Jenny, who wanted to meet us in Fort Smith, I probably wouldn't see them again before fall.

It was good to again be seated in our canoe and pulling on those paddles after our hectic and sometimes discouraging interlude in Flin Flon. Only a couple of miles above the bridge we arrived at Birch Portage and found a wide log skidway along the right side of the river. Crossing the lake in the Birch Portage Indian Reservation, we noticed the picturesque cabins of the settlement. We were able to paddle right on through the set of rapids about five miles upstream before lining the third set at the bend in the river.

We set up camp early on a beautiful little island at the bend in the river where it again swings back to the north. Our camera crew filmed a camp sequence during the evening which included the catching of several walleyes, or pickerel as they are called in Canada.

Wednesday, 14 July

DAY 89

We all started the day with a delicious walleye breakfast, getting off to a late start because of a downpour of rain and heavy winds from the northwest. Before nine we had paddled up through the fast water at Corneille Portage, where we entered Mirond Lake. Then the skies cleared but there was no abatement of the wind as we nosed our way up through the twelve mile length of Mirond, continually hugging the shore or ducking behind some of the many islands, to keep out of the huge waves which were sweeping down the lake.

In early afternoon we arrived at Pelican Narrows and were disappointed to find the Hudson's Bay store closed. We took a short break for a Coke and snack, then continued on into that headwind, working our way across seven-mile-wide Pelican Lake.

By four, we had arrived at Medicine Rapids. While I built a little fireplace, the others all did some fishing and in a few minutes, eight nice walleyes were frying on the griddle. As soon as our meal was completed, eighteen more of those fine fish were pulled from the eddies just below the rapids. Those fish, however, would be taken out with the film makers, who by the way had exposed considerable more film as they had accompanied us up the Sturgeon-Weir.

Medicine Rapids was where we separated. The camera crew, along with our son Philip and Jim

Pieke, said their goodbyes and headed back toward their vehicle at Hanson Lake Road. From there, Philip would accompany Bob McKee back to Michigan. Clint and I, alone again, lined up past the rapids and continued upriver, where we soon came to three more sets of rapids with good portages on the right.

Late in the evening as we paddled through Grassy Narrows along the Woody Lake Indian Reservation, three hungry sled dogs silently eyed us from a nearby island. In a few minutes we passed two more little islands with sled dogs imprisoned on them. It had long been Indian custom to stake out their dogs near the water or to put them on an island for the summer, where they would feed them about once each week. As autumn approached, however, they would feed those dogs every day to again fatten them up in preparation for a long, hard winter's work on the trap lines.

We set up camp on a point near the south end of Wood Lake. It was gratifying to learn that we had progressed thirty-two miles into the strong headwinds during the day.

Thursday, 15 July

DAY 90

My built-in alarm clock went off right at three-thirty. We wanted to make an early start and try to gain some lost time. An hour later, following a cold breakfast, we were underway facing a light headwind. Enjoying a colorful sunrise, we powered our way along the twelve-mile length of Wood Lake as all signs indicated that we should expect more rain. Three hours later as we worked our way across marshy Pixley Lake, our meteorological observations came true as showers moved in an continued off and on throughout the day.

Upon entering Pixley Lake we noticed a change in scenery. The water appeared stale. There was very little current moving through the narrows and it was as though we were moving through a big swamp. Wood Lake had been the final large lake we would traverse on the upper Sturgeon-Weir. A very attractive lake with its smooth, glaciated islands, it offered many inviting campsites along the high and dry wooded shores.

Finally there was Lindstrom Lake leading right up to the famous Frog Portage. The rainy morning called for some serious navigating as Lindstrom contains a multitude of islands and deep marshy bays. There was a good trail leading over into the Churchill River. The portage was also fitted up with pole ramps and rollways for the big, motor-driven freighter canoes.

"I can see why they named this place Frog Portage," said Clint. "That marsh back there around those lakes should be a great place for frogs."

"I think it was originally called 'Frog Skin Portage.' I don't remember the details, but I think Alexander Mackenzie said something about it in his book. I'll see what I can find when we set up camp tonight."

With that we embarked on Trade Lake and headed up the Churchill River. On the south side of the island as we neared the Grand Rapids, we met an Indian family at their summer fishing camp. There was an amazing amount of water shooting down those rapids and we realized that the Churchill was a mighty big river.

Three miles more and we arrived at Keg Falls, where we held to the right, portaging up past the falls and entering Keg Lake as the skies began to clear. At six we stopped for a combination lunch and supper, then moved on again until we were interrupted by a float plane which landed nearby and taxied up to us. It was my friend Gib McEachern who was also the manager of Athabaska Airways. "I was flying by and saw you fellows down here, so thought I would drop in to see how you were doing," he said. After a short visit, he took off and we soon arrived at Island Portage, crossed that and finally set up camp on a rocky point on an island about three miles out into Drinking Lake.

With a nice fire going and a wind to blow the insects away, we relaxed and I dug my Alexander Mackenzie information out of my pack. Here is what he said about Frog Skin Portage and Trade Lake.

> The **Portage de Traite** *(Frog Skin Portage)* received its name from Mr. Joseph Frobisher who penetrated into this part of the country of Canada in the spring of 1775, where he met with the Indians on their way to Churchill, according to annual custom, with their canoes full of valuable furs. They traded with him for as many of them as his canoes could carry and in consequence of this transaction, the lake received and has since retained its name of Trade Lake.

Then he says that when the Crees first arrived in this area, they either destroyed or drove back the Chipewyans,

> . . . whom they held in great contempt on many accounts, but particularly for their ignorance in hunting the beaver, as well as in preparing, stretching and drying the skins of the animals. And as a sign of their derision, they stretched the skin of a frog and hung it up at the Portage.

219

"So there you have the story as told by Mr. Mackenzie." It had been a good day in spite of the rain as we had moved fifty miles.

Friday, 16 July

DAY 91

We slept fast and were back on Drinking Lake shortly after sunrise. A couple of hours later we stopped at Drinking Falls Lodge and had a very good breakfast of pancakes, bacon, potatoes and coffee. Then it was across Nistowiak Lake. We could hear the roar of Nistowiak Falls off to our left. "I wish we had time to go over and see those falls," Clint said. "But we better not take time for that."

"Maybe the next time through. It sounds like there must be a lot of water pouring down through there."

"Sure does. The Montreal River drops more than fifty feet back in there below Iskwatikan Lake. I remember reading somewhere that according to Sir George Simpson of the Hudson's Bay Company, Lac La Ronge had a fur trading post from 1782 until about 1830 and by that time, the fur and game animals had all been killed off in the surrounding area."

We soon paddled into Drop Lake, portaged Stanley Rapids and arrived at Stanley Mission, Saskatchewan, before noon. Shortly after our arrival, Gib McEachern dropped in. He showed us around the settlement of about eight hundred people. We had lunch together at the local restaurant. In Stanley the Hudson's Bay Company has competition from the Co-op store. We bought a few supplies and visited the old Anglican church, across the river from the settlement. The mission is the oldest building in all of Saskatchewan and was still in use with its parking lot for canoes along the river bank.

In the afternoon we moved on through Mountain Lake, over the portages and into Otter Lake. It was beautiful canoeing country with lots of islands in the lakes, with their irregular shorelines. The lakes were full of fish and the trees, mostly conifers, were larger than we had found before entering the Churchill.

We passed one small island, not more than fifty feet long and half that wide, with seven husky puppies imprisoned on it. They appeared to be in good condition and well cared for.

More and more Indian camps were in evidence. Almost every island or point had some sort of shelter. White tents were the most numerous. Some had split fish hanging on smoking racks with smouldering fires below and fish nets often hung nearby to dry.

Late in the afternoon, Gib again splashed down nearby, turned off the engine and with door open, invited us to swing into Missinipe to join him for supper. He promised us the best steak dinner we'd had in our lives. It would be slightly off our course but we just couldn't turn him down. We arrived at the settlement by seven-thirty and received a royal welcome from Gib. He introduced us to several people, including the owner of the lodge, Bill Charrin. We also met Gib's wife, Karen, who was the radio operator at the base for Athabaska Airways. Gib had arranged for rooms with showers for us as well as a feast which included the steak, with all of the trimmings. Once we had finished our supper, Gib asked, "How would you two like to go for a little plane ride?"

Naturally we jumped at the opportunity and were soon flying back downriver as far as Stanley Mission, enjoying and taking aerial photos of the river and lakes we had just paddled up through. Gib asked all kinds of questions about our journey and was interested in about every detail. He even offered to call Jenny the next day from La Ronge to inform her of our whereabouts. He was terrific!

It had been a good day. As we turned in, Clint remarked, "This was one fun canoeing day!"

Saturday, 17 July

DAY 92

Bill Charrin and Gib were up early to prepare our breakfast and see us off. They would take no pay for either our lodging or meals. "I have a hunch that Gib arranged and paid for it all," I remarked to Clint, as we paddled on toward the bridge.

We portaged Otter Rapids along the right at the bridge where the highway now crosses the Churchill River. This is now a year-round road which leads to the south end of Reindeer Lake with a branch road leading up the west side of Wollaston Lake.

While crossing Devil Lake, Gib came flying over, circled and passing low in front of us, made an air drop consisting of some vitamins, other medication and a book he had told me about. "Good ol' Gib," Clint said, as we picked up the waterproof floating package and the plane soon disappeared over the trees in the southeast.

"Yes. He sure has done a lot of nice things for us."

An hour later we were getting hungry and stopped at a flat rock point which gently sloped from the forest down to the river's edge. Clint whipped out his fishing rod and before I had the fire started, he had brought in the first of seven northerns that he caught within a few minutes. I soon had the griddle hot and we enjoyed a delicious fish fry. That little flat point of rock made a very compact area from where the fish were caught, cleaned, fried and eaten all within ten feet of the water's edge. Clint was literally taking those fish out of the water and laying them on the griddle without moving a single step. The first fish was frying before he had caught the seventh one.

The temperature was about seventy degrees and even though the skies were overcast, we were so comfortable when we finished our meal that we just didn't want to hurry away. "There's only one thing wrong with this place," I commented. "It's just too good. Have you noticed, there are no mosquitoes here?"

"Yeah. This would make a perfect campsite. Too bad that it's not camping time."

The Rapids of the Dead above Dead Lake turned out to be three sets of rapids. We paddled up the first, waded and lined the second set with our tennis shoes on, and paddled up the third set. The water was warming up nicely, so wading by then was no big shock to our systems. In addition to those rapids, there was plenty of other fast water to negotiate before we arrived in Trout Lake.

About two miles out into Trout Lake we stopped for the night on an island. Once the tent was up, Clint asked, "Verlen, do you know how Dead Lake and the Rapids of the Dead came by their names?"

"No. I think I've read about it somewhere but I don't remember. Tell me about it."

"Well, according to Sigurd Olson, back in the days of the voyageurs there was a point near the foot of those rapids which was covered with human bones. There, an encampment of Cree Indians had died off from an epidemic of smallpox which had ravaged the tribes a few years earlier. The voyageurs named the place **Portage des Morts**, which translates to Portage of the Dead, and so the lake also became known as Lake of the Dead."

"Now I remember reading about that in Mackenzie's book." After a pause in our conversation, I said, "I think I understand why there is such a concentration of Indians along this river."

"Why is that?"

"This area appears to have an abundance of all kinds of life. The food chain must be complete. The water is murky, full of algae, bloodsuckers, crayfish, all kinds of small life and water bugs. Water plants grow profusely and there's all kinds of fish and waterfowl, as well as other birds and animals. The Indians have settled along this river system because of the plentiful supply of natural food."

"You're probably right," Clint replied.

At about eleven o'clock, the mosquitoes suddenly appeared in full force. We were driven into the tent to escape the hungry horde. As I was drifting off to sleep, I recalled that during our crossing of Dead Lake, we had met a young couple in a high-ended canoe. We had stopped and talked with them for a minute. The woman's first words were, "We've been out with our canoe for two weeks." When we told them where we had come from since mid-April and where we intended to go, I'm sure we must have ruined their whole day.

Sunday, 18 July

DAY 93

We moved on through Trout Lake and negotiated the rapids by paddling up through the channel on the right. Next came Birch Rapids with its good trail on the left.

Lunch time found us on a rocky island in Black

Bear Island Lake where Clint caught more fish. We also had a can of pork and beans, deviled ham, bread, hot cocoa, coffee, pudding and fig cookies. It took a lot of fuel to keep us going. While we enjoyed the food, we cooked up a large kettle of mixed dried fruit for future meals.

During the afternoon we took a shore break on another small rocky island. Clint fished again and caught a nine-pound northern pike and several smaller ones which he promptly released as we chose not to carry them along. In western Bear Island Lake a power boat with a small middle aged man and his Indian wife with a teenage son pulled up alongside us for a chat. They lived on an island in the lake and told us that they had a couple of older married children. The wife's only complaint was that she kept running out of tobacco. Unfortunately, we couldn't help. Their nearest store was down in Lac La Ronge.

Clint took charge of the maps from that day on. I was pleased about that, as I had been doing all of the navigating. It was seven-thirty by the time we arrived at Silent Rapids. There, Clint fished once more off the rocky island along the left shore and caught both walleyes and northerns faster than I could fillet them. With enough fish for two big meals, we lined up those rapids, crossed over to the right shore and proceeded to enjoy another delicious fish supper before we crawled into the tent early to escape the swarms of mosquitoes which had moved in on us.

Monday, 19 July

DAY 94

Shortly after embarking we moved up alongside a huge and powerful whirlpool, which was just below a short bend, where the river had narrowed down to only about a hundred feet. By pouring on all of the power we could muster, we were able to keep advancing along the extreme outside of that silent swoosher and continue on up the river.

"It would have been a real surprise, to be coming downstream around that point and drop right into the eye of that whirlpool," Clint remarked.

"I guess some canoeists wouldn't have the power required to pull up and get out of that one," I replied. We were enjoying another very fine canoeing day, with temperatures in the seventies. At Needle Rapids we picked a mixed pan of strawberries, raspberries and gooseberries, which we saved for lunch. Those berries were just beginning to ripen and were the first of many we would pick from then on.

Soon we headed out across island-filled Sandfly Lake. Birds entertained us all the way across. First it was a pair of pelicans. Eagles soared overhead or rested on a tree stub. Arctic terns chattered as they looked us over and circled only a few feet above. Ducks with their young broods frequently skurried away as we passed islands. There were a few gulls but not as many as we had seen earlier on the journey.

Indians were lifting gill nets and taking out their fish. We tried to talk with a couple, but it was difficult due to the difference in languages. We were seeing lots of them in their summer camps. The whole Churchill River valley had a fishy smell about it. We often passed points where fish had been cleaned by the hundreds. In some of those places the shore was lined with the guts and skeletons of fish. There just weren't enough of the scavenger-type birds such as gulls to keep those places cleaned up.

Lunch on an island found Clint fishing again off the rocky shore and catching walleyes on practically every cast. The fishing on the Churchill was fantastic with fish to be caught everywhere Clint tried. The only bait he used was a medium-sized yellow and red dotted daredevil.

Near the center of Sandfly Lake we met a pair of the few canoe paddling campers we were to meet that summer. They were Jim Klatt of Decorah, Iowa, and George Watson of Springfield, Missouri. Those two were paddling down the river and were on a two hundred and eighty mile journey from Ile a la Crosse to Otter Lake, which would take them six weeks to complete. They thought they were on a pretty long trip until we told them about what we were doing. They were astounded. We cautioned them about the whirlpool on downriver.

Rounding the point just below Belanger, we came across a fat and sassy mother mink that apparently had a den of youngsters on a small, rocky island. That mink was very nervy and it was evident from her actions that she was trying to keep us from invading her domain.

The settlement of Belanger is a thing of the past and only one old building was still standing. On up the river we met two Indians who were paddling a big, square-stern canoe, but not by choice. Their motor had broken down. With only one paddle, they had made another one from a dry spruce log. They were on their way to Black Bear Island Lake and at the speed they were moving, they would certainly be at it for another day or two.

By camping time we had crossed the entire north end of Pinehouse Lake and arrived at the foot of Snake Rapids. The loons had been noisy all afternoon, and during the evening they put up a terrific fuss. Those noisy loons were telling all creatures, including a couple of weary canoeists, that bad weather should be expected on the following day.

12

THE UPPER CHURCHILL RIVER

> *I want to go back to my lean, ashen plains;*
> *My rivers that flash into foam;*
> *My ultimate valleys where solitude reigns;*
> *My trail from Fort Churchill to Nome.*
>
> — *Robert Service,*
> ***I'm Scared of It All***

Tuesday, 20 July

DAY 95

We slept in as thunderstorms were sweeping the area. We were well protected from the strong winds by a high river bank. Finally, we decided to brave it and were underway before eight-thirty, facing three miles of fast water up past the Snake Rapids. The two-mile-long portage trail was on the right. By pouring on the power, we were able to paddle up along the left side of those rapids almost all the way. The only place we had to wade and line the

228

canoe along was for about a hundred yards at the middle drop and then less than that at the upper set of rapids. We covered that three miles in one hour. Not bad! Certainly we saved at least an hour by not portaging.

Along the west side of Sandy Lake we met three men who were doing some survey work for a mining company. We stopped at their camp which was set up in a low, swampy area and visited for a while over coffee and cookies. They asked us to stay for lunch but we had to move on. They had learned that we were low on a few supplies, so they gave us a pound can of much-needed butter and a pound of lard.

The wind was really whipping up when, at a little before two, we stopped for lunch. Then it was on up through the rapids below Dreger Lake without getting out of the canoe. Then across that lake where we observed our first baby loon riding on the back of its mother.

Leaving Dreger Lake we moved on through a cut-off called the Grass River, which shortened our route by about five miles. "We are in the Marshes of Haultain," Clint remarked. "At least that is what Sig Olson called this area when he came down through here, a few years ago."

"This certainly is one huge marsh!"

We made it through the Grass River channel even though part of the time we were pushing our way through cattails, marsh grass and water lilies. We pulled some of the cattails to try their roots for food. They weren't bad tasting and they were about the consistency of cabbage hearts.

Back on the main river again, we soon met three canoes. It was a group of men from the vicinity of Edmonton, Alberta. They had put in at Buffalo Narrows and were heading down to the Otter River. We chatted with them for a few minutes before moving on. That was the most canoes we had seen since we left the Boundary Waters Canoe Area.

Verlen gathers cattails for food

There was a steady current for the next dozen miles with the river continuing to flow through that huge swamp. As we moved on toward Knee Lake, I began to wonder if it was going to be another night for us to camp in the mud and willows. There were huge flat areas of open marsh with few trees but thousands of birds. Arctic terns soared, wheeled and dipped, keeping up their constant chatter of 'tee-ar' or 'kip-kip-kip-tee-ar.' Flocks of snipes, sandpipers and yellowlegs skittered and ran everywhere. Occasionally, a solitary sandpiper would circle over us for a close look, then return to its tree top, all the time continuing its incessant, shrill 'weet-weet-weet-weet' without letup. There were ducks everywhere as well as a few gulls and pelicans.

On the right as we entered Bentley Bay of Knee Lake, we saw a cluster of cabins. We were passing the Elak Dase Indian Reservation. We kept on going and much to our surprise, only about a mile beyond the settlement we found an island which looked as though it could make a good campsite. It was already past nine so we decided to stop for the night.

In the ninety-five days since we had left Lachine, Quebec, our camp chores had become somewhat routine. This is the way it usually worked out. After selecting a campsite, we would both unload the canoe together, then haul it out of the water and usually turn it upside down and tie it to a tree or a very secure anchor. This is an important habit to develop. No matter how high and dry or secure you may think the canoe is, it should always be tied to something solid. In remote country, that action could prevent real grief.

Back in the sixties, four of us camped on a point of land in the bush country of Ontario. We had pulled the canoes up into a shallow depression when a sudden squall came up and as we were inside our flapping tents trying to hold them down, the wind picked up both canoes and blew them up over a ten-foot-high ridge of rock and out into the lake. We had some bad moments before we found them twenty-four hours later on the opposite shore, slowly being chewed up on the rocks. We were lucky. If it had been a really big lake, our bad moments might have been more like bad days.

With the canoe secured, Clint would immediately proceed to select just the right spot to put up the tent and lay out the foam pads and sleeping bags inside. While he was doing this, I would be gathering firewood, building a fireplace if rocks were available, getting a fire going, and proceeding to get a hot meal. Very rarely would we make camp early enough to allow for fishing, for a fish supper. Quite often it would be dark by the time

231

we stopped. Then usually the first thing we would do was both scrounge for enough firewood for supper and breakfast because firewood can be difficult to find in the dark. Then we would go about our other chores. Clint got very good at putting up the tent even in the dark, taking into consideration level ground, bumps and lumps, wind direction and bugs. If he couldn't find what suited him, he'd work a spot over until it did. He was also an expert campfire cook, and occasionally we switched around. But when we were in a hurry we each were faster at our thing. I got so I knew where everything was in the kitchen pack and food bags, and even in the dark I seldom had to use a light, other than the campfire.

There are all kinds of campfires. Ours was nearly always a cookfire, being smaller and more neatly contained, usually built up with rocks for a fireplace to control the heat and wind and for a more convenient cooking area. In rock country, gathering rocks for a fireplace is as automatic as gathering firewood, and usually takes even less time. The key to a good rock fireplace is finding a good chimney rock. A flat face rock eighteen by twelve inches or more, standing on its end will act as a chimney, funneling the smoke away from the cook. We always used only "squaw" wood, that is, whatever dead, dry wood could be obtained without using an axe or saw. On rare occasions, to fit the fireplace we might have to use a saw, once the wood was gathered.

Starting a fire under any condition (even a downpour rain) is the test of your skill. It gets to be a matter of personal pride to never have to use more than one match. If you have to use two, you feel as though you have failed. We learned to carry a roll of birch bark wedged up in the bow of the canoe for use when all else failed.

We developed a loose system that suited us and kept things going smoothly. There seems to be an unwritten camp rule that the cook never has to wash the dishes. Neither of us liked to wash dishes, so we usually tried to keep them to a minimum. Our cup and spoon were considered personal items that each took care of himself. Nobody touched yours but you, and we kept them in our personal bag. We didn't have dishes. We used large aluminum soup bowls instead. If we had oatmeal or stew, one of us would divide it equally between the bowl and the pot, and the other would choose which one he wanted — that way, neither could feel it wasn't divided fairly. And, when you are hungry enough, you would be surprised how sharp eyed and greedy you can be over a tasty portion of food. Another thing, the cook should never have the habit of sampling his food before it is divided. A lot of choice tidbits can disappear that way. The other guy is sure to notice, with a certain amount of discontent.

We had a relaxed, easygoing system to all of our camp chores—which was really no system at all. We each did whatever he wanted to do. There was never any schedule of assignments—no one told the other what he should do, not even a "you do this and I'll do that." Yet everything got done quickly and efficiently, and our camp lifestyle had a smooth natural flow. There were only the two of us, and if one of us was doing one thing, it usually was obvious what the other should do. This probably would not work as well in a group of more than two.

How well you put your campfire out and how neat and unspoiled you leave your campsite will reveal what kind of outdoorsman you really are. A person should never build a fire in a woods or on humus soil. But if on rare occasion one should have to, they should be extra cautious about putting the fire out. A dead root can be burning underground or the humus can be burning down deep and you wouldn't know it unless you stirred the fire site with a stick while pouring water on it.

A very good habit to develop is to take one last good look around the campsite after everything is all loaded up and you are ready to shove off. Make sure you have left nothing behind, not even as much as a gum wrapper. Leave nothing behind you except foot prints and ashes.

Wednesday, 21 July

DAY 96

We started the day with a cold breakfast of stewed fruit with leftover pancakes and syrup. I had left the pancakes overnight in a pot with a tarp and canteen on top of them. Somehow the mice found them, chewing a hole through our good nylon tarp to get at them. We ate what pancakes the mice couldn't handle.

Embarking before six we moved on across Knee Lake as the rain began to fall. Then it was back into the river where we paddled through Knee Rapids, holding to the left all the way. At Crooked Rapids we waded and lined for less than a hundred yards. That was the only time we were out of the canoe in that six-mile stretch of fast water where according to our maps, the elevation above sea level changes by twenty-seven feet.

Lunch time found us in Primeau Lake where Clint again decided to fish, bringing in both wall-eyes and northerns. With our lunch we also tried some Labrador tea which was plentiful along the Churchill. There was not a lot of flavor in it, but it certainly was stimulating. We decided that it might be even better if it could have been dried and crushed as the Indians used to do.

We were beginning to get out of the Canadian Shield country which we had enjoyed so much, and moving through a flat, wooded area with lots of

Young bald eagles along Churchill River

swamps. We would soon be leaving the rocky Shield country for the balance of our journey.

I spotted a bald eagle's nest in the top of a large spruce tree near the river bank. There was a still taller spruce about fifteen feet away, so I climbed the tallest tree with both cameras and photographed two full-grown juvenile eagles in their nest.

Once across Primeau Lake we hustled on into Dipper Lake passing the Dipper Rapids Indian Reservation. Then it was across Dipper Lake to Pine River, just below Dipper Rapids. We found a good short portage and re-embarked just above the main drop. That left two more smaller sets of rapids to ascend. We hit the first one hard and managed to pull up through its drop of about eighteen inches.

The current was pulling us out toward the center of a horseshoe dropoff, which I didn't notice as I continued to push furiously ahead. Clint saw what was going on and yelled out with excitement, "Hit it! Pull harder! We're losing ground! We're being sucked over and will be going down backwards!"

I glanced around and saw the danger. Then pulling together with all the power we could muster, we finally pulled away from that drop and out of danger. The next drop was a fairly easy one and once above that one we called it a day.

Thursday, 22 July

DAY 97

Underway before eight, we worked our way up through the steady current of the upper Churchill. We found that Deer Rapids was actually two separate drops in the river, about a mile apart. Then it was Leaf and Drum Rapids with a total of five drops. Clint and I turned on full speed and made it up through all of those rapids with paddle power, except for about a hundred and thirty yards. There we hopped out into the river, wearing our tennis shoes, and waded along towing the canoe on a line behind us. We also paddled up the Patuanak Rapids.

By pushing along steadily we had covered the sixteen miles from Dipper, through the last ripple of Drum Rapids, in less than four hours. Both of us had checked the time. "I wouldn't have believed that it was possible," I remarked.

"We certainly made fantastic time coming up through there."

Since leaving Needle Rapids below Sandfly Lake, we had made only one portage. That was the short one at Dipper. We had made it through the toughest stretch of the Churchill, gaining one hundred and fifteen feet of altitude while doing so. Paddling, wading and lining were much faster for us than portaging.

The wind was coming out of the south by the time we entered Shagwenau Lake. Arriving at the settlement of Patuanak by two o'clock, we shopped for groceries at the Hudson's Bay store, then sat out on the dock in front of the store and lunched on a can of cold pork and beans along with cookies and pop. The town of Patuanak is situated on a peninsula and is in the Wapachewunak Indian Reservation. The place had a population of about six hundred people, most of whom were members or descendants of the Chipewyan tribe.

Then came the quarter-mile carry across the reservation enabling us to avoid Shagwenau Rapids and shorten our route by about four miles. That put us into Lac Ile-a-la-Crosse. Battling the headwinds we paddled south to Halfway Point, along the west shore. There up in the brush is where we made camp.

Friday, 23 July

DAY 98

For the first time since leaving Flin Flon, we slept a full eight hours. The strong southeast wind combined with a downpour of rain had slowed us down. A heavy surf was pounding Halfway Point. We were chafing at the bit to move, so before nine we carried our outfit over to the north side of the point, loaded up, snapped the spray cover down and pushed off. Five or six strokes of the paddles and we rounded the tip of the point into the full force of the wind.

Heading on down the shore line we rode up and down over some huge swells. Frequently a roller would break over the bow, splashing over me and the spray cover. "We wouldn't have been able to even be out here, without this spray cover," I yelled. We continued to battle the wind, rain and waves. An hour later, we noticed that the wind's velocity was dropping and by noon the rain had stopped.

Lunch time found us on Sandy Point, near the place where Lac Ile-a-la-Crosse bends around to the northwest into the Aubichon Arm of the lake. Walking around the point to exercise our legs, we found lots of ripe raspberries, gooseberries and Saskatoon berries. There were also plenty of wild roses and it looked as though there would soon be a good crop of rose hips.

"It looks like there's another storm brewing in the northwest," Clint said.

Glancing in that direction, I answered, "Sure is. I hope it isn't moving this way."

Within a few minutes, we had rounded Sandy Point and as we headed up the Aubichon Arm, the wind again picked up. This time it was coming right out of the northwest and the storm was once more moving in on us. We struggled on, nosing into that strong headwind all afternoon but making little progress. We gave it up for the day on a small sandy point opposite Watchusk Bay.

While I went for a walk and feasted on raspberries, Clint tried fishing again from along the shore but only managed to catch a few small pike. That evening our talk was again of the voyageurs who used to paddle the waterway along in front of our camp. We talked of the Frobishers, who first explored the route into Lac Ile-a-la-Crosse in 1776.

"Just think of that," Clint said, shaking his head. "There are probably few people in the United States who realize what was going on way up here during the Revolutionary War. As I recall, it was on July 2 of that year that the Continental Congress passed a motion made by Richard Henry Lee of Virginia, that the colonists ought to be independent. Then on July 4, 1776, they adopted the Declaration of Independence."

"It's difficult to comprehend that those fur traders were exploring this far into the interior even before there was a United States." I then pulled from my personal bag the copies of pages from Alexander Mackenzie's book, and read about how the Indians met each spring in the Ile-a-la-Crosse area. Here is what it said:

> *The time of rejoicing was but short, and was soon interrupted by the necessary preparations for their annual journey to Churchill, to exchange their furs for such European articles as were now become necessary to them. The shortness of the seasons, and the great length of their way requiring utmost despatch, the most active men of the tribe, with their youngest women, and a few of their children undertook the voyage, under the direction of some of their chiefs, following the waters already described, to their discharge at Churchill Factory, which are called, as has already been observed, the Missinipi, or Great Waters. There they remained no longer than was sufficient to barter their commodities, with a supernumerary day or two to gratify themselves with indulgence of spirituous liquors. At the same time the inconsiderable quantity they could purchase to carry away with them, for a regale with their friends, was held sacred, and reserved to heighten the enjoyment of their return home, when the amusements, festivities, and religious solemnities of the spring were repeated.*

"The Churchill River was then called the Mis-

239

sinipi, wasn't it?"

"Yes. That was the Cree name for it. The voyageurs later called it the English River before it finally became the Churchill."

"Then after 1775, the Indians no longer had to make that long journey to Hudson Bay?"

"No. Their annual journeys just about ended after Joseph Frobisher intercepted them. It's explained in Mackenzie's book. Here is what he said about it:

> *"It was about this time, that Mr. Joseph Frobisher, one of the gentlemen engaged in the trade, determined to penetrate into the country yet unexplored, to the north and westward, and, in the spring of the year 1775, met the Indians from that quarter on their way to Fort Churchill, at Portage de Traite, so named from that circumstance, on the banks of the Missinipi, or Churchill river, latitude 55. 25. North, longitude 104. West. It was indeed, with some difficulty that he could induce them to trade with him, but he at length procured as many furs as his canoes could carry. In this perilous expedition he sustained every kind of hardship incident to a journey through a wild and savage country, where his subsistence depended on what the woods and the waters produced. These difficulties, nevertheless, did not discourage him from returning in the following year, when he was equally successful. He then sent his brother to explore the country still further west, who penetrated as far as the lake of Isle a la Crosse, in latitude 55. 26. North, and longitude 108. West."*

"Portage de Traite was what we called Frog Skin Portage, wasn't it?"

"That's right. And from then on the Northwesters came up into these waters to trade, building those trading posts, or forts along the way. The volume of business of The Company, who were still operating down on Hudson's Bay, really dropped off for several years. Eventually, the H.B.C. also came into the interior to trade. The North West Company had just about cut off the supply of furs which formerly had gone to Churchill from this area. Then finally, in 1821, the two fur trading giants merged into what was to become the present-day Hudson's Bay Company."

Saturday, 24 July

DAY 99

At the upper end of the Churchill River, where it flows out of Churchill Lake, is a fifteen-mile stretch known as MacBeth Channel. Mid-morning found us nosing up through the channel and again facing a wind from the northwest under cloudy skies. The wind swung to the west and increased in velocity by the time we had entered Churchill Lake. There, with spray covers snapped into place, we found the going quite rough until we arrived at Buffalo Narrows, a little after noon.

Buffalo Narrows, Saskatchewan, was a settlement of about thirteen hundred people, most of whom were Chipewyans. We had a good roast beef dinner in the restaurant for the price of $1.85. Then it was to the 'Bay' and the Co-op stores where we purchased ample grub to take us all the way to Fort McMurray, Alberta. I tried to telephone Jenny, but there was no one at home. She must have been out shopping, so I walked over to the Department of Transport station and sent her a radiogram, letting her know where we were.

ONE INCREDIBLE JOURNEY

Just before leaving town at three-thirty, we stopped back at the restaurant for a beef sandwich and pop. Then it was on into Peter Pond Lake and straight west for about seven miles to get around the Thompson Peninsula. A strong squall line hit us as we rounded Fleury Point but we hung in there until we arrived on the lee side of Sandy Point.

Looking to the north it was easy to see that we could go no farther. The main body of Peter Pond Lake was solid with windswept white caps as far as we could see and that was a little too rough for us. Three Chipewyan gentlemen with a big wooden fishing boat with two motors were already waiting out the blow on Sandy Point by the time we arrived. They were from Dillon, the settlement at Peter Pond Indian Reservation. For the next two and a half hours, over two pots of tea and several pilot biscuits, we chatted with them. They supplied the fire and pilot biscuits while we supplied the tea and the pot.

They gave us a lot of information as we swapped stories. They pointed out a nearby monument to a young conservation officer who died in a plane crash near the point in 1959.

The wind began to die down some by mid-evening and our Chipewyan friends departed for home. We, however, decided to camp there on the point and try for an early start the next morning. Here is a short quote from my diary, written at ten P.M. --

> There are plenty of good Saskatoon berries around here, as well a some blueberries and raspberries. What's more, there are a lot of sand flies. As I write this from the safety of the tent, the hum and buzzing of the insects outside is almost a roar. We are also being treated to a chorus of bird songs and sounds. It's very comfortable and enjoyable in here. I have really been enjoying this

trip. No part of it has been dull. Every day is exciting and different. It's still daylight outside but we have noticed that the days are getting shorter.

Sunday, 25 July

DAY 100

The wind blew all night and the water was still very rough when we embarked at eight. It was slow going into the face of the northwest wind. We made a stop at Old Fort Point to do a little exploring and found where the old fort had once stood as well as where a cabin had recently burned.

Then it was on to Willow Point where we beached the canoe on a fine sand beach about five miles east of Dillon. Clint and I debated the pros and cons of whether to follow the shoreline around or to go straight across the big part of Peter Pond Lake. We both wanted to make the traverse as the shoreline route would be ten miles longer, but the seas on the lake were much too rough for us to make the gamble. So we waited, did some exploring, picked more delicious berries and listened to the music of the surf smacking up on the beach. It was also a wonderful place just to loaf on that sunny day while the wind held the insects at bay.

We found an Indian foot trail running parallel to the shore about fifty feet behind the willows. "We certainly are in Indian country," Clint remarked as we walked back on the beach.

"That's for sure! Have you noticed that we don't see many Indians in canoes? They all travel by motor boat."

"That's one thing that has changed since the

days of the fur traders. Then of course they also stay in more permanent-type settlements than they used to. Years ago, they followed the caribou, traveling up into the barrens each summer."

While waiting for a change in the wind we started talking of voyageur Peter Pond, who first traveled up through the lake which now bears his name. "He was indeed a colorful character. He was born near Milford, Connecticut, fought in the early days of the War for Independence and then entered the fur trade at Detroit and later traded throughout the midwest. Then when he was thirty-five years of age in 1775, he set out from Fort Michilimackinac with two canoes and eight men for Canada. From Grand Portage they headed for Cumberland House which at that time was the farthest outpost of civilization.

"The H.B.C. post at Cumberland House had been built the previous year to compete with the independent traders such as Pond who had been putting a crimp in the monopoly of The Company. The Indians, of course, were overjoyed to see the fur traders come into their area as up until that time they'd had to haul their furs nearly a thousand miles down the river to Fort Prince of Wales on the shore of Hudson Bay.

"On his trip from Grand Portage, Pond received a taste of the North Country's unforgiving nature. A wild August snowstorm caught his party as they were crossing Lake Winnipeg. That storm cost him four men and one of the canoes. Then in September, a local Indian chief forced him to give up most of his remaining provisions before they allowed him to pass. It was late October before Pond and his three survivors finally reached Cumberland House. He quickly built a small fort only a short distance from the Hudson's Bay fort, which had been constructed there during the previous year by Samuel Hearne. Competition was keen at the confluence of the Saskatchewan and Sturgeon Rivers for the next several years.

"While at Cumberland House, Pond made a discovery that did much to open the frontier even farther into the northwest. Through his close association and good relations with the Cree Indians, he discovered a product known as pemmican. Inasmuch as canoe travel to distant places such as Grand Portage usually required much of the summer, available food supplies had long been a serious limiting factor. What was needed was a compact, nutritious and easily preserved source of energy. Pemmican, a concoction of dried buffalo or deer meat mixed with berry tallow and bear grease was just the answer. The ever-resourceful Peter Pond adopted pemmican as his main traveling food and this he also bought from the Indians. From then on he and his men could substantially extend their range and so they set up a supply line of outposts stocked with this non-perishable and easily stored, high-energy food.

"That allowed him to seek out the fabled Northwest Passage across the continent to the Pacific Ocean, which explorers had already been searching for for over two hundred years.

"When the North West Company was organized in 1778, the wintering traders wanted to open up new territory to keep ahead of the H.B.C. Peter Pond was sent to Lake Athabaska which, according to explorer Alexander Henry, 'was a country hitherto unknown but from Indian reports.' So Pond, along with four canoes and sixteen nervous voyageurs, was going where no white man had ever before been. To them, it might as well have been the end of the earth. They followed the Churchill River to its source and eventually they crossed Lac la Loche and found the old Indian trail which had been in use for uncounted centuries. They followed it across the awesome thirteen-mile Methy Portage and down the Clearwater River. There the pioneering group again launched their canoes and followed that roaring stream down to its confluence with the Athabaska River. Then about two hundred miles north, just before they entered Lake Athabaska, Pond built a winter camp.

"The Chipewyans were overjoyed to see a white trader come into their midst. According to Alexander Mackenzie, they gave Pond a fantastic price in furs for the trade goods he brought. Before the following spring he had accumulated twice as many furs as his canoes could carry. And best of all was the superb quality of the beaver pelts traded. Those were superior to any that had ever before been shipped through Montreal to the felt makers of Europe. Those Chipewyans were honest people, too. The furs his canoes couldn't carry out with them were stored in his winter huts and they were still there, untouched and in perfect condition, when he returned the following autumn."

"That certainly is interesting. Didn't Pond have something to do with talking Alexander Mackenzie into continuing his search for the Northwest Passage?"

"Yes, he did. In 1784 young Alexander Mackenzie was sent by his partners to take charge of their post at Ile-a-la-Crosse. Then the following spring Pond and Mackenzie made the long trip to Grand Portage together with their loads of furs. Mackenzie was deeply impressed by the fact that Pond was almost certain that the waters flowing out of Great Slave Lake led directly down to the Pacific Ocean. While in Grand Portage that year, Mackenzie was assigned to Athabaska, to replace Pond, who wanted to go back to Connecticut after a thirty year absence.

"Fired with a secret goal of finding that Northwest Passage, Alexander Mackenzie made the return trip to Pond's old post in a record-breaking fifty-two days."

By early afternoon the wind died down. We embarked and were paddling in a dead calm before we

A trapper's 'rat' canoe

completed the eighteen-mile traverse to the mouth
of the La Loche River. Starting up the La Loche we
found very little current. It was nearly a hundred
yards wide near its mouth with lots of grass and
water lilies. The area resembled a big swamp.
Coming to some higher ground as we approached the
junction with the Kimowi River, we made camp in the
home of millions of mosquitoes. There we stumbled
across a small canvas-covered 'rat' canoe with a
bear skin in it. It probably belonged to a local
trapper. We put the canoe into the river and took
it for a trial run before returning it to the exact
spot where we found it.

247

ONE INCREDIBLE JOURNEY

D A Y   1 0 1

We were harassed by one terrific swarm of mosquitoes as we broke camp and headed on up the river
that dreary and misty morning. Our insect problem
continued all forenoon as we struggled on upstream.
The La Loche River was alive with every sort of bug
and insect imaginable.

In places water weeds with ten-foot-long stems
floating on the surface nearly choked the river
completely. In several places the bow of the canoe
would ball up with the long grass and bring us to a
stop. Then we would back up, push the ball of
grass to one side with the paddle, and again proceed. During the first two hours it was one shallow rapids or obstruction after another and usually
with not more than a hundred yards between them.

"We need to hurry along as much as possible,"
I reminded Clint, "as this is the day we are scheduled to again meet cameraman Phil at the far end of
Methy Portage. I know we won't make it today, but
for certain he will be camping over there tonight."

"If he beats us there, that would really be a
switch," Clint replied. "Every time before, we
have had to wait for him and my guess is that we'll
probably have to wait for him over there again."

The La Loche River is small, being not much
more than a creek above its confluence with the
Kimowi. There were at least thirty small, shallow
riffles or rapids. We lined and waded the places
that we couldn't paddle or pole. After those first
couple of hours we discovered that we were moving
through a huge swampy area with one snakey turn
after another. We were going more back and forth
than ahead against the slow but steady current.

We met no traffic along the way but we did see
several used campfire spots and also passed another
old dilapidated and abandoned canoe along the

shore. Then we found a four-foot-high spot on the river bank for the lunch break, but that still didn't get us away from the insects.

In early evening we came to another series of rapids where wading and lining were again required for about a half mile. At that same time a big black thunderstorm hit us with lots of wind and a downpour of rain which soon blew over. Then as we neared Lac La Loche, someone had put a stone dam across our creek. Next it was under a foot bridge where the trail between the settlement of La Loche and the Indian reservation crosses. All along the river we had found numerous ducks of many varieties with broods of ducklings of all sizes.

Our big moment of the day came when we finally broke through the last weeds and out into Lac La Loche. We were both happy to be finished with that little river. Nearly every day had its big moments for us along with the challenges and satisfactions of accomplishment upon which we thrived.

We were met by a group of Chipewyan children as we paddled up to the dock at La Loche that evening. They escorted us all the way through town to the restaurant where we had another good steak supper. We bought but few supplies as we only wanted the necessities to carry across Methy Portage.

La Loche was a settlement of about fifteen hundred people and we were told in the restaurant that ninety-nine percent of the population were natives of the area. The settlement has recently been connected by a road from Buffalo Narrows and the outside world. We must have been quite a curiosity, judging from the way the people looked at us. We were even escorted back to the canoe by our new-found friends.

Inasmuch as we prefer not to camp near a settlement, we paddled on up the lake, and by ten o'clock found a much-used grassy campsite on the west end of the island in Lac La Loche Narrows.

That place was also the residence of millions more of those very hungry mosquitoes.

Tuesday, 27 July

D A Y   1 0 2

We paddled to the northwest, heading for Wallis Bay and the little creek which leads to the portage. Before nine-thirty we had found the creek. As we moved along there was no noticeable current. The creek became narrower and narrower as well as bushier and bushier. It was also crooked. We wondered how the voyageurs could have made it through there with their big canoes.

A little more than a mile up the stream we came to a beaver dam. Just to the left of that we found the beginning of the famous Methy Portage. Within a few minutes we had unloaded and moved our canoe and gear to the site of the old post at the top of a little hill. We needed to sort and repack things for the long and arduous thirteen-mile haul across the height of land to the Clearwater River.

The present day take out place was quite brushy but the original trail was very easy to see, even though it was beginning to grow up with brush, and tree limbs were closing in on it. We had an early lunch using as many canned goods as we could consume. Then after several last-minute adjustments, at eleven-thirty we shouldered our equipment and headed off down the long trail. It was a gorgeous, warm, sunny day, ideal for a hike but after the first hour with that one hundred and seventy pound load on my back, the remainder of the day was not too comfortable.

Methy Portage is definitely a well-worn trail. We were surprised that it hadn't grown in more as it has seldom been used in recent years. The route

leads through an area covered with a young growth
of jack pines but the trail is still there, deeply
worn into the ground. As we trudged along that
afternoon our thoughts were of the famous men of
the past who had walked that same trail, men like
Peter Pond, Alexander Mackenzie, George Simpson and
Roderick McKenzie to mention only a few. Then
there were the hundreds of other voyageurs who
hauled the tons and tons of furs, trade goods and
canoes over that trail year after year.

The insects gave us a bad time as we struggled
along. They followed the canoe in swarms. The
black flies flew along, mostly on the outside of
the canoe and the mosquitoes swarmed along on the
inside. We hung in there, trying to ignore the
sweat and pain until we arrived at Rendezvous Lake,
having completed nearly nine miles of the Methy
Portage. By then darkness was settling in and we
were both ready to call it a day.

Wednesday, 28 July

DAY 103

We were off to a late start as we had caught
up on some much-needed rest. It was only about a
mile across the lake. The portage take out place
was not too well marked but once located, we were
back on a good solid trail. We loaded our packs
and the canoe on sore shoulders, aching backs and
hurting feet and were once more underway to cover
those final four miles.

The trail was more crowded with brush than the
southern section. We moved along through a thick
stand of young trees, which made it quite bothersome to keep the canoe moving. The footing was
solid and the trail reasonably level until the

final couple of miles. Then slowly it began to descend until finally in the last mile it took an abrupt drop and from then on it was really downhill.

At that point we made a stop. Looking down across the Clearwater valley the scene was breathtaking. As far as the eye could see, both to the right and to the left, that huge valley lay before us with its high and beautiful wooded ridges of hills. It was one of the grandest spots for scenery we had seen on the journey. It was also one of the most significant because from there on we would be going downhill with the rivers flowing in our direction. That was to be something we hadn't experienced since entering Lake Winnipeg.

The insects again pestered us all along the way with no breeze getting through the thick stand of trees. I really did sweat, mostly from the pain during those last four hours on the trail. I can truthfully say that never before in my life had I been more insect bitten in one day, but for some strange reason there was a deep satisfaction and enjoyment in it all.

We soon shouldered our loads and followed the ancient trail which drops more than six hundred feet of elevation in that final mile. That turned out to be the toughest part of the portage, toting our loads down that long, steep hill. But knowing that the end of Methy Portage was so near, made it bearable.

13

THE RAPIDS
OF THE DROWNED

> *Not by power, nor by might,*
> *But by my spirit saith the Lord.*
>
> — *Zechariah 4:6*

There was activity down on the riverbank. We could hear voices long before we broke out of the trees and into the clearing. As our steep trail leveled out at the bottom, there was Phil, movie camera on tripod, grinding away. It sure was good to set that canoe down. Clint was close behind slipping out of his packs.

Standing there to catch our breath for a moment and looking around, we saw the two boys that Phil had hired as guides and helpers. They were Mark and Phil Jean from Fort McMurray. We also met Dan Stein from the University of Saskatchewan and his crew of archaeologists who were doing excavation work along the river bank. Phil and the boys had flown in and landed in a wide spot upstream with a rented canoe, arriving two days ahead of us.

While Clint and I rested and lunched, we chatted with the group, filling them in on the more recent days of our travels. Dan Stein said, "If my group can dig up enough facts here, there is a good chance that the old post may someday in the future be reconstructed. At least, we hope it will be." We told them that as we had portaged down the trail from the hilltop, we had descended nearly seven hundred feet and now we would paddle down the rivers for nearly seventeen hundred miles to descend the next seven hundred feet.

Then, reluctantly at first, we did some filming sequences which Phil had planned. Finally at six in the evening, we shoved off into the waters of the Clearwater River, which we would follow for eighty miles to where it flows into the Athabasca at Fort McMurray.

We had progressed only a few miles when we pitched our tent where a short portage trail crosses an island in one of the sets of rapids. We were tired and needed some sleep to recuperate from our activities of the past couple of days. Sometime after we were asleep, Phil and his two boys came straggling along. They were making a lot of noise while trying to find the portage in the dark. I grabbed my flashlight as I jumped out of the tent. When they came ashore, we discovered that Phil had been fishing at a rapids as they came down and had caught one big northern pike. That monster certainly weighed more than thirty pounds.

I soon had the campfire going again and fed the hungry travelers.

Thursday, 29 July

DAY 104

It was nearly seven by the time our camp began to stir. As usual, I had been awake a couple of hours earlier but it was great to comfortably lie there and listen to the natural sounds including the murmur of the nearby rapids, the whistling of ducks' wings as they flew nearby, and the songs of the birds.

The five of us had breakfast together while Phil did some filming and Clint and I hobbled around camp, limbering up our sore muscles. The two of us soon broke camp while Phil and the Jean boys remained behind to boil up that huge fish for future meals. They knew they were going to have to hustle as Phil needed to arrive in Fort McMurray ahead of us. He said that they would paddle all night if they didn't overtake us by evening.

Clint and I hustled right along. It was wonderful to be moving in the direction the water was flowing. The current of the Clearwater was neither as fast nor the water as clear as we had expected. There were a few sets of rapids to negotiate early in the day but only one of importance once we had crossed the provincial border into Alberta.

By mid-forenoon we arrived at Whitemud Falls. There several sulfur springs bubble up into the river and there is a buildup of very unusual pinnacle rock formations. We later learned that the local people used to drink water from those springs for health purposes. Holding to the right we found a small channel. We took it and decided we had made a mistake as we scraped, scratched, bounced and banged over numerous drops. Then to our surprise we found ourselves below Whitemud Falls without portaging.

Along the shores of the river there were large grassy areas without trees, then there were areas

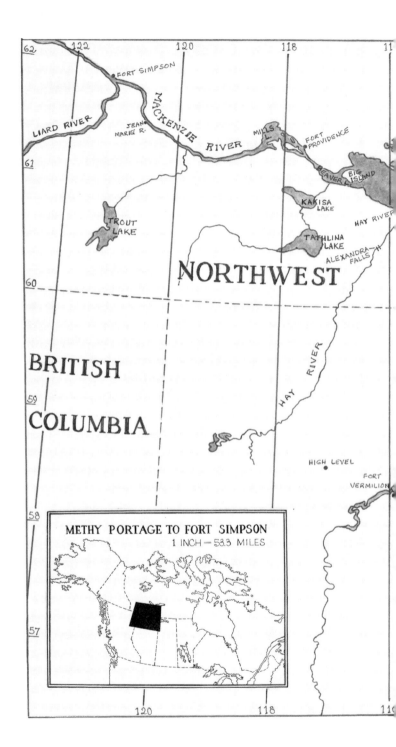

256

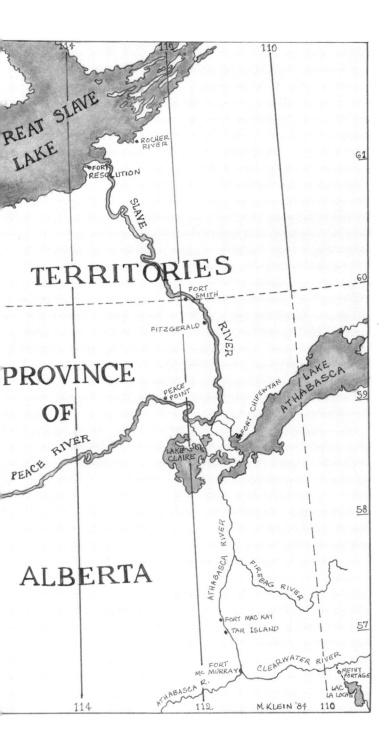

GREAT SLAVE LAKE

ROCHER RIVER

FORT RESOLUTION

SLAVE

TERRITORIES

FORT SMITH

FITZGERALD

RIVER

PROVINCE

OF

PEACE POINT

FORT CHIPEWYAN

LAKE ATHABASCA

PEACE RIVER

LAKE CLAIRE

ALBERTA

ATHABASCA RIVER

FIREBAG RIVER

FORT MAC KAY

TAR ISLAND

FORT MC MURRAY

CLEARWATER RIVER

METHY PORTAGE

ATHABASCA R.

LAC LA LOCHE

M. KLEIN '84

61

60

59

58

57

heavily forested followed by more grassy open areas. We were enjoying our descent of the Clearwater.

Only a few miles below the junction with the High Hill River which flows in from the north, we found a nice campsite on the right shore. After supper, Clint did a little fishing but to no avail. With a nice breeze blowing up the valley, insects were no big problem so we kept the fire going and talked. "What time do you think Phil and those two young men will arrive here tonight?" I asked.

"We should be so far ahead of them that it's unlikely they will catch us this side of McMurray."

"You may be right. Clint, while you were fishing I looked over my copies of pages from Alexander Mackenzie's book and found that I have his description of Methy Portage."

"Wonderful!" he said as he seated himself near me, upwind from the fire. "Read it to me."

"Methy Portage was known as Portage La Loche back in those days. It says,

> *The Portage la Loche is of a level surface, in some parts abounding with stones, but in general it is of entire sand, and covered with the cypress, the pine, the spruce-fir, and other trees natural to its soil. Within three miles of the north-west termination, there is a small round lake, whose diameter does not exceed a mile, and which affords a trifling respite to the labour of carrying. Within a mile of the termination of the Portage is a very steep precipice, whose ascent and descent appears to be equally impracticable in any way, as it consists of a succession of eight hills, some of which are almost perpendicular; nevertheless, the Canadians contrive to surmount all these difficulties, even with their canoes and lading.*

The Rapids of the Drowned

This precipice, which rises upwards of a thousand feet above the plain beneath it, commands a most extensive, romantic, and ravishing prospect. From thence the eye looks down on the course of the little river, by some called the Swan river, and by others, the Clear-Water and Pelican river, beautifully meandering for upwards of thirty miles. The valley, which is at once refreshed and adorned by it, is about three miles in breadth, and is confined by two lofty ridges of equal height, displaying a most beautiful intermixture of wood and lawn, and stretching on till the blue mist obscures the prospect. Some parts of the inclining heights are covered with stately forests, relieved by promontories of the finest verdure, where the elk and buffalo find pasture. These are contrasted by spots where fire has destroyed the woods, and left a dreary void behind it. Nor, when I beheld this wonderful display of uncultivated nature, was the moving scenery of human occupation wanting to complete the picture. From this elevated situation, I beheld my people, diminished, as it were, to half their size, employed in pitching their tents in a charming meadow, and among the canoes, which, being turned upon their sides, presented their reddened bottoms in contrast with the surrounding verdure. At the same time, the process of gumming them produced numerous small spires of smoke, which, as they rose, enlivened the scene, and at length blended with the larger columns that ascended from the fires where the suppers were preparing. It was in the month of September when I enjoyed a scene, of which I do not presume to give an adequate description; and as it was the rutting season of the elk, the whistling of that animal was heard in all the variety which the echoes could afford it.

This river, which waters and reflects such enchanting scenery, runs, including its windings, upwards of eighty miles, when it discharges itself in the Elk River, according to the denomination of the natives, but commonly called by the white people, the Athabasca River, in latitude 56. 42. North.

At a small distance from Portage la Loche, several carrying-places interrupt the navigation of the river; about the middle of which are some mineral springs, whose margins are covered with sulphureous incrustations.

"Verlen, that certainly is interesting. Apparently the portage and the river have changed but little since Mackenzie traveled through here."

Friday, 30 July

DAY 105

We broke camp at eight but Phil and his young men still had not arrived. There was, however, a slim chance that if they did paddle all night as he had planned, they might have passed us in the darkness, not seeing our camp.

Clint remarked, "If they did move after dark, I guess Phil found out that night time paddling is not all moonlight and romance."

"Yeah. In this river night time navigation would be difficult. They would have bogged down on some of those sand bars with those millions of mosquitoes."

Rounding a bend we surprised a half grown black bear down at the water's edge. We managed to get right up along side of him in the fast current before he saw us. The bear 'woofed' and scrambled up the twenty foot steep bank and looked back at us through a screen of brush.

At noon we passed the mouth of the Christina River flowing in from the south. Its waters appeared to be murky and brownish in color. Then an hour and a half later we arrived in Fort McMurray and were met at the dock by Al Furneux of Contact Airways, the same people who had flown Phil and the Jean boys into Methy Portage. Al drove us the half mile into town, to a restaurant where we had a big steak dinner.

Then Bernard Jean, editor of the **McMurray Courier** and owner of Jean's Gift Shop, and his wife met us for a visit and an interview. They also arranged for us to go on television at 7:30 that evening. They took us to the RCMP office and introduced us to Corporal Dan Rumpel who was most helpful with information on the Athabasca River.

We expected to find only a thousand or two people living in Fort McMurray. We were surprised to see a much larger town. Bernard Jean told us the population was more than six thousand. That was largely due to the nearby Athabasca tar sands. The Canadian Oil Sands Company, Ltd., were mining and producing a grade of oil known as sin-crude. The product is then further refined and they end up with products like kerosene, gasoline, naphtha, sulfur and coke. The city is at the northern terminus of a railroad and a highway was being built, so they are now connected to Edmonton and the outside world by both road and railway.

The Jeans even loaned us their automobile to go shopping for groceries. I telephoned Jenny and she said she was still planning to meet us in Fort Smith, three hundred and fifty miles down river from Fort McMurray on 5 August. That phone call certainly was the highlight of my day. It's truly great to be in love and to be loved.

Phil and the Jean boys finally arrived at four thirty. We would meet him next at Fort Chipewyan if all went according to plan. We had another steak supper, then it was back to the canoe and we were soon down on the Athabasca River with its faster current. At ten in the evening we set up camp on the east bank, about eight miles north of the city.

Saturday, 31 July

DAY 106

Our tent sat right on the river bank only a few feet above the water. Sometime before dawn the natural silence was shattered by the roar of a diesel engine approaching. It sounded as though a locomotive was barreling down on us. We poked our heads out of the tent flap to discover that a string of barges was being pushed up the river by a tug boat. The morning dawned calm, warm and foggy. It felt as though summer had arrived as we broke camp to get out on the river away from the swarm of mosquitoes. There we breakfasted, as we drifted, on cookies and chocolate milk.

About twenty miles north of McMurray we passed the huge processing plant and refinery at Tar Island where they are digging up the Athabasca tar sands and turning them into petroleum products. A little later we passed historic Fort MacKay on the west river bank opposite the Indian Reservation of the same name.

We stopped for lunch along the east bank but had difficulty in finding a place to disembark. The whole river bank seemed to be wet with oil-soaked sand.   It was an outcropping of the oil-impregnated shale and probably the heat of the day brought more oil to the surface.   I went for a walk, exploring for about a quarter mile and found a patch of ripening rose hips.   Harvesting several, I munched on them while continuing to walk around.

The dog days of summer had apparently caught up with Clint.   He seemed to be angry with the world.   He seldom spoke to me that day.   I didn't mind the silence but it did cause concern.   Maybe he wasn't feeling well.   I had been enjoying the journey immensely.   It had been all I expected and more, with every day so full and interesting, but the fact that I enjoyed things didn't appear to make my partner any happier.   I didn't learn for many days what the problem was.

We were having a calm day with temperature in the eighties.   We paddled steadily to keep ahead of the insects which moved in on us whenever we slowed down or stopped.   The river current was becoming slow and sluggish and for some reason we were unable to make the desired mileage.

In mid-afternoon out of the balmy breeze from the trees on shore a hundred yards away, came drifting a fairy-like thread of spider web, settling on my lap as we paddled along.   Soon a baby spider, no bigger than the period at the end of this sentence, was briskly building a web between my knees as we continued along.   Fascinated, I watched him for more than an hour without moving my knees as construction work continued.   Later as I stepped out of the canoe, the web was ruined and the little spider disappeared.

For the past few days, due to the mosquitoes, we had been stopping for supper a couple of hours before camping time, before those nuisances really closed in.   It would have been almost suicidal to have attempted to prepare a hot meal when we stopped that night.   We selected a sandy beach along a willow-covered island near the mouth of the

Firebag River. There we were met by a real swarm of hungry mosquitoes which were particularly vicious. We put up our tent that night in record time to escape the hungry horde.

Actually the mosquitoes and other insects did not make life as miserable as it may sound. The insects did not cause us to use head nets or repellent at any time, although we carried both in case of extreme emergency. I disliked the repellent even more than the mosquitoes. I had learned to develop an attitude of tolerating certain discomforts for the greater joy of our journey.

Sunday, 1 August

DAY 107

It was another cold breakfast, this time inside of the tent. It would have been rough outside as the mosquitoes were like a storm cloud. We fought them for another half hour after embarking, killing them off or outpaddling the survivors. Fortunately, we had a good tail wind. Without that breeze, putting ashore for any purpose was getting to be a dreaded ordeal.

Prior to one o'clock, we found a high, sandy bank on the east shore. We were at the abandoned Embarras airport. I made up a batch of salmon patties. There was also a Ranger station at the south end of the airport. Even that was abandoned. We were finding a lot of vacant or abandoned property across the north, especially Indian houses and occasionally entire settlements. The Canadian welfare program is changing the Indian way of life.

It was almost too hot for paddling in the bright sunshine. I checked the thermometer and it registered eighty-eight degrees. We pushed steadily on and a couple of miles upstream from the fork of the Embarras River, we found a neat white house along with a couple of smaller ones. It was the only store along the two hundred miles of river between Fort McMurray and Fort Chipewyan. The place was operated by a woman who happened to be in McMurray at the time.

We stopped to get something to drink and met seventy-one year old Andrew Dahl, who was looking after the place until the owner returned. He told us that the lady was trying to sell the business so they were low on supplies. The only thing Mr. Dahl had to drink was cold water, right out of the open well with a dip bucket about twenty feet down to the good cold water. That drink was the best one we'd had since leaving Lake Superior. We bought a two-gallon plastic jug, filled it, and carried it along with us as the water from the Athabasca, with all of its silt, oil and trash really wasn't fit to drink.

Mr. Dahl told us the river had been ten to twelve feet higher only a couple of weeks before. A flood had caused extensive river bank damage as it spread over the whole country until it was one big lake all the way to Lake Athabasca, fifty miles away. He also told us that in the wintertime, the water level in the river drops an additional fifteen feet. Mr. Dahl said that he lived in a little log shack about six miles downriver and that he had run a trap line for the past twenty years.

Just before nine we stopped for the night at a house on the north riverbank, completing a seventy-mile day. The place belonged to Melvin Hanson, who was a commercial fisherman during the summers. We pitched our tent in his yard. He had six sled dogs staked nearby. Melvin told us that we were forty miles from Fort Chipewyan by way of Fletcher Channel.

The Athabasca River, where the country flattens out, was very similar to the Saskatchewan in size, current, dirty water and vegetation, with sandy and willowy shores on one side and often a cut bank that was badly eroded on the other. There were many floating trees in and along the water's edge.

Monday, 2 August

DAY 108

I had been sick during the night and was still feeling bad when we set out at eight in the morning. We wasted no time in breaking camp as the ever-present mosquitoes again harassed us unmercifully. We were in for another hot day as the temperature stood at sixty-eight degrees before we departed and the wind was blowing out of the southeast.

I had eaten some tainted peanuts the previous evening and feeling bad early in the morning, had tried everything in our first aid kit. First it was aspirin. Then came the Alka Seltzer. When that didn't help, it was the Sorbex. All to no avail. I was unable to paddle. My muscles were too sore and weak. Clint paddled alone most all morning. Just before noon we put ashore on a log jam. That is where everything came up. I began to recover almost immediately and resumed paddling. As the hours went by I continued to recover and was soon feeling hungry again.

Entering Lake Athabasca our channel was shallow and weedy. We dodged trees, logs and stumps for a while as we moved out into the lake. We could see higher ground in the direction of historic Fort Chipewyan where we finally arrived at four on that hot afternoon.

The settlement had a population of nearly

eighteen hundred people, mostly Chipewyans and Crees. It was a rough, frontier-type town and is the oldest established settlement in the Province of Alberta. We headed for the Pineland Inn, where we had a hearty meal. I had fully recovered. John and Theresa Inglis, owners of the Pineland, were interested in what the two of us were doing. When we told them about our journey, we were given a free meal. Inasmuch as we were having to wait for Phil, we decided to put up in the hotel for the night. We also had two other reasons for staying over at the Pineland. One was that for one night we would be free of mosquitoes and the other was that we were both badly in need of a good hot shower.

When Phil arrived that evening, he was anxious to look up Pastor Art Hoehne of the Fellowship Baptist Church, a friend of the Bernard Jean family in McMurray. Pastor Hoehne went out of his way to befriend us and helped us in every possible way, driving us around town, introducing us to some of his people and he even gave each of us a dried and very lightly smoked whitefish. That was our introduction to dried fish. It was delicious. From then on we frequently enjoyed a mid-afternoon snack of dried fish and hot tea.

Tuesday, 3 August

DAY 109

There were several movie sequences that Phil needed to shoot in Fort Chipewyan. By the time he was finished it was mid-afternoon so we were off to a late start. I was again back to normal and feeling great.

Early in the day I visited with Horace Wylie,

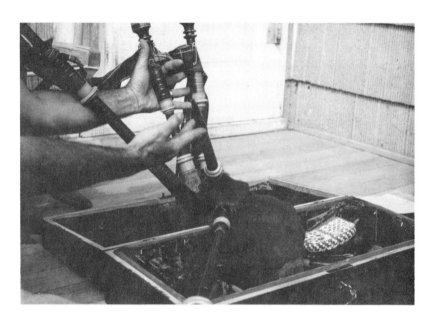

The bagpipes of Colin Frazer

a great-grandson of Colin Frazer. Mr. Wylie invited me into his house to see the old books, memos and the bagpipes which had belonged to his great-grandfather. Colin Frazer, of course, became famous as the assistant and bagpipe player to Sir George Simpson, Governor of the Hudson's Bay Company in the early nineteenth century. Mr. Wylie told me that he was also a relative of Simon Frazer.

Phil engaged sixty-nine year old Bill Flett with his flat-bottomed skiff with eighteen-horse-power motor to move himself and his camera equipment down to Fort Smith, N.W.T. In that way he would be there and waiting for us as we came through the rapids between Fitzgerald and Fort Smith. Bill Flett is a mixture of Chipewyan and

Scottish. He said that his ancestors were some of the earliest settlers of Fort Chipewyan.

Late that afternoon, we moved on downriver, passing the inflowing Peace River and down the Slave River for a total of only forty miles that day.

Wednesday, 4 August

DAY 110

This was to be our first full day of paddling down north on the Slave River. Our plan was to stop at a rapids at the mouth of Ryan Creek, twenty miles downstream, and have a hot breakfast. Clint was in a good mood again, and he promised to catch enough fish for our meal. We were underway by six but faced a brisk headwind all forenoon. Our planned three-hour wait for breakfast turned out to be four and a half hours because of the wind. When we finally arrived at the rapids, Clint was unable to catch even one fish, so we made up a double batch of pancakes for our late brunch. As Clint gave up the fishing, he said, "There's one good thing about this north wind. The mosquitoes didn't bother me. I don't see how any fish could survive in this dirty river water anyway."

Dense smoke from a forest fire covered the area around noon. Apparently a fire was burning somewhere to the northwest of us. We hoped the burn was not in the Wood Buffalo National Park, which borders the Slave for many miles along the west bank. By three, the wind was losing some of its velocity and we were making better time. We enjoyed watching three bald eagles circling above and looking us over. Ducks and geese were again becoming plentiful.

ONE INCREDIBLE JOURNEY

Phil had Bill Flett drop him off at the settlement of Fitzgerald that evening. Phil was then
going to hike down to Fort Smith and meet us the
following day at The Rapids of the Drowned. Just
beyond Fort Fitzgerald, the Dog River flows into
the Slave from the east. We made camp on the right
below the confluence on a nice rocky shelf overlooking Cassette Rapids. Our campfire felt good as
the weather had turned cool. That night we knew we
would sleep well after a full day of good exercise
and with the music of miles of big rapids roaring
in our ears. As we turned in, a red full moon was
rising over the tree tops. We both agreed that
tomorrow, with all of those rapids, should be an
interesting day.

Thursday, 5 August

DAY 111

We attempted something that very few people
had done in the twentieth century. We were going
to try to follow the route of the voyageurs down
through the eighteen miles of rapids between Fort
Fitzgerald and Fort Smith. There are four major
sets of rapids in that stretch. First were the
Cassettes, just below our camp, followed by Pelican, Mountain and Drowned. Most people take out on
the left at Fort Fitzgerald and have their gear
trucked down the road to the lower end of the
Rapids of the Drowned, where they put back into the
Slave beyond Fort Smith.

Traveling under our own power, the truck was
out of the question and we didn't relish the
thought of an eighteen-mile portage, so we would
follow the exact route described by Alexander Mackenzie, down the right side of the river.

The Rapids of the Drowned

At rising time rain was falling so we were off to a late start under dull, grey skies. We held tight to the right shoreline and descended the first drop of Cassette Rapids. Then it was into the little channel that passes the main part of the rapids. Soon we made a short portage on the left and after about a mile there was another portage on the right of nearly a quarter mile. Those two portages took us around the Cassettes. Both were very brushy and difficult to follow, as were all of the portages that day.

We enjoyed some good fast water for the next five miles, which took us down to Pelican Rapids. Again we entered a small channel along the extreme right and soon had a most unusual experience. We found the same log jam that Alexander Mackenzie described in that same channel back in 1789. I'm sure, however, that in the one hundred and eighty-two years since then, the log jam had grown considerably in size. We were forced to portage more than a quarter mile to bypass that huge pile of sticks. Then a little later came one final portage and we were down on flat water for another four or five miles.

Mountain Rapids is divided into four parts. The first is really a waterfalls with a short portage tight to the falls on the right and under the power line. Then there were three other short portages with lots of fast water between. Mountain Rapids was a very impressive sight and the roughest of the four. On our second portage we put back into the river too soon. The rushing and turbulent force of the water carried us around a rocky point. While fighting the severe turbulence we shot right into the eye of an unseen whirlpool, hitting it dead center. It was a real live one, spinning 'round and 'round. The bow went under as we went down into it and hitting the other side we had powerful forces working on both bow and stern in opposite directions at the same time. For a split second our twenty-one foot canoe very nearly rolled and it seemed like we were about to lose it. Speedy, instinctive counteraction on our part was the narrow margin that saw us through. We both pulled hard on the paddles and were soon free of that powerful spinning vortex of water. We stopped and looked at each other, without a word of comment realizing that it had been a very close call. Our God watches over us and we were at that moment very aware of it. Had we upset, there would have been but little chance of survival from that turbulent, crazy, raging water. The place is notorious for not giving up the bodies it claims.

Mountain Rapids was by far the most difficult of our portaging during the day. None of the portages were marked. In fact, we never found a portage trail. We just worked our way through and along as best we could. Probably back in the early days there was one trail which bypassed the entire series of turbulent waters of Mountain Portage. When we pulled out to make the fourth portage and not knowing it was the last one, we sat down on a big flat rock and replenished our fuel supply with pork and beans, kippered herring and cans of apricots and orange juice. At that place, looking upstream, the roaring river was more than a mile wide and our view was of a beautiful series of falls, rapids and hills as far as the eye could see.

Suddenly, after shooting a few smaller drops of the river, we were once more on flat water. Then within an hour, after crossing the sixtieth parallel, we arrived at the famous Rapids of the Drowned. "This one sounds scary to me," Clint remarked as we approached it.

"I know the feeling. I've heard that down through the years, this one has taken the lives of many people."

"Let's not take any chances! We might better portage."

Approaching along the extreme right, we paddled through some preliminary fast water, passing the upper set of islands. Then it was around a sharp bend and into the right channel. At a point where we could see straight ahead to the end of the channel, which looked like a narrow chute of rapids and waterfalls, we promptly put ashore. We portaged along the flat rocky shoreline for nearly a quarter mile and all of a sudden we were below that granddaddy of all rapids. The whole day had been a very satisfying and worthwhile experience. Clint and I were pleased to have descended those rapids under our own power.

We crossed the river to Fort Smith, Northwest Territories and soon made our way to the Pinecrest Hotel, where my Jenny was waiting.

Friday, 6 August

DAY 112

Phil Pemberton had arrived in Fort Smith early in the morning. He awoke us before nine to pick up some film and a check which Jenny had brought along from Lansing. He was anxious to get out into Wood Buffalo National Park to film some of the wild life. He planned to meet us again at Hay River, down on Great Slave Lake.

Jenny and I toured Fort Smith on foot. There were a number of interesting things to see. We were in a picturesque community, built mostly along the north side of the sixtieth parallel. It is an important link on the Mackenzie River system. Fort Smith was established by the Hudson's Bay Company in 1874 to tap the fur country of the Slave Indians, who were later forced on downriver by the advancing Crees. It served as the capital city of

273

ONE INCREDIBLE JOURNEY

Northwest Territories until only a few years before our arrival, when the seat of government was transferred to Yellowknife.

Fort Smith is the home of Grandin College, named after a pioneer bishop of the Oblate order, and serves students from all parts of Northwest Territories. We also visited the Cathedral of St. Joseph, a most impressive church. The population of the city was about twenty-five hundred, and consisted mostly of Indians and Metis.

There was a modern Hudson's Bay store as well as Kaeser's store, owned and operated by the Mayor of the city, Paul Kaeser. Then there was a good drug store, a covered ice arena and several Federal, Territorial and local government offices. The streets had very recently been hard surfaced.

Saturday, 7 August

DAY 113

We were enjoying our layover at Fort Smith's only hotel, The Pinecrest. The city is located on the edge of the huge Wood Buffalo National Park, home of North America's largest herd of buffalo, numbering about fourteen thousand animals.

Walking around again, we spent considerable time on the high bank of the Slave River, overlooking the beautiful Rapids of the Drowned. In the Bay store, I bought a fiberglass patching kit to repair our canoe. The bow was badly chewed up from all of the rapids Clint and I had negotiated. I had taken pains to make sure it was well built and adequately reinforced in wear areas. I had used prime Sitka spruce wood strips with extra layers of glass cloth below the water line and high quality epoxy resin. It had been holding up remarkably well.

We were unable to work on the necessary repairs as it was raining part of the day. We did, however, go over our other gear, sharpening knives, sewing on buttons, laundering camp clothes and repacking our bags. Clint shopped at the Bay, restocking our food supply.

Fort Smith seemed to have its share of misfits, rejects and riff raff. The Pinecrest's restaurant, beer hall and lounge appeared to be the center of it all. We became well aware of the large, belligerent and alcoholic native element with their many troubles and frequent fights. During the evening a cab driver suffered a heart attack in the hotel parking lot. The evening before, as we were sitting in the restaurant eating supper, a fight broke out between a drunken Indian and the Chinese manager of the establishment, who had objected to the drunk's foul language. In the skirmish that raged over half of the restaurant, the Indian had one ear bitten nearly off. Bleeding profusely, he was hurried off to the doctor for needed repairs.

Sunday, 8 August

DAY 114

We slept in again after talking until nearly dawn. The sun came out, drying the canoe from the rain of the previous day, enabling me to patch the bow where the rocks had chewed through to the bottom layer of cloth. It was pretty well scarred with several other deep scratches along the bottom. We had hit and scraped numerous sharp rocks, even hitting some head on, which stopped us completely. We expected that the rivers ahead would be easier on our trusty canoe. At least we hoped they would be.

In the afternoon Jenny and I visited the comprehensive museum of Northwest Territories, housed at Grandin College. There we saw many old curios and antiques of the early days, current native arts and crafts and dozens of other interesting displays.

Clint was anxious to continue our journey down the Slave so this would be our final evening in Fort Smith. That turned out to be another very short night.

14

GREAT SLAVE LAKE

> Do you fear the force of the wind,
> The slash of the rain?
> Go face them and fight them,
> Be savage again.
> Go hungry and cold like the wolf,
> Go wade like the crane:
> The palms of your hands will thicken,
> The skin of your cheek will tan,
> You'll grow ragged and weary and swarthy,
> But you'll walk like a man!
>
> — Hamlin Garland,
> **Do You Fear the Wind?**

Monday, 9 August

D A Y   1 1 5

The three of us walked down the long, steep hill from the Pinecrest Hotel to the river that cloudy morning. We slid the canoe back into the water just below the Rapids of the Drowned at the

277

point where we had disembarked the previous Thursday evening.

Jenny and I said our goodbyes. If all went according to plan, we would next meet in a little more than two months. I didn't like to leave her there all by herself. She would have to wait in Fort Smith until Wednesday to catch the next plane going south. She had a tremendous burden of responsibilities at home, with so much happening and the usual variety of problems that comes with a family of teenagers. That would have been a big load for two, let alone one woman. And I must say, all around she did exceptionally well. How she could have found the time and go to the trouble to travel nearly six thousand miles to visit me, I do not know, but it certainly was just what I needed.

As Clint and I paddled away, I looked back and my heart came up in my throat. There on the shoreline at the foot of that high cut bank hill, stood a lone figure, looking forlorn and lonely and trying bravely not to cry. She appeared so small against that huge hillside, my sweetheart, my woman, my wife, a very real part of my own self. I swallowed hard, blew my nose, brushed the blur from my eyes and paddled on. As we became but specks of flashing paddles in the vast, dim distance of the mighty Slave River, another small speck trudged slowly up the long, steep path to the top of the hill, thinking, longing and aching. Parting is such sweet sorrow. It's great to be in love.

We paddled along in a quiet, pensive mood all through the day, passing Sawmill Island and numerous other islands. Finally, just before nine in the evening, we encamped on the island just beyond the final Grand Detour bend as the river swings to the north again, having moved fifty-four miles since morning. It became clear as the day progressed, that the Fort Smith sojourn had been a long layover for Clint as he mentioned that he hoped we would have no further lengthy delays.

Tuesday, 10 August

DAY 116

We were underway by seven, facing a light head wind which continued nearly all that day. The scenery was becoming somewhat monotonous as we moved on down the wide Slave River with its cut banks topped with spruce and popple or marshy shores covered with tag elder or willows.

Lunch time found us stopping on the west bank in an area recently burned over. We had some of the fresh fruit and nuts that Clint had purchased in Fort Smith. We were trying to eat a nutritional balance. It looked like the fire which had burned right to the river's edge had happened only a few days before we arrived. We could see smoke on downriver, and late in the afternoon we came across some fire fighters camped in an area that had escaped the burn. Ahead of us the fire was still raging out of control along a twenty-five mile front. A helicopter was using a cable and bale bucket to shuttle water to the fire. They told us there were nearly a hundred and fifty men fighting that fire. We paddled along in the smoke for hours and at times the fire was burning right along the river bank.

During the evening as we moved along the east side of Long Island we came across a large family of Indians camped on the high riverbank. Stopping to visit, we learned that earlier in the day, they had killed three buffalo and had been working on butchering and packing them to their camp. They lived up the river at a place called Hook Lake and would have to make three more round trips to pack out all of their meat. It caused me to wonder—if they are citizens of Canada, then it would seem they should have full and equal rights to that citizenship—no less and no more. Special privileges because of race is a policy that cannot possibly continue to work forever.

Then a little later as darkness was settling in, we saw the silhouette of two long-legged birds, making an odd cry as they walked across a sandbar island. Clint identified them right away as sandhill cranes. We speedily made camp on a wide spot below a high bank as a thunderstorm moved in on us. The storm was of short duration and probably helped very little in slowing down the forest fires. Thus ended a seventy-five mile day.

Wednesday, 11 August

DAY 117

Early in the day a heavy fog blanketed the area and made navigating difficult. We could see nothing at times but tried to keep the near shore in sight most of the time. Within an hour a breeze came up out of the north improving our visibility. The breeze soon became a strong headwind and we really had our work cut out for us. By mid-afternoon, there were times when even with hard paddling and with the current helping, progress became almost impossible.

The Slave River out of Fort Smith is big and wide and slow, no rapids, no fast water, no boulders, very much the same scenery all the way. If you didn't like to paddle you might call it dull or uninteresting. I wouldn't want to have missed any of it. To me, every single stroke was adding up to an interesting and exciting adventure. Sitting there in the canoe, I had plenty of time to think as we paddled along. I calculated and recalculated the push we were receiving from the current and yesterday it figured out to only about one mile per hour assist to our normal flat water speed.

We were seeing bald eagles nearly every day and lots of signs of moose and bear. However, those animals were seldom seen by us. With the steady native traffic on the river, most of the game had been spooked. The people travel by power boats in going from place to place and just about every boat carried either a rifle or a shot gun, sometimes both, with which they shoot about anything that moves.

Ducks and geese were plentiful but very wild. We had not seen or heard a loon since leaving little Rendezvous Lake on Methy Portage.

Slave River splits into at least a dozen channels in a delta system as it enters Great Slave Lake. We were watching for Nagle Channel, about twelve miles long and the shortest route to Fort Resolution. It was easily found by a large pile of sawdust close to shore just before it forks off to the left. The logging camp seemed to be recently abandoned. Just before reaching it, we hit our roughest water of the day in a long, wide stretch of the Slave River where the wind was particularly strong, creating big, deep water-type swells. That made us all the more happy to arrive in Nagle Channel. It is a small channel with little current, and is lined with a good stand of spruce and popple, which cut off the wind. The change was so sudden that it seemed unreal. As we neared Great Slave Lake, we came across an old, abandoned steam-fired tug boat, stranded part way up on shore. Everything removable had been scrounged out of it.

Nagle Channel goes out in the lake by way of a shallow weedy bay. The last mile or so is completely bare of trees on both sides, with nothing but marsh grass and cattails. The wind was strong there. Long before we could see the lake we could hear the ferocious roar of distant breakers. When we paddled out of the mouth of the channel we were met by white caps but the really mean stuff was breaking at least a mile out, apparently over a shoal. It was getting late, so we decided to make camp and face our problem the following day. We paddled back up the channel and tried to find high enough ground for a tent. We almost settled on a wind-whipped tall grassy spot but in tromping around to make a campsite, we found that water was rising in the grass. We decided to buck the white caps and go across Nagle Bay to where we could see some high timbered ground, across the point from Fort Resolution.

That was a good decision. There we found an old, heavy duty dock. Above and back in the trees we were able to set up a sheltered camp where we were somewhat protected from the wind. It had been a good day. We had progressed another sixty-five hard earned miles.

Thursday, 12 August

DAY 118

What a welcome we had to Great Slave Lake!?

The wind howled and threatened all night, bringing with it a driving rain that beat upon our tent for hours. In between those sounds was the steady, ominous roar of the distant surf on the edge of the bay, nearly two miles away.

We were somewhat intimidated to sleep in that morning. We found we were able to analyze the situation right from our sacks. It is surprising how much you can learn about things around you just from sounds and noises. Every morning before I opened my eyes, my sense of hearing would be feeding my mind vital information about the day. Long before I took a look outside the tent, I would know a lot about the weather and water conditions and about the animal life, such as singing birds or a flock of geese flying over, a coyote howling or a mouse trying to get in our food. If there was a wind of any kind, I even learned some about surrounding vegetation. It seems that a man's senses become much more sensitive and acute when they become necessary to his existence. Your senses begin to automatically register the things essential to your well-being, without your having to consciously turn them on. Senses and instincts that have been dulled by disuse or misuse of modern living suddenly become awakened and alive!

The rain began to let up before nine. We soon learned there was some sort of road between Fort Resolution and the dock near our camp. We were across a point about a mile and a half north of the settlement. As we loaded the canoe for an attempt at the lake, a man drove up in an automobile. He asked where we were from and where we were going.

Early in the journey we enjoyed answering those questions, but now it was becoming a real chore. We had found there were no easy answers. If we told them the truth without a lengthy explanation, they plainly didn't believe us. Some would clam up and hardly talk to us at this insult to their intelligence, others would just change the subject.

The man also remarked that it was the strongest blow of wind they had seen on Great Slave Lake that summer. Then he added, "A windstorm of this type usually blows for three days." That wasn't what we needed to hear.

We cautiously started paddling out across Nagle Bay, towards Moose Deer Island, about two and a half miles out. This island and shoals protected the bay from the really big waves. But the bay was still mean with wind-whipped white caps and spray.

We stopped on the lee side of the island, to figure out if there was some way we could keep going. The wind was coming from the north, blowing into Resolution Bay, so there would be no advantage trying to paddle along the south shore. We figured it would be better to traverse the bay. It was about twenty-five miles across with a couple of islands along the way.

The first island was about ten miles out, but looking out across the rough waves with unstable cloud formations, it looked a lot farther!

We stalled around awhile not wanting to quit and yet not wanting to go out into the storm. We pulled ashore and scouted the island and watched the breakers crashing over the near shoals. At eleven A.M., we thought the wind was dying down a little, so we snugged our spray skirts up around us and pushed off to make the big traverse. Immediately we were into some pretty big swells, but handling them very well. About two miles out, the wind that we thought was dying down had only been resting up for a bigger blow! The huge swells started to crest on top, sometimes washing across our canoe. It got to be too much. Without any argument we headed back to the south side of Mission Island Peninsula.

We put ashore in a little bay where the water was very shallow for the final hundred yards, and it was good to be ashore. The point of land was well wooded as is most of the south shore of Great Slave Lake. The lake bottom along there was a soft silt and the action of the wind and waves made the waters along the shore very muddy. It was the only water available, so the water we used was heated and boiled. Then we would let the mud settle to the bottom of the pan and carefully pour off the clear top water into another pan.

While we hung out our wet things on the branches and bushes to dry, Clint experimented with some brown sugar and bannock. It was very good. Later he tried his hand at stew and dumplings. The dumplings didn't hold together, but they were eatable. We gathered some cranberries and rose hips to combine for a sauce. They tasted great, but did require a lot of work and a lot of cooking time to be tasty. Upon scouting the area, up the shore a short distance from our camp we found several large, strange-looking limestone slab fireplaces about three feet high by six feet long. They were loosely laid up and hadn't been used recently, but we could tell that they had once been fired to intense heat. We couldn't imagine what they had been used for. Possibly they were the old cooking fireplaces at the stopping points of the voyageurs.

   We progressed only six miles that day as the wind howled on.

Friday, 13 August

DAY 1 1 9

   The wind shifted to the southeast sometime during the night. It looked as though we might be able to paddle on. As we puttered around getting things together, waiting for the lake to calm down, the wind switched to the west and became stronger, so we were still windbound. It was the third day for that storm.

   While Clint hiked the four or five miles along the shore eastward to the settlement, I caught up in my journal and did some personal chores such as taking a wash basin bath and trimming and scrubbing my beard with hot water and soap. I think Clint wanted a change in company and I was happy to be alone. We were fighting off a bad case of 'tent fever.'

   At about noon the wind died down so I started preparing to shove off as soon as the waves calmed down. I knew Clint would be hurrying back when he noticed the drop in the wind's velocity. A couple of hours later, I spotted him about a half mile away, walking along the shore. As I watched, I noticed two other men following along about a quarter mile behind. When he arrived, I asked him what he had done in town, that he was being followed. That surprised him. He looked back and they were heading right for us. It turned out that they were young officers of the R.C.M.P. detachment in Fort Resolution. They had followed Clint all the way from town, apparently suspicious of this strange character who had drifted into the settlement from out of nowhere with some wild tale about canoeing across the continent. They were courteous and friendly, although one of them did ask a lot of clever questions, and kept his billy club in his hand. I'm not sure he ever was quite convinced of our story.

We took them up the shore and showed them those strange fireplaces, but they didn't have any answers either. The clever one never did seem to relax his guard, and always kept a comfortable distance from us. I had just taken a bath, so I don't see how it could have been my B.O. I thought they were a couple of outstanding police officers.

It was three twenty in the afternoon when we embarked. We had decided to be brave and make the twenty-five mile traverse of the bay. The wind was still calm but the waves were very large and steep. We had to head straight into them. Sometimes we'd hit one wrong and it would drop the canoe with a slam and a splash that slowly got us wet. It kept getting better as the hours rolled by. We met a couple small boats of commercial fishermen pulling their nets, which they hadn't been able to do for the past three days.

Our strategy on Great Slave Lake was the same as on Lake Superior, that is, to just keep right on paddling day or night, if conditions were right. Early in the night we had a quarter moon, with a beautiful and interesting display of northern lights and falling stars. Shortly after midnight as we were making a seven-mile traverse across another bay, it clouded up and a fierce quartering crosswind hit us from out of the south. Almost immediately, heavy white capping waves started pounding and bouncing us around. For the next two hours our work was really cut out for us as we struggled toward shore. We really got drenched. Some of the waves were breaking over the bow up to my armpits and tossing us around like a bucking bronco. In the darkness it was all exaggerated by not being able to see what was coming at us. The canoe would rock, and I would grab for the water with my paddle and get nothing but air, and nearly fall out of the canoe. Another time I'd grab for the water as the canoe was going into a wave and my paddle would plunge in up to my elbow! For a while there, I would have preferred to have been some place else! It was with a real sigh of relief that we finally gained the protection of Sulphur Point and pulled ashore on a long rocky beach.

Saturday, 14 August

DAY 1 2 0

It was after two in the morning. We were soaking wet and cold as we hurriedly built a big fire to warm up and try to dry out.

By the time we got through eating, I was attracted by our unusual fire. Instead of burning down, it seemed to be burning more intensely. The whole fire had sunk about a foot into the stone bank. That mystified us. Poking the fire with a long stick trying to figure out how the stones could be burning, we found that the shore was lined with one huge long pile of logs and driftwood, nearly ten feet deep. Over the top of the pile, a layer of gravel and stones had been pushed by the shifting lake ice at breakup time. In the darkness we had mistaken this for a solid stony shoreline and had built our fire about halfway up it.

We were alarmed to discover that huge pile of driftwood was on fire beneath the layer of stones. Close to the driftwood, all along the shore was a heavy stand of mature spruce. We had the potential makings of a forest fire!

We both grabbed cooking pots and started running back and forth throwing water on the fire. After considerable running around I saw that we were losing the battle, so I grabbed a long stick with a hook on the end, and started raking away the stones and pulling out logs and pieces of wood and throwing them in the water. For a while it looked as though we had lost control, but after two hours of frantic fire fighting we finally had every last ember put out. In the struggle, soot and ashes had covered us from head to foot and we had dug a hole in that beach of stones and driftwood ten feet in diameter and three feet deep.

By then the sun was up and we were ready to go back to paddling. We left there experienced forest fire fighters, and a little bit wiser in woodsmanship.

Strangely, we found a nice tailwind had developed with gentle swells coming at us from the north, ninety degrees to our route. As we cruised along enjoying the beginning of another day, the tailwind kept getting stronger, until it was causing white caps ahead of us, at the same time the big swells from the north were getting bigger and bigger. That puzzled us. Why should the big wave action be coming at us from an entirely different direction than the wind? Something big had to be happening out in the lake.

By the time we got to Breynal Point , the lake was getting vicious. The swells had grown to a hundred feet between crests and curling on top. At the same time we were following smaller waves coming from the east, and we had two sets of waves, one from the east, one from the north, both creating white caps. Our situation was compounded by a shallow shoreline that caused the big swells to turn into a roaring, ocean-type surf, which was breaking a quarter mile offshore. As far as we could see down the shore it all looked the same. There was no way a canoe could survive going ashore through that surf. We began to get a trapped feeling. We had to do something. Water was steadily coming into the canoe around our canoe covers and spray skirts from the waves breaking over us. I prayed and paddled, doing both desperately!

Coming around Breynal Point we spotted a partially submerged island that the waves were breaking over, but which gave a small protected harbor behind it. This appeared to be our only salvation.

We were several hundred yards out beyond the shoals when we turned in towards shore. This put the big swells to our stern. Back in Flin Flon we had lost our rear spray cover. The stern of the canoe was, of course, low cut and of a racing style, only twelve inches high. Now we found ourselves in a situation where the water could pour into that seventy-four inch opening behind the stern seat. As long as we kept moving forward we never did have water come over the stern, and it wasn't bothering us then except that we were committed to moving forward, and we had to be right about our course of action.

This now was the wildest, trickiest moment of the storm. Those huge swells would come up under the stern, lifting it up and giving the canoe a shove forward, but as each swell was moving much faster than we were, it would continue on under the canoe, lifting it up until we found ourselves uneasily sitting on top of the peak looking out over the whole raging mess and being somewhat distracted at that moment by the swoosh of the breakers around and sometimes over us. This was followed by a sinking, sliding feeling and the next thing we knew we were down in the valley looking up at the huge monsters, and they do look huge from the seat of a canoe! For a split second we gazed in awesome wonder at how we had survived that one, but there came another, and another. We were too busy to absorb the full appreciation of the predicament. It was an impressive experience. All the time we tried to keep paddling steadily along, not losing sight of our objective. At no time did we ever feel out of control, but needless to say we were very careful, like men walking a tightrope. At all times we were very conscious and respectful of the tremendous forces at play around us.

By carefully choosing a weak spot in the surf to one side of the island, we managed by the grace of God to slip through and back around behind the island to the main shore where we pulled out at an ideal campsite, nicely protected from the wind. Right across the sand point through a thick stand of small trees, were the worst of the breakers. We enjoyed safety and shelter up close to that raging storm.

We were so wet that the water dripped out of our clothes when we stepped from the canoe. My first reaction was to thank the good Lord for seeing us through another tight spot. It's always so good to know the He hears and cares.

That was twice in one morning that I had been drenched to the skin. We built a big fire and changed clothes and scattered all the wet stuff around to dry out. Then finding a spot sheltered from the wind, we stretched out on our sleeping pads in the bright, friendly sun and slept until noon. We woke up hungry, but a big stack of pancakes smothered with syrup and washed down with hot cocoa soon fixed that.

Great Slave Lake was giving us a rough time. To that point we had moved only fifty miles. Hay

River was less than thirty miles away but it may as well have been three hundred. We were in one of our best camps, enjoying that comfortable feeling of being all alone in the far north. Seeing the storm continuing to rage, we put up the tent in the afternoon and caught another nap so we would be prepared to paddle again that night, weather permitting.

We did our usual scouting the area around our camp, up and down the beach each way a mile or two, and also back in the bush. Somehow, exploring around our campsites made me feel more comfortable and more like it was our very own!

Sunday, 15 August

DAY 121

The wind and waves raged on all night but snug and warm in our little sheltered tent, that storm was like music to a wilderness lover's ears. Sleeping in was pure pleasure, but we couldn't help having some nagging thoughts about moving on. Already the nights were getting cooler and we knew that fall was just around the corner.

Breakfast was a large order of pancakes. Clint seemed extra hungry and I was glad to see it. Making pancakes sometimes depended on the convenience of making a fireplace for the griddle. At some campsites it is difficult to find adequate rocks that would hold the griddle. Ideally, I needed flat-surfaced rocks that would hold the griddle level about eight inches off the ground. I also needed a tall, flat-faced rock, placed upright in the rear to act as a chimney to funnel the smoke up and away from the cook and to reflect the heat onto the cooking.

While Clint was puttering around the cook fire experimenting with making bannock, I put my light personal bag on my back and took off inland for a more extended scouting hike of the area.

The land was quite flat, with a lot of muskeg and all well wooded or bushy, with no big timber. It seemed to be pretty much the same wherever I went. Unexpectedly, I came across several survey trails, with flags and numbered markers. Possibly they were planning to build a road. I also saw a couple large owls, and lots of grouse. Fresh meat would go good with our menu. As the fools hens were plentiful, I threw a lot of sticks before I finally got one. I skinned it out and put it in a plastic bag in my pack sack. I also kept seeing signs of bear and caribou as bald eagles circled overhead.

When I wandered back into camp late that afternoon, Clint had just come back from gathering a pail of low bush cranberries. They were just the thing to go with fresh roasted grouse! Clint simmered up a delicious pan of wild cranberry sauce while I slowly roasted the grouse on a stick turning and buttering it until done. We also made a pot of stew with dumplings and a pan of instant pudding to go with the fresh buttered bannock. To add to the occasion, we opened a can of apple juice. Out here on the shore of Great Slave Lake, that was a meal fit for a king!

After an early supper, I made a few extra bannock to take along the next day, hoping we would be too busy paddling to do it then. Windbound days contributed much to the overall enjoyment and satisfaction of the journey. We seemed to regard them as enemies to our trip, but used them as friends.

Clint was one of the best wilderness campers I'd ever been with. He seemed to do the right things around a campfire, and was an excellent cook. Being with the U. S. Forestry Service, he really knew his flora and fauna better than most.

When I crawled into my sack that night, I had a feeling, probably mostly from subconscious reading of weather signs, that the wind might die down during the night. So as I slept, a part of me remained sensitive to the sounds of the storm. Sometime along about midnight, I was awakened by a letup in the noise level of the wind and waves. For a few minutes I lay there in the dark, listening and analyzing the situation. With the comforting thought that we would soon be able to move on, I set my built-in alarm for three in the morning and went back to sleep.

Monday, 16 August

DAY 122

Eagerly we embarked before sunrise and headed west along the shoreline. The wind had changed and was blowing from the south. The low shore offered little protection so we battled a crosswind most of the day. There was no real problem from the waves.

By eleven we were paddling up the east channel of the Hay River towards the town of the same name. Hay River was a thriving, bustling settlement with a population of more than three thousand people. The main industrial and commercial activity was on Vale Island, which lies between the east and west channels of the Hay River where it flows into Great Slave Lake. An all-weather road connects the town to the outside world by the Mackenzie Highway and Alberta's Highway 35. A railroad from the south also terminates on Vale Island, making it the major port for all heavy traffic into Great Slave Lake and the Mackenzie River system. The post office and residential part of town are located about five miles upstream on the right bank of the river.

ONE INCREDIBLE JOURNEY

We were in one of our planned mail pickup points so we paddled on up the river to the post office. I received a couple of letters from Jenny and Clint picked up one from her too. Those letters sure made my day. While in town we again picked up a few more supplies. We were looking for Phil as he was supposed to meet us in Hay River. In asking around, we learned that he had been seen in town. On our way back out to the lake, we spotted him on one of the docks. We spent about an hour taking a few movie shots, and arranged to meet him next in Fort Providence.

Further on and tied up at one of the last docks, we spotted the twenty-six foot "North" canoe used by the Northwest Territories team in the big three-thousand-mile Canadian Centennial Canoe Race from Rocky Mountain House, Alberta, to Montreal, Quebec, in 1967. We stopped and looked it over. It had about six inches of water in it and appeared as though it was no longer being cared for.

We resumed our journey along the south shore of Great Slave Lake by five p.m., heading for Fort Providence and planning not to stop until we arrived there. The entire length of the route along that shore was shallow, frequently rocky with sand bars and sometimes with boulders, making it difficult for night time travel. Early in the evening it started to rain and continued most of the night. Little did we know then that we were in for one of those difficult and trying overnight paddles.

Late in the evening we put ashore at Point de Roche and had our supper. There had been a recent encampment of Indians nearby. Clint had been quieter than usual for the past few days and hadn't said much since leaving Hay River. It seemed that he was trying to endure something he didn't like and I could feel the tension! I must have been a little dense because, try as I might, I just couldn't comprehend what it was that was bugging him.

15

THE MIGHTY
MACKENZIE

> I know the trail I am seeking,
> It's up by the Lake of the Bear:
> It's down by the Arctic Barrens,
> It's over to Hudson's Bay;
> Maybe I'll get there, — maybe:
> Death is set by a hair...
> Hark! It's the Northland calling!
> Now I must go away....
>
> — Robert Service,
> **The Nostomaniac**

Tuesday, 17 August

DAY 123

We were wet, cold, and hungry as we stopped again at about two on some unknown island for more fuel and to warm up and try to dry out a little.

It was hard to get a fire going in the rain for all the wood we could find in the dark was thoroughly wet. We heated up a can of pork and beans, and ate our bannock along with a big canteen of hot cocoa. Then we tried to catch a quick cat nap. I sat on a log near the fire, on one end of the nylon tarp and pulled it back up over my head and down over the front of me and went to sleep. Just then the rain increased to a downpour.

In less than an hour it slowed down to a drizzle. Then I lay down on the log with the tarp over me. That was great. It was almost luxurious to be able to stretch out and sleep. After twenty or thirty minutes the knots and ridges of the log began to reshape my back, waking me up. I was somewhat refreshed and ready to go. A more accurate translation would be to say that the misery of trying to sleep any longer on that log in the rain, in cold wet clothing, was worse than the misery of paddling in the dark, banging into boulders and running into sand bars!

Some time later, the sky began to lighten with the coming dawn and the rain let up. By then we had passed Point Desmarais, which is considered the beginning of the Mackenzie River. There was some current but it didn't look very much like a river as we moved along the mainland shore south of Big Island. It was weedy and so shallow that often the canoe dragged along on the bottom even though we were a half mile off shore. Then a strong headwind picked up and it was slow going. We decided to angle across Beaver Lake to the north shore, and when we arrived at a point five miles west of Willow Point, it was early afternoon and time for dinner. The entire eleven-mile crossing was surprisingly shallow with a noticeable current between the huge patches of water weeds.

Apparently our delays were bothering Clint more than I realized. Especially the ones such as Flin Flon and Fort Smith when Jenny came to visit me. While eating our meal, I remarked, "Now that we're off that big lake, we should be able to really move down the Mackenzie."

"I hope so."

"We lost more than three days of paddling time because of those storms on Great Slave Lake."

"Yeah! We wouldn't have had those three windbound days on the big lake if you hadn't wasted all that time in Fort Smith. We could have just as well been down here before those big winds hit."

"Well! That's probably true," I replied, "but it was important that Jenny and I get together. You know, Clint, she's carrying a terrific load. Besides all of the complicated problems of seven teenagers, more critical events have happened at home this year than at any other time in our lives. She also has the problem of explaining me, and how her husband could go off and leave his wife and family for the entire summer."

"You're probably right."

"People at home are thinking that Jenny has a neglectful and irresponsible man, to do a thing like this. Then there's the psychological stigma of her husband being considered a backslider, neglecting his family, his church and his Christian duties. That's too much of a load for her to carry alone. But she has been doing an exceptionally wonderful job of it and I'm terrifically proud of her."

"I never thought of it that way."

"You see, Jenny is facing all of those problems alone and I really should be at home to share the load. She and my family are a lot more important to me than this trip, and it's very important to me that she doesn't develop any bad feelings about our journey, due to my neglect of not being there when she so needs me. You see, Clint, I actually owe it all to her, that I'm even here at all. I couldn't have been away like this without her wholehearted consent, support and encouragement and her wonderful attitude of wanting me to do my thing. She is willing to pay the price so that I can be here with you. Jenny and I are extremely close and sensitive to each other."

"I'm glad you've explained it to me. I just didn't realize what you've been going through. I guess we haven't been communicating very well, have we?"

"Not too well. I'll try to do better about expressing my thoughts from now on."

"Me too!" Clint replied.

Our discussion sort of cleared the air and it appeared that Clint's attitude had changed completely. It taught us an important lesson in the value of communication.

We moved along the north shore of Beaver Lake and down into the river still facing the headwind. Early in the evening we crossed the Yellowknife branch of the Mackenzie Highway, as the free ferry shuttled cars and trucks from one side of the river to the other.

"Probably some day there will be a bridge crossing the Mackenzie here," Clint commented as we paddled past the ferry while it unloaded at the dock on the northeast shore. As we approached Meridian Island, keeping to the right, we entered Providence Rapids. The current picked up speed and in less than thirty minutes we had descended the final three miles, arriving at Fort Providence by eight.

Phil had seen us coming down the rapids and was out to meet us with camera grinding away. Also out to welcome us ashore were great swarms of black flies. "You two must have had better luck with the big lake, this side of Hay River," Phil said.

"That's right, but Great Slave Lake certainly is not what you would call good canoe country," I replied. "It required some mighty hard pulling on the paddles and this end is shallow and weedy. We didn't see another canoe anywhere on the lake."

Wednesday, 18 August

DAY 124

Phil Pemberton again had several filming sequences to shoot which used up the early part of the day, we left him just before eleven-thirty and headed on down the Mackenzie. It was one of those perfect days, ideal for canoeing. As we crossed Mills Lake, near the south shore, an unusual thing happened. In a light breeze from the north, hundreds of spider webs came drifting from across the six to eight mile expanse of the lake. Where they came from was a mystery but they were a nuisance in our beards.

Mills Lake was the final one in the Mackenzie River system. From there and for the next thousand miles, it would be river travel all the way to Arctic Red River. Our schedule allowed us sixteen days to cover the distance. "Let's try to make this thousand miles in record time," said Clint, as we were leaving Mills Lake.

"I'm all for that! That's my kind of a challenge," I replied. Then I added, "But we should remember, we're not in a race. We should take time to enjoy this part of Northwest Territories as we go along."

"I'd like it just that way. Weather permitting we should make good time down through here. At least we don't have to waste any more time with Phil until we again meet him in Arctic Red River."

"That's right. If this weather holds, let's plan to paddle right on through the night."

"Excellent!" Clint replied.

It was after eight in the evening when we stopped for a supper of beef stew and dumplings, a substantial meal as we wanted plenty of fuel in our tanks for the all night run. Then pushing along again, we enjoyed the evening as a pair of loons flew over and a group of ducks paid us a compliment and almost landed in our canoe as darkness began to settle in. Those were the first loons we had seen since crossing Methy Portage. We thought it also meant that once more we were in good fresh water. Certainly the water was much clearer than any we had seen in the Athabasca or Slave below Fort McMurray.

After dark we met a couple of barges being pushed by tug boats. It was a perfectly beautiful night. The stars were bright and the northern lights flared and flickered across the skies.

Thursday, 19 August

DAY 125

We stopped for a shore break just before two in the morning, pulling up on a place with rock ledges similar to many areas in the Precambrian Shield country. Building a fire was essential, not only for warmth but also to smoke away the horde of mosquitoes. Following a quick snack, we laid our sleeping pads on the ground well away from the fire and unrolled our sleeping bags. I put some big sticks on the fire and crawled into my sack. Clint was already snoring and most likely I joined him in a duet within the next few minutes.

We slept nearly three hours, until five o'clock. I was comfortable even though the temperature was a cool forty-two degrees. Our sleeping bags were wet from the heavy dew. "My four inch sleeping pad is absolutely perfect," I remarked as I rolled it up. "It's one of the most ideal pieces of camp equipment I've ever used." Then as I slipped into my L. L. Bean light cut shoepaks which were finally wearing out, I said, "These boots are the most ideal footwear I know of for all around canoeing. I'm going to hate to part with them. They have been so comfortable."

I think Clint was getting enough of my rambling on as he finally said, "It's a lucky thing that you brought them along." Then he added, "It's tough getting up. I certainly enjoyed sleeping under the stars. The mosquitoes didn't bother me much either."

"No. I've always noticed that whenever the temperature gets down around forty degrees, those pests are no problem."

With breakfast out of the way we embarked at six, enjoying a light to brisk tailwind. It was one of those days, almost too good to be true. Eighty-five miles out of Fort Providence we finally reached the point where the river stopped looking and acting like a long lake and became a river as it narrowed down and the current picked up. Until then there had been only about a half mile per hour assistance, to our paddling, from the river. Before lunch we saw another pair of common loons, proof that we were back in the real wilderness once more.

While going past the settlement of Jean Marie River we watched a most unusual sight. We saw a lone man paddling away from the settlement and heading down river. We were traveling along the opposite side of the river and were mystified. At first we took the lone paddler to be an Indian, yet that was very unlikely as Indians seldom if ever energetically paddle. They seem to prefer outboard motors. This fellow was still paddling steadily after an hour. Finally we came alongside and it turned out to be a young blondheaded university student, Dick Mans, from the Netherlands. He had been in Yellowknife where he had worked to earn enough to buy a sixteen-foot white fiberglass canoe and the necessary camping gear. He was paddling solo and on his way to the Arctic Ocean all by himself. At the time we thought that to be a most

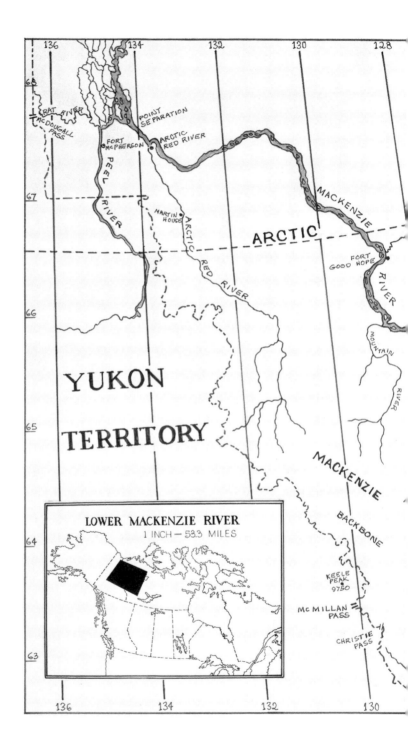

YUKON

TERRITORY

LOWER MACKENZIE RIVER
1 INCH — 58.3 MILES

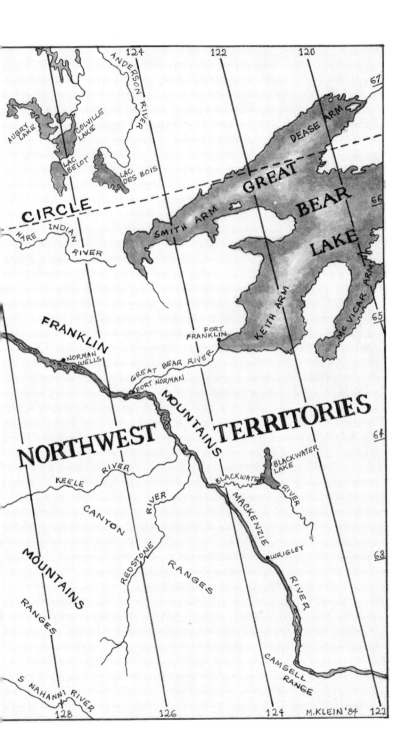

CIRCLE

GREAT BEAR LAKE

DEASE ARM

AUBRY LAKE

COLVILLE LAKE

LAC BELOT

LAC DES BOIS

ANDERSON RIVER

HARE INDIAN RIVER

SMITH ARM

KEITH ARM

MC VICAR ARM

FORT FRANKLIN

FRANKLIN

NORMAN WELLS

GREAT BEAR RIVER

FORT NORMAN

NORTHWEST

MOUNTAINS

TERRITORIES

KEELE RIVER

CANYON

REDSTONE RIVER

RANGES

MOUNTAINS

RANGES

S NAHANNI RIVER

BLACKWATER LAKE

BLACKWATER RIVER

BLACKWATER

MACKENZIE RIVER

WRIGLEY

CAMSELL RANGE

M.KLEIN '84

67
66
65
64
63

124 122 120

128 126 124 122

unusual thing to do. This incident added fuel to the dream that had been germinating within me of the special magic of solo canoeing and the need for proper canoe design and equipment. Within the next few years I moved on to designing and building solo canoes and paddling one on my 28,000-mile 'Ultimate Canoe Challenge.'

Rounding the bend where the river again swings west toward Fort Simpson we enjoyed a fifteen mile stretch of fast water before arriving there at ten in the evening. Fort Simpson is situated on an island at the junction with the Liard River. The population of the town was about nine hundred people. The only business place open was the new motel and restaurant. There we had a good supper and were able to buy a loaf of bread and a couple of cans of pork and beans before heading down river in the darkness. About five miles beyond, we set up camp and were soon enjoying some much needed sleep. It had been a one hundred mile day.

Friday, 20 August

DAY 126

We were on the river by six-thirty and it was another unbelievably beautiful day with little wind and the temperature moving up to seventy degrees by noon. For lunch we had large servings of pancakes with corn syrup. They always gave us extra amounts of go power.

After running afoul of a few sand bars in the river, we finally learned to follow the navigation markers. In places those Mackenzie River sand bars were nearly as big as the river itself, often stretching on for miles.

The Nahanni Range of mountains came into view

from nearly thirty miles away and for several hours we were treated to a spectacular sight. We were getting into country where there were mountains and hills all around. We were enjoying some of the best scenery we had encountered on the journey. We remained close to mountains throughout the day and should be near them for many days to come.

Several rain showers moved through the area during the afternoon but fortunately only one of them caught up with us. At supper time we put ashore on a point along the right shore directly across the river from where the North Nahanni River joins the Mackenzie. There the scene was gorgeous with Lone Mountain and Nahanni Mountain to the left of the inflowing North Nahanni, and Mt. Camsell to the right with a colorful Northwest Territories sky for a backdrop.

Rounding Camsell Bend we moved on to the north down the wide slow river with its numerous islands as darkness began to settle in. Clint was having trouble staying awake as had often been the case whenever he was short on sleep. That was a problem which seldom bothered me. I could get by on very little sleep as everything was so interesting to me that my mind usually remained active. We were still paddling along at midnight.

Saturday, 21 August

DAY 127

We finally made a difficult landing along the east shore at one in the morning. Quickly we pitched the tent and crawled in to escape the bloodthirsty mosquitoes. Little did we know then that it was the final time on our journey when the mosquitoes would give us a bad time. Certainly we had suffered enough from them for one summer. Both Clint and I must have many, many blood relations up there now. We slept fast and were up and at 'em by six. In the daylight we soon identified the location of our camp. We were opposite the east side of McGern Island and about six miles south of the mouth of Willowlake River.

We were back on the river by seven. During the forenoon we watched several flocks of ducks going south up the river. They were larger groups than any we had seen earlier in the summer. Many flocks numbered up to a hundred. Clint always perked up at the sight of water fowl. He understood ducks, geese and shore birds as well as anyone I have ever met, going to great lengths to identify and thoroughly explain each species sighted. I learned a lot from him. "Those ducks must know something that we don't," he remarked. "There may be a bad storm brewing up north or maybe they're just reminding us that winter's not very far away."

"I hope they're wrong about that!"

A little later we saw a flock of twenty sandhill cranes go by. They were also heading to the south. "This really looks bad for us. Those birds wouldn't be flocking up like that and heading south unless they had a good reason," Clint said.

The skies clouded over before noon and a strong north wind began to blow in our faces just before we arrived at Wrigley. We had planned to stop there to restock our food supply at the "Bay" store, but the town had disappeared. All we could see was about a dozen abandoned houses and some old shacks with no one in sight, so we kept on paddling. All of the houses had been partially destroyed with roofs ripped off, windows broken out, and doors smashed. We noticed that most of the abandoned cabins we had seen along the route had suffered the same fate. It appeared that someone had enjoyed engaging in malicious destruction.

Abandoned cabin along the Mackenzie River

Consequently we continued on down the river and would be on short food supplies until we reached Fort Norman, one hundred and sixty miles away. Eventually we learned from an R.C.M.P. officer in Norman Wells that Wrigley had been moved and rebuilt about four miles upstream.

It was tough going that afternoon. Even while we were in the fast water stretches below Wrigley, we could only move about two and a half miles per hour by really pouring on the coal and expounding maximum effort. It was difficult canoeing all the remainder of the day. Often in the strong gusts we would be brought to a standstill, not moving forward at all. At ten in the evening we gave it up for that day, selecting a campsite well above the river along the west shore.

While cooking supper I remarked, "I certainly hope this wind calms down before morning!"

"Yeah! Me too. It sure was difficult to make

any progress this afternoon. My arms and shoulders feel like we had been in a canoe race and had been struggling for hours to keep the lead."

"Do you realize , Clint, that we moved nearly fifty miles in the first six hours this morning and in the nine hours since lunch, with all of that heavy paddling, we only progressed another twenty miles?"

"No wonder I'm tired! One good thing about this wind is that there are no mosquitoes around here tonight."

Later as we relaxed near the campfire, Clint sat gazing out across the river in the direction of mile high Cap Mountain when he said, "It's a thrill to be here and know that we're looking at the same scenery that young Alexander Mackenzie peered at when he moved through here in 1789."

"It certainly is! I was thinking about that this morning."

"I can't help but wonder what his thoughts were as he explored this river. I'll bet every time he rounded a bend to the west, he optimistically was thinking, 'could this be the place where we head down to the Pacific Ocean? I sure hope so.' Then every time the river swung to the north a wave of pessimism must have swept over him."

"Yes! Peter Pond had told him that this river most likely had its outlet in or near Cooks Inlet which is now in Alaska. Mackenzie was determined to find that Northwest Passage. He was also convinced that going down this river would lead him to the Pacific."

"What a disappointment it must have been when he learned the truth and had to retrace his route all the way back up to Fort Chipewyan. He had tremendous responsibilities from the outset. How many people were in his party as they went down through here?"

"Let me glance at my pages from Mackenzie's

book and we'll get it right.   Here it is.   This is what he wrote--

> *The crew consisted of four Canadians, two of whom were attended by their wives, and a German; we were accompanied also by an Indian, who had acquired the title of English Chief, and his two wives, in a small canoe, with two young Indians; his followers in another small canoe. These men were engaged to serve us in the twofold capacity of interpreters and hunters. The Indian was one of the followers of the chief who conducted Mr. Hearne to the Copper-Mine river and had since been a principal leader of his countrymen who were in the habit of carrying furs to Churchill Factory, Hudson's Bay, and till of late very much attached to the interest of that company. The circumstances procured him the appelation of the English Chief.*
>
> *We were also accompanied by a canoe that I had equipped for the purpose of trade, and given the charge of it to M. Le Roux, one of the Company's clerks. In this I was obliged to ship part of our provision; which, with the clothing necessary for us on the voyage, a proper assortment of the articles of merchandise as presents, to ensure us a friendly reception among the Indians, and the ammunition and arms requisite for defence, as well as a supply for our hunters, were more than our own canoe could carry.*

"So apparently, they had two North canoes, Clint, plus the one small canoe belonging to the English Chief.   In all there must have been at least sixteen people in his party."

"That is interesting!   Let's see, I'm trying

to recall the name of the guide who conducted Samuel Hearne on his Coppermine Journey. Matonabbee! Does that sound right to you?"

"That's right. Chief Matonabbee," I replied. With that the discussion discontinued and we soon crawled into the tent.

Sunday, 22 August

DAY 128

The north wind continued all night but calmed down to a gentle breeze before noon. We had a good seven hours of sleep before shoving off around seven-thirty under cloudy skies. We met three more flocks of sandhill cranes heading south. "There's a feeling of fall in the air this morning," I quipped.

"Yes. If this is fall already, it certainly was one short summer."

Clint's hands had been swelling and bothering him on the long, hard days we were putting in. "How are your hands today?"

"Not much better. They're puffed up again and my fingers are numb."

"Mine are a little swollen too but they don't bother unless I think about it."

The Mackenzie was definitely a big river, with high banks and cliffs. The high water line was at least twenty-five feet higher than the water level upon which we paddled. There were big hills with gullies between and mountains in the distance. The McConnell Range was to our east and the Mackenzie Mountains at a greater distance in the west.

We enjoyed a good current with but little headwind and were making time as we passed the confluence with the Blackwater River, flowing in

from the east. Rounding the bend where the Mackenzie swings west for a few miles, we stopped for
lunch on a high bank along the right shore.
Packing our food to the top of the hill we enjoyed
a panoramic view of the vicinity as we lunched and
took pictures. The hill was almost a mountain,
nearly seven hundred feet above the river.

"Distances are deceiving up here in this big
country, Clint. Have you noticed how hard it is to
judge distances?"

"Yes. I had no idea how far it was to the top
of this hill when we started up it. I hear that
it's even more difficult to judge distances out in
the barrens."

"I like this comfortable feeling of roominess
where a man can stretch his arms back over his head
and not poke someone in the eye."

A huge section of the south side of the hill
had slid part of the way down toward the river. It
looked as though it might be sliding a few more
feet, each wet spring, forest and all. There were
cranberries, labrador tea and ripe rose hips
growing profusely over much of that hill. We har-
vested and munched on several of the rose hips and
I took time to carve Jenny's and my name in the
white bark of an aspen tree before returning to the
river.

Another fierce wind came sweeping down over
the hills just as we were ready to step into the
canoe. It turned the river into a froth within a
few minutes. When the wind blows against a strong
current it looks like the wind is trying to roll
the water up like a big roll of carpet, making
white capping waves with spray blowing back over
the top. The only way we made any progress at all
was to hug the shoreline thereby missing the best
of the river's current. The north wind blew
strongly through out the remainder of the day making for very tough going.

We met another heavily loaded tug boat pushing

eight barges upstream that afternoon. We kept plugging away until ten in the evening, but once again due to the wind, had to settle for a seventy mile day. Our camp was on the east bank opposite the inflowing Redstone River.

Monday, 23 August

DAY 129

It rained most of the night so we slept in and didn't break camp until after ten. The weather continued cold, wet, windy and miserable all day long. We had our tent set up on a mud flat which had been dry the evening before but over night the area had turned into a sea of mud.

The cold north wind blew on, combined with a steady rain. At lunch time it took nearly a half hour to get a fire started. We were soaking wet and to make matters worse, running very low on food. All of our oatmeal, sugar, pancake flour, canned goods and bread had been used up. The only food left to eat was potatoes and powdered milk. We found ourselves in that situation because we had passed Fort Simpson late in the day when everything was closed and thinking we could restock at Wrigley, we had gone on. Then when we couldn't find Wrigley, things became critical, so we went on short rations. I told Clint, "I tend to think of myself as a human engine that requires certain care with regular maintenance and fuel, continually having to put more gas in the tank depending somewhat on the mileage and power output required." When we finished our meal of potatoes and warm milk there in the rain, certainly our fuel tanks were far from full.

The river current had been strong. In the first four hours we had averaged eight miles per hour in spite of the wind. It seemed like we had chased spring half way across the continent but suddenly we were trying to beat fall.

A few miles out of Fort Norman we saw fires burning on the east river bank. They resembled steam geysers. We quickly went ashore to examine them and found lots of pieces of coal and some material resembling peat on the shore. There were also pieces of red rock looking like burned brick.

The current was slower in the afternoon. At twenty minutes after ten we pulled ashore at Fort Norman. A man stood there looking out across the river into the twilight. We told him about our food shortage. Immediately he took us to the home of the manager of the Hudson's Bay store. The manager graciously offered to open the store for us. We accepted the offer and were indeed happy to stock up on food and other needed supplies. I even bought a pair of Indian Bay rubber boots to replace my worn out L. L. Bean shoe paks.

We pitched our tent on the edge of the settlement on a high cut bank and were soon enjoying some much needed food. Weatherwise, it had been one of our most miserable days of the trip. Everything was wet that night but when things are difficult, strangely I become stimulated to overcome whatever the obstacle may be.

Tuesday, 24 August

DAY 130

Fort Norman is located at the confluence of the Great Bear and Mackenzie Rivers, the former flowing in from the east from Great Bear Lake near Fort Franklin. It is a sizeable river and of course increases the size and power of the Mackenzie.

ONE INCREDIBLE JOURNEY

A barge arrived at the settlement very early in the morning with its engine noises and bright lights to disturb our sleep. For nearly two hours the unloading process continued just below our camp and dawn was breaking before quiet was restored.

The same cold, rainy north wind greeted us as we broke camp at seven after cleaning the mud out of the canoe and re-arranging our packs to make room for our new supply of food. The waters of Great Bear River appeared to be less silty than those of the Mackenzie as we crossed its mouth just below Fort Norman. The Mackenzie has a huge shore line, often more than a hundred yards from the waters edge to the main bank. There are no trees between as everything has been scoured clean by the annual spring breakup of the ice, leaving its shores rocky and desolate.

By noon we had passed the Halfway Islands and soon stopped for lunch on a low rocky shore. Just then the sun came out for the first time in several days. We spread all of our wet things on the rocks to dry. While we feasted and relaxed the wind calmed down to a gentle breeze and it was amazing how that nice warm sunshine improved our spirits. The Norman Range of mountains, paralleling the river, six or eight miles to the east were gorgeous to gaze at. They were completely covered along their higher elevations with snow which had fallen while we were receiving all of the cold rain.

It was good going in the afternoon as we moved down river. As we approached Norman Wells, we saw Phil Pemberton's signal flag up on shore, tied to the root of an upturned tree. It was a piece of fluorescent pink surveyors tape. We pulled in and sure enough, a still smouldering campfire was there, close to the road. But where was Phil? We went on into the settlement and finally learned from the R.C.M.P. that Phil had waited there for us for three days. He had left town that afternoon, catching a ride by jeep to Inuvik. He had left word that he would meet us at Arctic Red River.

"That certainly has to be one long ride in a jeep," the R.C.M.P. officer said. "It will take at least three days to drive the more than eleven hundred miles from here to Inuvik."

"If Phil lingers very long up there, we may arrive in Arctic Red River before he does," I responded.

Norman Wells is a town of more than four hundred people. It lies on the east side of the river, across from the terminus of the Canol Heritage Trail, a jeep or truck trail connecting with the Alcan Highway, out of Watson Lake or Johnsons Crossing in Yukon Territory and over the Selwyn Mountains through Macmillan Pass.

We had an excellent supper at Mackenzie Mountain Lodge. Then leaving Norman Wells at eight thirty in the evening, we paddled on for twenty-four miles during the next four hours and encamped on an island in the dark. It had been a seventy-six mile day.

Wednesday, 25 August

DAY 131

We slept in and finally embarked at eight that showery morning. The weather had improved and the winds were calm. Moving down river we enjoyed the scenery as we were surrounded by mountains of all shapes and sizes. The taller ones were snowcapped.

Right after lunch Clint and I hiked up and along the nearby mountains. The view from up there was wonderful. We both like to wander around and explore. Usually, however, we go in different directions as he and I are each very independent and find no necessity for each other's company to be able to be happy. This hike, however, was really stimulating as we could see over to the Mackenzie Mountains in the west. We found plenty of luscious ripe fall rose hips. I like their pleasant bland taste. We both consumed a lot of them whenever we found them.

Back down on the river we enjoyed the antics of the Arctic terns as they flew out for a look at us whenever we entered their territory. We could hear them talking as they approached. They would circle around, usually twenty to thirty feet above us, and chatter their familiar, harsh and high-pitched "Tee-ar, kip-kip-kip Tee-ar."

"Terns certainly are plentiful in Canada. We have been seeing them nearly everywhere we go up here," I said.

"Yes. Arctic terns are gorgeous birds, so graceful in flight. We have been seeing them since we hit the Churchill River."

"I thought we saw them first down in Lake Huron."

"No. Those were common terns and a few black terns. Those birds don't summer this far north."

"I didn't know that."

"That's right. These Arctic terns are well known for their long migrations. They spend their summers up here along the lakes and rivers of the far north where the sun shines nearly the clock around. Then in September, they will migrate southeast over Newfoundland, across the North Atlantic, south along western Europe and Africa, and down to Antarctica, where they spend the winter months. There the sun shines the clock around while we in the northern hemisphere are having our shortest days. Then in March these terns reverse their route back to the Arctic, traveling as much as twenty-two thousand miles in their annual migrations. They see more daylight than any other living creature as they are in both the Arctic and the Antarctic during the longest days."

"That certainly is interesting."

At seven in the evening, we rounded East Mountain point, opposite the inflowing Mountain River, and there just ahead was Sans Sault Rapids. Looking ahead and doing a little maneuvering, we shot through on the left with only fast water and a few riffles, however we could see quite a respectable rapids along the extreme right. Then a little later we stopped and talked with the captain of a tug boat which was tied along the west shore. He told us about another rapids down at the beginning of the Rampart Narrows, which is only noticeable during periods of low water.

We paddled on until after midnight and then had difficulty in finding a dry and level spot for our tent. It had been an enjoyable seventy-five mile day and slowly but surely we were making progress. However, we still had a long, long way to go before winter arrived.

16

ARCTIC RED RIVER

> *I've stood in some mighty mouthed hollow*
> *That's plum full of hush to the brim,*
> *And watched that big husky sun wallow*
> *In crimson and gold and grow dim.*
>
> — *Robert Service,*
> ***The Spell of the Yukon***

Thursday, 26 August

DAY 132

It rained most of the night so once more we were off to a late start. The rapids above The Ramparts came into view by nine. We shot them very close to shore on the right. There was no danger in the spot we selected. Farther out those rapids appeared to be much wilder.

The Ramparts of the Mackenzie

The Ramparts are spectacular, sheer limestone cliffs rising straight up from the water's edge for from one to two hundred feet. Passing the mouth of the Ramparts River flowing in from the west, behind Spruce Island, we soon entered the narrows where the water flows somewhat slower and is very deep.

A mile or two above Fort Good Hope an Indian family had set up a fish camp with lots of fish drying and smoking. We stopped for a short visit and bought four smoked herring which were excellent eating. We arrived at the Hare Indian settlement before noon. A man from the Fish and Game Division showed us around town and was most helpful. We checked in with the R.C.M.P. and then had a big steak dinner at the new restaurant which was operated by Al Wilson and his wife. He said, "I have been around these parts for a long time. We recently moved up here from Inuvik."

Apparently, people who live along the Mackenzie regard the whole river as their local area and a move of three or four hundred miles is considered to be 'still in the same neighborhood.' Al Wilson also told us that the main church in town was the Roman Catholic.

We bought another supply of food at the Hudson's Bay store as well as a pair of long johns in preparation of the anticipated cold weather. I mailed a news letter to Darwin Gilbert in Lansing and telephoned Jenny. A seventy-one year old Indian gentleman came up and talked with us. Earlier, he had seen us going by upstream and remarked, "No Indian would paddle like that. Hareskins don't have to work that hard anymore."

Clint and I were impressed with Fort Good Hope and its friendly people. We thought it was one of the better settlements we had visited at that time. However, when I canoed down the Mackenzie in 1982 on our Ultimate Canoe Challenge journey with Steve Landick, things had changed. We found none of the old familiar faces. By then a fancy new school system had been built for the settlement with a population of nearly four hundred and fifty people. I was told in no uncertain terms that "white people are no longer welcome!" That was shocking! We couldn't imagine what had happened or how a settlement could change so much in only eleven years.

Later, through many inquiries with the R.C.M.P., the H.B.C., the Fish and Game Division people, and others, we learned more about the Fort Good Hope situation. It appears that the antagonistic attitude toward the whites began to build after the Indian Brotherhood was formed about fifteen years ago. During the early years of the Brotherhood, they began hiring Marxist-type lawyers from the University of British Columbia as advisors, using Federal funding to pay these attorneys.

Judge Thomas Berger's Pipeline enquiry did a lot to divide the natives from whites. Their hostile attitude toward whites is far from justified; consider that most of the Indians at Fort Good Hope are living in government low-rental housing, paying ridiculous rent that includes oil heat, electricity, garbage removal, water, etc. If they don't have the monthly rent they get it from their social worker who is another native. Her bill for February, 1984 alone was more than $21,000. Of course all medical work is free, including air fare to the hospital, dental work, glasses, etc.

The beautiful and expensive school with a large gym, built there recently, was named T'selei after an old-time Indian chief. Education is paid, for the students, right through the University level. There are also adult education upgrading classes given, and students are paid to attend. There is a Hostel to keep children from the area, and for those who want to leave Good Hope for awhile to live in the bush.

The people enjoy all kinds of government grants, paid for by the whites' taxes. Very few natives in Good Hope pay any taxes. A few summers ago there were twenty-six funded projects going on at the same time.

The Good Hope Indians do not seem to appreciate the free educational opportunities they have been given, and it is not surprising that most of the kids say they don't like school. They don't like any kind of discipline, apparently never having experienced any at home. This complete lack of discipline, incidentally, is the main reason they don't remain in school to complete their education and cannot stay on a job once they have quit school.

ONE INCREDIBLE JOURNEY

The Good Hopers are Hareskin Indians, a branch of the Chipewyan nation. Their present chief is Charlie Barnaby.

Now, back to our journey. It was past two when Clint and I again headed on downriver. Below Fort Good Hope at the junction with the Hare Indian River, we started seeing more Indian fish camps. Some were like small tent villages. At that time, a one hundred twenty-five pound bale of dried fish sold for $15.00, at the river bank.

We arrived at the Arctic Circle at eight-fifteen. We did not find a monument or sign marker signifying the fact. Stopping there for supper, we enjoyed and photographed a beautiful sunset in the Ross light before again moving on. At about that time some rocks and a pile of gravel began to slide down the steep face of the hill, splashing into the river right beside us. "This wouldn't be a very safe place to camp for the night," Clint quipped.

In most places, the riverbanks are steep with a shallow slope of a hundred yards or so above the water. Most of the way these shorelines had been swept clean by the action of ice and high water. In places boulders and stones were well packed down, almost as though laid by a stone mason. Often the banks were cut and continuously eroding away with trees and rocks sliding down into the river.

We had entered the land of little sticks. There were no big trees. A small spruce tree older than your grandfather is likely to be no taller than he was. We soon moved again. The current in many places did not take up the entire width of the river. The Mackenzie was more like a river within a river. For the best speed we learned that we should follow the navigation markers, even though many times it was not the shortest distance between two points. There were lots of sand bars to trap us whenever we tried to take a shortcut, especially in the dark.

322

DAY 133

The skies were cloudy when we broke camp but cleared by ten as we moved down past the numerous islands of the area known as The Grand View. The Mackenzie remained wide, up to four miles in width in some places. We passed several more Indian fish camps. It seems August is the time of year for drying fish for winter use. Much of it would be used to feed the sled dogs. We noticed all along that the Indians tended to do all things in season when it was the easiest and most convenient for them.

At lunch time we stopped where a small, un-named creek joins the Mackenzie. There were a couple of old, vacant cabins to explore. One of them had been wallpapered with old newspapers dating back to 1934. We prepared good old salmon patties for lunch. The hot sun had warmed things so well that by the time we finished our meal, we decided to do a much-needed task. Namely, to do up our laundry and take a bath in the river. Then while the clothing dried, we each went for a walk in the bush.

We had our shirts off most of the afternoon doing a little sunbathing to replenish our sun tans for we knew there most likely would be but few more opportunities that year. There was a definite feel of fall in the air. It was much like an Indian Summer day. Spider webs as well as certain fine weed seeds floated along on their dandelion-like vehicles of fluffy down. Many of the birches were turning the color of gold.

At different times during the day we saw Indian canoes with outboard motors moving up or down the river. Many were loaded with whole families or occasionally young couples. Late in the afternoon we watched a fox running along on the riverbank.

Still going strong at midnight, we wanted to knock off at least seventy miles before making camp.

Saturday, 28 August

DAY 134

Can you imagine what it's like to be wading down the middle of the mighty Mackenzie River at two in the morning, on a black, moonless night, a mile from the nearest shore? Well, we can! We found ourselves trapped in shallow water over a huge submerged sand bar. In the darkness we floundered around and whatever direction we tried, the canoe would go aground.

"This is ridiculous!" Clint said, each time we ran aground. Finally, I stepped out into the river and by feeling my way along the bottom with my foot and a paddle, I towed the canoe with a line until we eventually found deeper water. By then I had had enough! We headed straight for the nearest shore and pitched the tent to get a short night's sleep. We slept fast. Three and a half hours later dawn had broken and we were soon underway once more on what turned out to be a day of continuous drizzle.

The high point of the day came in late afternoon while we were having a rest break along the west shore. The sightseeing passenger boat **Norwega** came upstream around a bend, close along the shore, and stopped to talk with me. Clint had been having more trouble staying awake as we paddled along, so he had gone tramping out through the bush in an attempt to wake up. This same boat had passed us more than a week earlier going downstream from Hay River to Inuvik. Apparently by then nearly everyone up and down the river knew who we were and where we were headed. The moccasin telegraph had

The **Norwega** pulls in to talk with us

been in action. We were becoming a tourist attraction on the Mackenzie River. I felt a little like
a bear must feel when being gawked at. Some people
aboard were probably asking, "What is it?" I ran
along the shore taking pictures while the passen-
gers waved and hollered at me. Finally I sat down
on a big rock and just looked at them. When they
decided that I wasn't going to perform any more,
they headed on south.

Stopping for supper a couple of hours later,
we feasted on pork and beans with a can of ham.
The early voyageurs out of Montreal were called the
'pork eaters' because of the salt pork they carried
and consumed. They could have called us the 'pork
and bean eaters'!

Shortly after midnight we encamped only
thirty-eight miles upstream from Arctic Red River.

DAY 135

We slept for nearly five hours before sliding the canoe back into the river. Twenty miles above the settlement of Arctic Red River, we entered the Lower Ramparts. They differ from the limestone Ramparts or cliffs in the vicinity of Fort Good Hope, the former being of shale and hard clay and also very high and spectacular.

Arctic Red River was a most welcome sight as Clint and I rounded the bend east of town and came paddling up to Phil Pemberton's bright orange tent pitched on a low sand bar on a point of land across the Arctic Red River from the village. It had been one of those cold, blustery early winter type mornings and we had looked forward to getting off the river for a while. Just past noon we nosed our canoe into the mud and driftwood of the shore and headed for a still-smoldering campfire, but Phil was not there.

Kicking the burned off pieces of wood back onto the fire to revive it, we warmed ourselves while discussing the important things of life. Number one of which was something to eat. We were hungry and our fuel tanks were nearly empty, having paddled since breakfast into a strong north wind. We scrounged some hard tack and jam from among Phil's supplies. Gulping them down, we unloaded our canoe, pitched our tent beside Phil's and put away our gear. Then we headed for the settlement across the smaller river in search of Phil. The last time we had seen him was at Fort Providence, eleven days earlier and nearly a thousand miles upriver.

Arctic Red River was to be the last trading post on our route, until Old Crow, Yukon Territory, and that was about four hundred miles up and over the mountains along a devious and uncertain route.

The Hudson's Bay store in Arctic Red River

So we wanted to replenish our supplies before continuing our journey.

Arctic Red River was another Indian settlement with a population of ninety-four, including the six white people. It is strategically located high above the confluence of the two rivers in the foothills of the mountains, two hundred miles above the Arctic Circle. There is an exceptional view overlooking the outside curve of the final bend of the Mackenzie River where it swings to the north before sprawling out all over the map into its fantastic delta to flow into the Arctic Ocean.

At the time of our journey the settlement and the native culture remained very much the same as it was in the beginning. That, however, was about to change. Since then a new road called the Dempster Highway has been completed running from east of Dawson, Yukon Territory to Inuvik by way of Fort McPherson and Arctic Red River.

327

Crossing the river we docked our canoe below the Catholic church which was up a steep hill. We stopped and talked with the priest and had a good visit. He had seen Phil earlier in the day and thought we might find him at the Hudson's Bay store up on the next higher hill. Eventually we found our missing cameraman in the home of the Bay store's manager. They were talking with a couple of other young fellows who were doing some kind of government fish and wildlife survey and research work.

We took care of important matters first, such as picking up a good supply of food, a new pair of rubber boots which are so popular with the natives of the north, and the only new windbreaker jacket in the store. We also bought a single barrel shotgun and shells to take along, in case we needed to supplement our food supplies while going over the summit.

With that taken care of, next came the movie sequences which Phil had planned. We were invited to have supper at the home of the Bay store manager where we had a grand time swapping stories and information about the area.

One of the stories we heard was about the Mad Trapper of Rat River, the very river which Clint and I would be ascending a couple of days later on our way up to McDougall Pass. The Mad Trapper's real name was Albert Johnson, who in reality was neither a trapper nor a madman. The news media had picked up the story and called it the Mad Trapper story as they spread it across North America.

Johnson lived in a cabin on the Rat River about seventy miles from where we were talking that evening. He was a solitary man and a little peculiar, but certainly no madman. Johnson was addicted to interfering with the trap lines of the trappers of the area, as he didn't take kindly to people trespassing across what he considered to be his own private property. His victims finally reported him to the R.C.M.P., who of course are the law of the north. The Mounties soon set out up the Rat River to investigate.

"How long ago was that?" Clint asked.

That was in the fall of 1931. When the police reached the cabin they were unable to find anyone around so they returned to their post in Aklavik. There they armed themselves with a search warrant and finally arrived back at the Johnson cabin on New Year's Eve. They soon discovered that the wanted man had converted his home into a barricaded strong point during their absence. Approaching, the two constables were greeted with a burst of gunfire, which seriously wounded Corporal King. As the temperature was forty-five degrees below zero, his partner decided to make the long trek back to Aklavik with Corporal King riding on the dog sled.

On January 9, the Mounties returned again to the Johnson cabin with a force of seven men and forty-two sled dogs. Using guns and dynamite, they were unable to find their man. Again the intense cold finally forced them to return to Aklavik as their quarry had fled. Then three weeks later, Johnson's tracks were picked up in the mountains, high up the Rat River where he was believed to be hiding out in the bush. This time the constables caught up with him. The shooting soon started and a Mountie by the name of Constable Millen was killed.

Shortly after that an early bush pilot named Wop May flew into the story. It seems May was in Fort McMurray when the R.C.M.P. sent out a call for a plane. May soon took off but the weather slowed him as he flew north and it took him three days to reach Aklavik. On the fourth morning he flew out to the police camp and landed on a frozen lake, near the spot where Constable Millen had been killed. Johnson meanwhile had struck out over the mountains through McDougall Pass, into the Yukon. The Mounties by this time were out for blood.

Wop May began the search immediately. Flying just over the tree tops he eventually picked up the Mad Trapper's trail along the Barrier River. Reporting back to the searchers' camp, he then flew Constable Millen's body out to Aklavik and returned with more food and supplies for the police.

Several days passed during which May flew up and down over those mountains searching for the fleeing desperado. On 14 February he picked up the trail again, dropping red streamers to guide the ground force. This time they found that Johnson obliterated his tracks by mingling them with the tracks of a herd of migrating caribou.

Another three days went by before May again picked up the trail. This time it was clear and traceable, leading toward the Eagle River, deep in the interior. May flew back and forth showing the route, as the police party converged on the area. Sergeant H. F. Hersey, driving the leading dog team, swung around a bend and straight into the muzzle of Johnson's gun. The Mad Trapper fired and Hersey fell, seriously wounded. The others closed in for the kill, and kill it was as they caught him on the ice of the frozen river.

The big problem then was Hersey, as by that time the weather had closed down with clouds in the tree tops. Did Wop May have the courage to attempt to fly Sergeant Hersey out, they asked. "That is precisely why I'm here and that's what I'm paid for," he replied. The wounded constable was carefully laid on the cabin floor, where Jack Bowen, May's flight engineer, tended him while May skimmed the trees and just above the river bottoms, much of the way not ten feet off the ice, bringing Hersey to the hospital in Aklavik. The doctors there said another half hour would have written off Hersey's chances for survival.

One more chore remained. May flew back to the police camp, bringing out Johnson's body to Aklavik for burial, then flew the body of Constable Millen out to Fort McMurray for shipment home. When pilot Wop May finally reached Edmonton, it was to find himself a continent-wide headline hero and a local celebrity.

That was only a sample of the many interesting stories we heard during the evening. I also called my wonderful wife at home in Michigan by radiophone for which I suffered an attack of homesickness.

To return the hospitality we had been shown, Clint and I invited the same gang over to our campfire on the sand bar point for a pancake breakfast the following morning. We paddled back to camp and as I was pressed for time, I stayed up most of the night getting out letters and catching up on my diary.

Monday, 30 August

DAY 136

We woke up to a cold drizzle of rain. Checking the thermometer the temperature stood at thirty-eight degrees with a wind out of the north. As the weather was so disagreeable we ended up by serving our planned pancake breakfast at the home of the Bay store manager. I felt rather awkward preparing breakfast in a kitchen. I know I could have handled it better over one of our campfires. It was a struggle but I'm sure we came out ahead in the exchange. We asked questions about the best route up the mountains. No one seemed to know much about it except to tell us it had seldom been done.

Most people who did go our route, we were told, flew up and over the summit by plane. Only a week before Charlie Wolf, who is widely known as 'The Gentleman Canoeist' and his partner from Fairbanks, Alaska were flown in to Summit Lake. We also learned that four other canoe parties had attempted to make it over McDougall Pass earlier that summer but only one had apparently accomplished the feat. That was four German youths, with one canoe and two kayaks. They had left Arctic Red River two weeks ahead of us and hadn't returned so presumably they had succeeded. Everyone whom we inquired of shook their heads and advised us not to try, telling us it was just too late in the season. They said winter would be nipping at our heels and reminded us that there had already been several freezing nights.

True, ducks and geese had been heading south, vegetation had nearly all turned color and many trees and bushes had dropped their leaves, but we felt we had no choice as we had traveled so far. We had to continue in an attempt to achieve our goal. They even told us about a spot up the Rat River at the foot of the mountains called Destruction City, where back in the early days, dozens of gold prospectors were stopped by the difficult passage. Most of them turned back, leaving behind piles of equipment and supplies. A few stayed, being trapped by winter and most of those never went any farther. The north was too much for them as several froze to death that winter. Clint and I hoped we would be able to cope with the difficult task ahead. We were confident we would make it.

Phil had met a knowledgeable young Chipewyan Indian at Fort Providence by the name of Tony Mercredi, and had arranged to have him assist Phil all the way over to Fort Yukon, Alaska. He had also purchased a used sixteen-foot Sears canvas canoe and was planning to accompany us up and over the summit. Looking at his equipment and considering the route, I was having some silent apprehensions, but things usually have a way of working out for the best.

Right after our late breakfast, Phil wanted to take more pictures. Consequently, it was noon before we finally paddled off down the river while

Phil and Tony stayed behind to film an Indian family sequence for the movie. He had also hired a man with a motor boat to ferry them and their canoe on up the route ahead of us for the first fifty miles, where we planned to overtake them. As the afternoon wore on, we didn't see them pass us.

The waters of the big river were pretty rough from the cold north wind which blew throughout the day, making progress slow. We followed along the left shore after passing Point Separation and entered the Mackenzie River delta, which extends for more than a hundred miles as it widens out to join the Arctic Ocean. Before five we stopped to prepare a hot meal, walking back into an alder and willow thicket to get some protection from the cold wind. It was surprising how we felt at a time like that. We were cold and wet, sitting in a damp thicket and thankful for our smoky fire and a little protection from the wind. Yet we were enjoying it!

We saw several more large flocks of geese heading south and Clint remarked, "We are probably in for some more bad weather. Those birds wouldn't be moving south in such large numbers unless something bad was moving in." A couple of hours later, we left the main part of the Mackenzie and headed west toward the Peel River past a small Indian settlement. Six miles to the southwest we set up camp in a willow thicket leaving our canoe out along the river bank where Phil would be sure to see it when and if he came along. Phil turned out to be the main topic of our discussion over our late campfire supper.

I started an interesting discussion when I asked, "Where in the world do you suppose Phil is?"

"I can't imagine," Clint replied.

"If he doesn't show up by morning, I wonder how long we should wait for him?"

"I wouldn't wait at all if it was up to me. Phil may be a nice fellow, but it seems to me that he's really taking advantage of you."

"Why do you say that?"

"Because you are paying for his entire trip and now he has even hired a guide. Did you think about how much more this is going to cost you?"

"Well, I did think about it, but I had no choice. I am committed to the completion of the movie. You know, Clint, that movie when completed is going to make us famous!" I kidded.

"That is ridiculous! Compared to what Phil is costing you, it's just not worth it, but that's your problem. My problem is all of the time we have wasted on your movie and by continually having to wait for Phil. And now with winter coming on, due to all of those delays, it begins to look like our chances of completing our journey as we had planned are very slim. I'm really beginning to doubt if we can make it before freeze up."

I didn't know what to say but finally I said, "I still think we can make it. You are right about all of those delays and I'm sorry about that. Let's keep plugging away. We may even surprise ourselves with the speed we make, once we get over the summit."

"I'm all for that," Clint replied.

Our discussion undoubtedly was good for our overall morale. It sort of cleared the air. We both realized we had our work cut out for us and best of all, we were still good friends.

17

CANOEING UP
A MOUNTAIN

> *This is the law of the Yukon,*
> *That only the Strong shall thrive;*
> *That surely the Weak shall perish,*
> *And only the Fit survive.*
>
> —— *Robert Service,*
> **The Law of the Yukon**

Tuesday, 31 August

DAY 137

We were off to a late start as it was not the kind of morning that would normally entice canoe travel. The temperature stood at freezing with a stiff, raw wind blowing out of the north bringing intermittent snow flurries interspersed with sleet. Phil and Tony had not shown up, so off we went eager to meet the difficult and unknown challenge just ahead. We were anxious to learn first hand the answer to the question, 'how do you canoe up a mountain?'

335

ONE INCREDIBLE JOURNEY

It was upstream on the Peel River that morning. In some places there was a brisk current. Along the way three sled dogs followed us along the bank for about five miles as the snow continued to fall. We began to worry about those dogs. Were we going to be stuck with them? We didn't relish the idea of being accused of dog stealing. Fortunately they were finally stopped by a sheer cut bank and that was the last we saw of them.

According to our maps, the entrance to the Rat River was gained by turning north on the Husky Channel of the Peel where it also flows into the huge Mackenzie Delta. Then about a mile down the Husky Channel the map showed we should make a sharp turn to the left, putting us in the south branch of the Rat River. So that was the route we followed.

Heading down the Husky Channel we soon came to a place where it was pretty well blocked by an island with six hungry black and white sled dogs on it. Turning into the Rat before noon, we found it to be very winding as it looped back and forth in every direction of the compass. After several hours of moving along, constantly keeping an eye on the map and checking the mileage, it began to dawn on me that something was wrong. We definitely were not where the map showed the river to be! Of all the places for a map to disagree with us! It was disconcerting to say the least. I can hardly think of a more confidence-shattering, ego-bursting place on earth than the vast Mackenzie Delta with its hundreds of multiple channels and thousands and thousands of pothole lakes, to find that we were probably lost.

Navigation would have been difficult even if the map had been correct that dark, blustery day as we were in an area of the continent where the compass variation was thirty-eight degrees east of true north. At our late lunch break in a marshy thicket, we discussed the situation, wondering just what we should do. We decided to push on to the west and north as long as we could find water to paddle in, all the while hoping to find the main channel of the Rat River. During our discussion, Clint said, "Maybe those people back in Arctic Red River were right. Maybe it is impossible to get through here this late in the season. The water is at its low stage, that's for sure."

Pushing on I found some comfort in the words of a song that kept running through my mind, 'My God Knows the Way Through the Wilderness.' I kept very close track of where we thought we were by tracing our route on the map, even though things just didn't look right. That task did get quite complicated and time-consuming, especially when we began going through dozens of small pothole lakes. Most were so shallow that we left a track of the canoe trail and paddle marks in the soft mud of their bottoms.

We kept on struggling along, mostly to the west until nine. By then we could see higher ground and some hills a couple of miles ahead. Deciding that we should lay over, I said, "Let's set up camp and maybe things will look brighter in the morning."

"That's a good idea. I've had enough for one day."

We had been leaving orange surveyor tape markers with date, time and initials for Phil and his guide to follow, but that evening we decided for sure that they could never catch us. "No motor boat could make it this far. Unless they had paddled all night and caught us before we left camp this morning, there was no possible way they will catch us in that sixteen foot canoe," I said.

"That's for sure!" Clint replied.

Right after supper we built a large campfire so that it could be seen, just in case. Once more we discussed our situation. It was unanimously decided that we had no choice but to continue on the next morning. I'm sure we were both relieved and pleased that from then on, we would push on at our former mileage-consuming pace, unhampered by trying to leave a trail for Phil and his guide.

Early that day we had talked about going back to see what had happened to Phil, but the agony of indecision soon passed as Clint reminded me, "The name of our game is to get to the Bering Sea."

"You are right," I replied. "For all we know, Summit Lake may already be freezing over."

Wednesday, 1 September

DAY 138

The mosquitoes were no longer a problem. In fact, we hadn't seen an insect of any kind in several days. Undoubtedly they would have been a terror in the delta country a few weeks earlier. The weather remained much like the previous day. Fortunately none of the snow was remaining on the ground at our elevation, but occasional glimpses of the Richardson Mountains showed plenty of snow at the higher elevations. Those mountains were only ten or twelve miles away in a straight line. Our route, however, by water and around a giant horseshoe, would require nearly sixty miles of travel.

It was our third day in the mud and slime of the huge delta and slime it was, in everything. Our canoe, clothing, gear, water and food were saturated with the gooey stuff as we worked our way to the northwest, keeping as near the west edge of the delta as possible. Finding our way through was difficult. We circled one large pothole nearly twice before we located the outlet. A mistake in navigation could have been disastrous. We had no one to ask for help except the Lord. Silently, that is what I did and at three-thirty we finally arrived entering the main channel of the Rat River. It was a good-sized stream and this proved to us that our maps were indeed wrong. We had crossed the delta on an uncharted channel.

Late in the afternoon as we rounded a bend to the left toward the mountains, we arrived at the first set of rapids. The river water was clear and clean, with sand or gravel shores. It was certainly wonderful after all of that mud and slime. We lined the first set of rapids and paddled a short distance to another. Then as we rounded the second bend to the left we moved past the northernmost point of our entire journey. The precise location of that point was 135°, 25 min. west longitude and 67°, 46 min. north latitude. Little did we know then, there would be no more paddling for us for quite some time. We faced a continuing set of rapids, lining on upriver for the next five miles to the foot of the first low mountains. By then we had waded and lined enough for one day so we set up camp on the right side of our route in a lovely scenic place.

It was with real joy and gratitude that in two and a half days since leaving Arctic Red River we had crossed the Mackenzie Delta and were looking up into the mountains. From there on it would be a whole new ballgame. We reveled in the scenic wonder surrounding us. There were beautiful fall colors and snowcapped mountains sprinkled with patches of small green spruce trees. We felt good about being there and celebrated the occasion with stacks of hot pancakes along with stewed apricots and hot tea. Those pancakes were so good that we consumed eight of them.

During the day we had been surprised to see a brood of young ducks, not yet able to fly. We wondered how they could grow up in time to escape the coming winter.

Studying our map, we saw that the Rat River

was coming down out of a box canyon which gradually increased in width until it flowed through a wide, flat canyon that was nearly two miles wide near our camp.

Thursday, 2 September

DAY 139

The weather was about the same and we were off to another late start because of the early morning sleet and rain, but our spirits were high. For breakfast we had more pancakes and baked an extra batch to carry along for lunch. Ours were no ordinary pancakes. They were highly fortified with a cup of corn meal and lots of powdered milk. At other times we added oatmeal or powdered eggs, or both, varying the recipe considerably. No matter how we fortified them, pancakes proved to be the best energy-producing food that we consumed on the entire journey. Clint and I were both nutrition conscious and took particular note of the effect of different foods on our systems. A bellyful of those pancakes gave fifty percent more energy than the biggest steak dinner we could eat.

The day gave us a sample of things to come as well as a reminder that we should stay alert and proceed with caution. It was evident before we broke camp that lining and wading would be necessary so we tied both of our quarter-inch nylon ropes together, giving us nearly forty feet of tow rope. I towed the fully loaded canoe while Clint guided the canoe out into the deeper water with a ten or twelve foot long pole. Usually we both waded in shallow water. That was easier going than the unstable gravel we found in most places just above the water line. Occasionally we would hand hold the canoe around tricky boulders in the numerous and continuing rapids. At those times, the water often came in over our boot tops.

Clint was using four-buckle overshoes and several pairs of wool socks while I wore the rubber knee boots with three pairs of wool socks. About ten minutes with our boots full of ice water was all we could endure at a time. Then we'd have to remove our boots, dump the water, wring out the wool socks and put them back on. I wore the same three pairs of socks all the way through there. On later mornings when they were frozen stiff, I crushed the ice with my hands to soften them enough to get them on my feet. At times like that there was of course a certain amount of discomfort.

Fortunately, I had with me a pair of rubberized work gloves. Those proved to be ideal for handling and pulling on the wet nylon rope all day, sometimes being yanked to a stop by a boulder, or pulling with all my might over submerged rocks, while Clint pushed whenever he could. Unfortunately, the shoreline varied continually. Sometimes we would progress less than a hundred yards along one side, being stopped by heavy brush, a high cut bank or a sheer cliff. There we would pick a spot where the water was best, maneuver the canoe heading out into the current, hop in and paddle furiously to ferry across to the opposite side of the river. At times, that was a little tricky! We repeated that process as much as seventy times in one day. This was where experience and team work really became important.

By continuous work we had progressed about five miles by one o'clock and were heading for an island which looked like a good spot for lunch and a warming campfire. There disaster struck! We were lining up a narrow channel and trying to maneuver around a log jam at a drop in the rapids when the rushing water caught the canoe partly sideways.

The force of the water pushed the canoe against a stub of a log and flipped it upside down and jammed it under the pile of logs. It was so sudden and unexpected we were momentarily stunned. It was one of those freak things that should never have happened. Our situation would be desperate if the canoe broke up and our gear went to the bottom in those powerful rapids. Everything would be scattered for miles along the bottom of the Rat River. We were in about the most remote and desolate spot we would be in on the entire journey. Certainly help would not be easy to come by.

Clint jumped in and grabbed the canoe and was reaching under and pulling things out as I rushed back around the log jam to help him. Suddenly a better idea dawned on us. We would try to pull the canoe out from under that pile of logs and turn it back right side up if we possibly could. Even though we barely managed to keep from being swept downstream, we heaved with all our might and miraculously succeeded. The spray cover had kept nearly everything in the canoe, and we were lucky. We only lost four cameras and film, our canned goods and a few miscellaneous small items.

There we were on a small gravel bar island, hurriedly pouring water out of all of our gear, food and supplies. Everything was soaking wet. At that time another heavy downpour of rain hit and it rained continuously without letup for the rest of the day. We pitched our tent right there and built a fire to try to dry some of our most essential things but that was almost impossible in the persistent rain. Fortunately, our extra set of clean clothes were in waterproof bags and our polyester fibre fill sleeping bags were only partly wet. I wrung a little out of mine to make it as comfortable as possible for sleeping. Then it took a while to wring more than a bucket of water out of my foam sleeping pad.

The way the weather was acting we could be in

for more trouble. Towards evening the temperature dropped and a freezing rain fell. "If this keeps up all night we may not be able to move in the morning," Clint remarked.

"We wouldn't go very far up this mountain in an ice storm."

For supper that night we had fried hardtack, which had been soaked in the upset and we didn't want to throw it out. We knew we were going to be short on food as we had lost so much canned food in the rollover. Along with butter and jam and hot tea, our fried hardtack tasted good.

It was a long way out, whichever way we chose. We soon decided that we should press on the next morning if at all possible. We were well aware of our predicament but I must say, somehow I was enjoying it. Instead of being discouraged, I had the distinct happy feeling that someone cared for me and with His help we would make it.

We crawled into our wet sacks that night in a soggy tent to sleep in damp sleeping bags on a wet foam sleeping pad as the cold rain continued. We were to wake up the next morning with water in the tent and it wouldn't have been too surprising if we had both had wet dreams.

Friday, 3 September

DAY 140

The rain stopped for a few hours in the morning and it warmed enough so that ice was no longer a problem. We breakfasted on cream of wheat which also was waterlogged, then repacked everything, loaded the canoe and headed on upstream. The water level of the river was rising rapidly and had nearly flooded our little island camp by the time we could get away. It dawned on us that camping on an island in the middle of a mountain river, during a steady rain, is not a good idea. We were wearing rain jackets and pants, the latter with rubber bands around the cuffs which often prevented the boots from filling, as I made quick steps through deep water. The farther we moved up the canyon, the steeper it became and the faster the water flowed.

The rains returned before noon. Following a quick lunch in the rain we continued to carefully work our way along the loose rocky slope at the base of the sheer side of the mountain. Suddenly rocks splashed in the river right in front of me. That put a little more haste in our steps as we kept one eye on the mountainside. Several more rocks came bounding down. It was an uneasy feeling watching a rock come at you from 'way up there and not knowing which way to duck because you didn't know which way that last bounce or two would send them. Several small ones hit the canoe but we managed to duck all that came our way. A little farther on, below another mountainside, a mud slide came slithering down to splash into the river only fifty feet ahead of us. There were no dull moments that day for every minute was an interesting and exciting experience.

We pitched our tent well back off the river on the highest ground we could find in the canyon. The river was still rising and by the time we finished supper it had risen another six inches. I glanced at the map in its waterproof case and found that we had progressed about five miles since morning. We crawled into the tent before ten to escape the continuing downpour. Everything was as wet or even wetter than it had been on the previous night, but we were adjusting!

Crawling into our cold, wet, clammy sleeping bags that night, with the river rising fast, we were fearful that it might flood the canyon. Before I dozed off, I found myself thinking of my honey back in Michigan, at home and snuggled up there warm and dry in our nice, soft, comfortable bed with clean, dry sheets. Then I began to wonder what was wrong with my head. What kind of a problem, I asked myself, does a man have that he would put himself into a spot such as we were in?

Saturday, 4 September

D A Y   1 4 1

When we awoke and popped our heads out of the tent, we were in for a shock. The water level had risen more than two feet overnight, submerging our campfire spot and coming to within a short distance of the tent. The canoe that we had beached, high and dry and tied to the trunk of an upturned tree, was afloat, tugging at the tow rope in the strong current. We rolled out and went to work immediately, first re-securing the canoe to a standing tree above the water's edge. Then as Clint was doing the usual morning camp chores, I prepared another big batch of fortified pancakes and brown sugar syrup, as the rain continued. While eating, I remarked, "These experiences in the box canyon of the Rat River will give us something to talk about when we get home."

"That's for sure! This weather is ridiculous! All we need now is for this canyon to become a solid river and we would have to take to the hills."

"If the water continues to rise all day we will have no other choice. I've been wet for so long now that I'm beginning to feel like a rat myself. Muskrat, that is."

The rain did continue all day, with the temperature in the afternoon hitting a not-too-sweltering forty degrees. One consolation was that it would be impossible to get any wetter. As long as we kept moving, we didn't seem to suffer from the cold too much, but whenever we made a stop, we would build a fire as rapidly as possible.

Late in the afternoon I could tell that Clint was having about all of the bad weather and all of the Rat River that he wanted. Whenever things didn't go too well for him, he would say, "This is ridiculous!" I didn't keep track of it, but I'm sure I heard that phrase at least a half dozen times during the afternoon.

It was a rough and difficult day for both of us as we progressed six additional miles. The water was well over the regular river banks, forcing us out into the brush which made for slow and tedious work. We saw several large trees, roots and all, come floating down the canyon which was growing narrower and narrower as we slowly moved onward and upward.

Sunday, 5 September

DAY 142

The Rat River was wild! We continued on upstream in thirty-six degree temperature on another misty morning. It had rained most of the night but finally it looked like we were getting a break in the weather. By noon the rain had stopped and we could dimly see the sun through the clouds.

I again slept well in my wet wool shirt and damp long johns, in my sleeping bag, using my soggy rolled-up jacket for a pillow. Each morning I would put all of those wet, cold, soaked clothes back on after again wringing more water out of them. It did take considerable determination and fortitude for both Clint and me to continue each morning, but we had no choice.

The river apparently crested during the night, as the water level was a couple of inches lower in the morning. Breakfast was more pancakes fortified with oat meal along with syrup and coffee. As Clint stood there eating his eleventh pancake, I heard him say, "Verlen, I think your cooking is improving. These are delicious!"

We had camped between the larger uppermost cliffs along the Rat. Due to the many days of steady rain, the mountainsides were loose and eroding with mud and rocks which frequently fell. The uphill climb of the river became even steeper and more difficult. By noon we were a mile past the junction with the Barrier River and the canyon walls were closing in as we waded and lined along, but they were no longer towering above us as they had farther back down the mountainside. At lunch with our fire spot only a canoe length from the river with its speeding current, we could hear rocks being rolled along the bottom of the channel.

Many of the rocks in and along the river bed, regardless of size, were lying loose and they often rolled over when we stepped on them. Even those weighing several hundred pounds could not be depended on. We had learned from previous experience that one must always expect every rock one steps on to roll and if that rock doesn't move at all, then that was a lucky step. The Rat contained more than its share of loose rocks. Frequently even though moving with care, rocks would roll over and spill us into deeper water.

Other than the flood, the biggest obstacle to our progress turned out to be just plain old brush. Due to the high water in the canyon and over the riverbanks, the willows, tag elders and popples often impeded our progress.

My pair of rubberized work gloves were just the thing for handling the tow rope. Otherwise my hands would have been cut and sore. The gloves were often full of water as were my rubber boots. By then, with four days of continuous soaking, both my hands and feet looked like prunes. They were, however, no longer causing me noticeable pain from all of the ice water, which at first had been so disagreeable. It was the same with sleeping in a wet, soggy tent on a sleeping pad that probably still had at least a gallon of water in the foam and a sleeping bag that was equally wet.

We had no dry paper towels or toilet paper but did keep our wet, soaked paper towels. Whenever we needed toilet paper, we hurriedly dried a couple of sheets over a campfire.

During our noon lunch break, Clint counted fifty-five cracks, blisters and abrasions on his hands. When he compared them to my prune-like hands, he decided that from then on he would also wear his gloves. Showers returned in the afternoon. I hadn't been able to dry the laundry that was done more than a week earlier, even though it was hung out by the fire on five or six different occasions.

We encamped early as the rain temporarily stopped, and built two fires. By the time we had gone to elaborate preparations to hang everything out to dry around those fires, the rain started again. I did manage to get my sleeping bag partially dried out at the noontime stop. All in all, we had the driest tent and sleeping bags that we'd had for a good many days.

Monday, 6 September

DAY 143

With the mercury standing at thirty-eight degrees we were off to a late start, lining and wading up the canyon. At breakfast we inventoried our remaining food and discussed our situation. The nearest place where we were certain additional supplies of food could be obtained was at Fort Yukon, Alaska, nearly six hundred miles ahead. There was a chance, however, that we might be able to restock in Old Crow, Yukon Territory, but we were unsure of that. We were down to the basics. The main meals would have to consist of Lipton soup with dumplings, oatmeal and pancakes. Gone were our peanut butter, cheese, jam, cocoa, candy and peanuts. We had discussed our food situation following our upset and decided we should eat well while going up the canyon, even if it meant we might be hungry while going downstream. We found that going up the Rat required a tremendous amount of energy, especially in the flood time of early winter. We hoped we would be able to make it.

Snow flurries showered down off and on all day. Most tree leaves had already fallen but some color remained in the bushes. The going was difficult until noon. Then suddenly the canyon widened out into a valley and the current slowed down. For the next couple of hours we moved along at good speed.

Naturally we were most anxious to reach the summit. Clint and I worried about the freeze up, especially with our canoe full of wet gear. The continuing adverse weather and rough going seemed to be getting through to us. Each day we were noticeably becoming more and more run down. To make it even more difficult, we were definitely suffering from a bad case of 'tent fever,' caused by having to be in such close and constant contact with each other, day after day. We were getting on each other's nerves! We were both concerned about our chances of finishing the journey. To say the least, it was a difficult time and I didn't really know how to cope with it.

At lunch break I finally said, "I guess it was a mistake for us to insist on waiting that extra week in Flin Flon so we could take part in their big canoe race. Had we continued on after a day or two there, we could have avoided the long delay of being windbound on Great Slave Lake and would have been up through here ahead of all this foul weather."

Grinning, Clint replied, "Verlen, your hindsight is better than your foresight."

"That's for sure!"

The tension was eased and we soon moved around a bend where the high mountains came into view. We were seeing lots of caribou tracks and occasionally crossed the trail of a moose as it walked along the river. That evening we set up our camp at the foot of Symmetry Mountain in a willow and alder thicket amidst a steady snowfall which melted upon hitting the ground. About two hundred feet up the slope was the line above which the snow was sticking and from there to the peaks it was a gorgeous scene. The water in our little river was crystal clear, a vast improvement from the flood of muddy waters we had encountered downstream. We were getting the feeling of being near the top, especially when looking back down the canyon and seeing tree tops extending below our line of sight.

We had made better mileage that day, knowing that once across the summit it would be all down hill for the remainder of the journey.

Tuesday, 7 September

DAY 144

The thermometer stood at twenty-eight degrees at breakfast time. Best of all, the day dawned bright and cloudless and the view was breathtaking. The snow-covered Richardson Mountains were all

350

around us. That was our first real view of them as they had been obscured for more than a week by the miserable weather. We were camped at the entrance to the whole range of higher peaks. The river ahead came flowing down out out of the midst of that range. When Clint looked upstream, he said, "That looks impossible," and I could understand his concern.

I spent some time fussing with my camera, trying to wipe it off and dry it out. We just had to secure some pictures in there to capture some of the gorgeous scenery. Finally I decided the camera was working, so loading it with film I shot some scenes, but we wouldn't know until much later whether or not I had been successful. "This has to be some of the most outstanding scenery we're likely to have on the whole journey," I remarked while preparing another big breakfast.

"It looks like we may finally be able to dry some of our wet things today, too," Clint replied.

Our spirits improved that morning as we pushed steadily on up the river, working our way around bend after bend between the peaks. Taking some extra time at lunch break we were able to air everything out and pretty well dry most items. We had been eating tremendous amounts of food and our remaining supply was running very low. "Maybe we'll be lucky and be able to shoot some game right close to the river," I said. We were keeping the shotgun handy, just in case.

We had been wearing our rain suits constantly since leaving Arctic Red River, and mine was worn out. The orange jacket had come apart at the seams and the pants were hanging in shreds with most of one leg gone. During the afternoon we made thirty-six crossings of the river from side to side to get where the walking looked best. Mentally and emotionally we were both tired. It had been a long trip and there was still a long way to go if we were to make it. The fact that winter was nipping at our heels didn't allow us much time to relax and enjoy the beautiful day, but it was a good feeling to know that we were finally nearing the summit.

Wednesday, 8 September

DAY 145

Snow was falling when we rolled out and we had lost our sunshine of the previous day. We had progressed only a short distance when we came to the junction of a creek flowing in from the south. Unsure of ourselves, we turned to the right and soon the river forked again. This time we took the larger branch, ascending that for a half mile before deciding we were going too far north. Carefully checking the map, we decided that we were in Fish Creek. A certain amount of trial and error sometimes becomes necessary in tight spots. Our 1:250,000 topographical map simply did not show all the small crooks and turns as we neared the top of the mountains.

Turning back downstream, we took the next most likely-looking fork which turned out to be Sheep Creek. Not sure, we ascended that stream through some rough going and inasmuch as it kept coming from the south, once more we decided we were going the wrong way. Back we came and finally took the smaller middle fork. It was a very unlikely looking Rat River, but there was no other choice. Right away we came to a narrow rocky cut about four feet wide, with a short turn in a treacherous rapids. It was a tricky spot to negotiate and in the attempt we nearly filled the canoe with water while pulling it up through a big shelf wave. Backing off, we emptied the canoe, crossed that little Rat and threaded our way tight to the shore up through the thick alders, wading in nearly crotch-deep water.

Moving on upstream for an hour and a half over gravel bars and around sharp turns, we stopped for lunch on a cold, wet, unfriendly inside bend of the river. All we could find was soaked willow and alder for firewood. I was in dire need of removing my boots, dumping the water and wringing out my socks. The teeth-chattering cold rain mixed with snow made things difficult but eventually things came under control.

From there the river leveled off and we paddled along for the next ninety minutes around bend after bend as the Rat grew smaller and smaller. "It will be fun to soon be going down a river and watch it grow larger and larger," I said.

Late in the afternoon we arrived at the very small Twin Lake. Our map showed that we should go through a couple of other lakes but we didn't find them. Once again our maps did not quite jibe with what we were seeing with the result that we turned up the wrong branch and wasted a couple more hours scouting to determine which way we should go. The time, however, wasn't all wasted as we found a luscious patch of blueberries which tasted good, even though they had been frozen. We tanked up on them.

Finally we were again on the Rat going southwest through Ogilvie Lake. Then it was Long Lake and on west up a very small creek that you could step across where Two Ocean Creek flowed in from the south. From there the Rat was choked with brush and beaver dams. As darkness was settling in we found a blaze on a spruce tree. We had arrived at the portage over McDougall Pass. We were on top. Hooray! It was good to be there!

We had made it from Arctic Red River in nine difficult days. Pulling everything out of the water, we made camp right there. Crawling into our sacks that night, it was a good feeling to know that once we were over this portage it would be downhill all the way to the Bering Sea.

18

FORT YUKON

And once again I curve and flow
To join the brimming river,
For men may come and men may go,
But I go on forever.

—— Alfred Lord Tennyson,
The Brook

Thursday, 9 September

DAY 146

More light snow fell during the night. We were out in the thirty-degree temperature by eight. I used the last of our pancake flour to prepare breakfast. We really savored that meal as the food supply continued to diminish. We decided to double haul the portage which turned out to be a rough and uncertain trail through tundra country, sparsely wooded with black spruce and alders. We carried nearly three quarters of a mile, right down to the shore of Summit Lake. While doing so we crossed the border between Northwest Territories and Yukon Territory.

Walking back along the trail, I remembered that James Bell had been the first white man through McDougall Pass back in 1846. I mentioned it to Clint and he replied, "That was exactly one hundred and twenty-five years ago, if my mathematics are correct."

"I think you're right. Then during the following summer Alexander Murray of the Hudson's Bay Company moved through here with supplies and built a post down at Fort Yukon."

Following the trail back into Northwest Territories, I checked on to the east and found that the portage trail actually started at the junction of Two Ocean Creek and the Rat River. Then completing the final trip across the portage, we were in for a pleasant surprise. Suddenly there stood Phil and his guide Tony. The four of us were mutually happy to make the connection. Especially Clint and I, as it meant more food and news from the outside world. Phil had heard of the difficulties we would have coming up the Rat and expected it would take us a lot longer and would therefore need extra food. He had brought a good supply when they had flown into Summit Lake two days earlier. We had a big meal of bannock right then and there.

Phil had traded canoes at Fort McPherson since we had last seen him, swapping in the little sixteen footer for a very adequate twenty-foot Chestnut Guide model. He had been told by Johnny Charlie, an old trapper who had traveled the area for many years, that we probably wouldn't make it to the summit. First there were the pot holes and multiple channels of the delta with low water, the old trapper had said. Then came the rains and the flood and he was sure that ascending the Rat canyon at a time like that was an impossibility. They were sure that if we ever did make it, we would be many weeks working our way up through there.

Filling us in on his experiences since we left him in Arctic Red River, Phil said, "The man with the power boat that I had hired to run us and our little canoe to the mouth of the Rat River didn't get underway that day. By the time he was finally ready that afternoon, he said, 'It's too windy to go today. We'll start out tomorrow. We should easily catch them.' So when we finally did head out the next day, we followed your marker flags and our motor boat man brought us as far as he could. Then Tony and I paddled along following your trail. In checking the date and time you had marked on those flags, we decided before the second evening that we were losing ground and could never catch you.

"Camping in the delta, we headed out the next morning. Once we made it to the Peel River, I decided to paddle up to Fort McPherson. Then that big storm hit so we stayed there for nearly a week. Then yesterday, I hired a bush pilot to fly us and our big canoe up here to Summit Lake. That's about the whole story."

"So that's what happened. We just couldn't imagine where you two were," I said.

"Oh, yes! Verlen, there's one thing more. You know, we had your new shotgun with us and before leaving Fort McPherson, I traded it for this 30-30 rifle and six shells. I thought we should have a rifle with us up here instead of a shotgun."

"You did? Let's see it." Phil handed me an old, beat up single shot rifle. It would not eject a cartridge by itself. We had to pick them out with the blade of a knife. To say the least, I was not especially overjoyed with the deal.

We took time to look around Summit Lake. It was an exhilarating and satisfying feeling to finally be on the top of the Richardson Mountains and in McDougall Pass. A team of wildlife research men were camped nearby on Summit Lake and had been in the area most of the summer. The two group leaders were Grant Lortie of Whitehorse, Yukon Territory, and George Caleb from Winnipeg. They had been hired by an oil company to especially study the habits and migration of the caribou herds, to determine what effect, if any, the big pipeline would have on wildlife. They told us that the tree line followed the river up through the mountains and that only a short distance away from the rivers were the barrens. Walking up one of the hills we could plainly see that the timberline did follow the river. In most places the forest grew only in narrow bands of a hundred feet or so on each side of the river. The rest of the countryside was barren except for the grasses, lichens and mosses.

The best of the fall colors were past and most of the leaves had fallen. Autumn had arrived only about ten days earlier. The weather was very similar to November in Michigan. It had been a sudden change to early winter. We hoped that by going west from Summit Lake and to lower altitudes we would be able to keep pace with the season.

The weather during the afternoon continued cold, cloudy and snowing so we decided to move on and try some downhill paddling. We started down the small creek leading out of Summit Lake with Phil and Tony following along in the Chestnut canoe. We were surprised to see three robins way up there. When I mentioned it to Clint, he cheerfully remarked, "That's one of the two reasons why the technical name of a robin is 'turdus migratorius.' It's because they migrate so far."

By seven thirty we had arrived at the junction of the Little Bell and Bell Rivers and set up camp in a nice willow thicket. That very evening a fat young moose came walking past our camp. Tony and Phil shot it. Then they worked until nearly midnight to butcher it out. That was our lucky day. It couldn't have been handier. It was almost like manna from heaven. Suddenly we had more food than we knew what to do with.

Looking out over Summit Lake
with Tony Mercredi and Phil Pemberton

Earlier in the evening around the campfire,
Tony remarked that before she died, his grandmother
had predicted that someday he would be someone
special and do something special because he was the
seventh youngest child in the family of twelve. He
seemed to believe it. I complimented him on that,
saying, "It's good for a man to believe in himself.
You probably are destined to be or do something
special in this world. Believe you are a success,
and you are, even if only to yourself. That's
where it counts the most, and fret not if the world
never recognizes the fact that you are special."

359

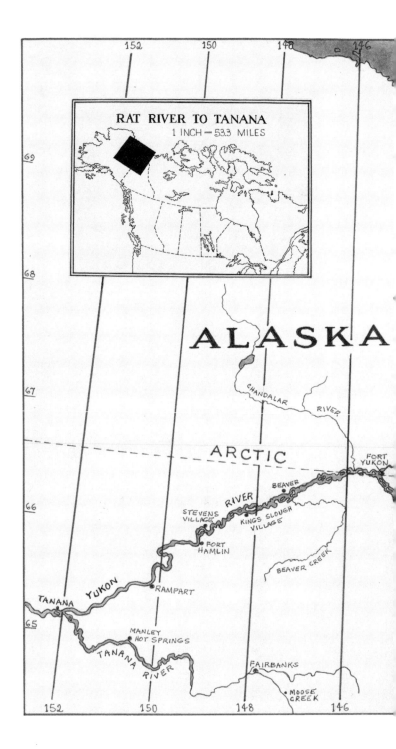

RAT RIVER TO TANANA
1 INCH — 53.3 MILES

152 150 148 146

69

68

ALASKA

67

CHANDALAR RIVER

ARCTIC

FORT YUKON

66

BEAVER

STEVENS VILLAGE

RIVER

KINGS SLOUGH VILLAGE

FORT HAMLIN

BEAVER CREEK

YUKON

RAMPART

TANANA

65

MANLEY HOT SPRINGS

TANANA RIVER

FAIRBANKS

MOOSE CREEK

152 150 148 146

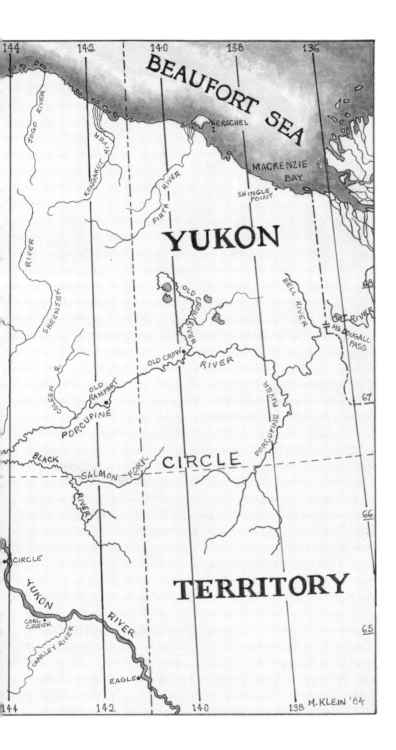

BEAUFORT SEA

HERSCHEL I

MACKENZIE BAY

SHINGLE POINT

YUKON

JOGO RIVER

KONGAKUT RIVER

FIRTH RIVER

BELL RIVER

RIVER

SHEENJEK

OLD CROW RIVER

OLD CROW

RIVER

BAT RIVER

McDOUGALL PASS

COLEEN R.

OLD RAMPART

PORCUPINE

PORCUPINE RIVER

BLACK

SALMON FORK

CIRCLE

RIVER

CIRCLE

YUKON

COAL CREEK

CHARLEY RIVER

RIVER

EAGLE

TERRITORY

68

67

66

65

M. KLEIN '84

144   142   140   138   136

144   142   140   138

Friday, September 10

DAY 147

I rolled out at eight to get a fire going. Clint soon followed. Then some time later, Phil came out to join us and finally at about the time the moose steaks were ready, Tony rolled out. It was another cloudy, thirty-degree morning but at least it wasn't snowing.

We spent the forenoon in camp, cutting, wrapping and packing the moose quarters into Phil's canoe. Along with the movie equipment and packs, the Chestnut was really loaded down. Then came another big meal of boiled moose tongue, fried moose heart, bannock, pears and pineapple juice before finally breaking camp. Clint and I were no longer hungry and believe me, that was a satisfying feeling. Phil and Tony were going to canoe along with us to Old Crow and possibly as far as Fort Yukon, consequently we would not set any speed records.

Before evening the mountains were being left behind. The sun came out briefly and Phil did some movies of the spectacular scenery. We climbed a high hill and enjoyed the view of the surrounding countryside with its rivers, small lakes, trees, tundra and snow. Back in the canoe we watched a cow moose along the shore. She couldn't decide what we were and hesitated before trotting back into the elders.

We progressed only twenty-five miles down the Bell River before making camp.

Saturday, 11 September

DAY 148

I rolled out at five-thirty to build a fire. Sounding the wake up call, "It's daylight in the

swamp!" and "It's time to rise and shine!" I
checked the thermometer, which again stood at
thirty degrees. Ice was forming along the shore.
Once again my suspicions were confirmed. A four-
man camp is always slower than a two-man camp, in
fact too slow. Three hours and fifteen minutes had
passed before we finally broke camp.

Some distance above La Pierre House, Clint and
I came upon a chocolate brown colored young bear
along the shore. Quietly we paddled right up to
him and he didn't spook until the canoe slid up on
the shore less than a canoe length away. We were
beginning to think he was there to greet us, then
suddenly he took off like a shot. Once more I had
missed a good picture with our inoperative cameras.

We almost missed La Pierre House, hidden back
in the brush near the right shore. It had been
closed for many years but still apparently was
being used by a trapper and occasional hunters.
Three buildings were still standing but a half
dozen others rotting away gave witness to the days
when it had been a bustling place located where the
portage route of the fur trade from the Mackenzie
River met the Bell. Recently archaeologists had
excavated what appeared to be the original site,
unearthing old logs and most likely valuable arti-
facts.

Preparing lunch we waited an hour for Phil and
Tony to come along. After eating we all pushed on,
wanting to reach the Porcupine River, fifty-five
miles downstream, before stopping for the night.
In late afternoon a bobcat swam across the Bell
ahead of us. Drifting up to the shore where the
cat disappeared, suddenly there it was, only twenty
feet away staring at us. As the cat finally
bounded away, Clint said, "Apparently the animals
through here so seldom see people, that they don't
realize how dangerous man can be to their
survival."

Even though we were still four miles upstream

from the junction with the Porcupine River, we stopped at midnight to find a campsite as we were both hungry and my feet were cold. Using the flashlight we went ashore in three different places before locating a good level spot thirty feet up on the riverbank. We were in a spruce grove with a carpet of caribou moss covering the ground. It was a cold night and we were fortunate to find a good supply of wood with which we built a large fire so that Phil and Tony would spot us when they came along.

Even with our late start that morning, it had turned into a satisfactory seventy-two mile day.

Sunday, 12 September

DAY 149

We were treated to an excellent display of northern lights while warming ourselves by the fire. Finally, before crawling into our bags at one thirty in the morning, we rolled several large logs on the fire as a signal to Phil and Tony.

Six hours later we were up again and wondering where they were. We had our breakfast and still no Phil. We were almost certain that they couldn't have passed us in the night as we had also left the canoe turned upright at the water's edge. Clint and I were ready to move out but assuming they were behind us, we busied ourselves making extra bannock and preparing some moose meat. Clint fixed some stew meat and hung some out in the smoke to dry. Then I fried some and we ate again.

Finally at ten thirty Phil and Tony came paddling down the river. Immediately I fried up a big griddle of moose meat, gave them some bannock and hot tea. They had spent the night about two hours upstream. They soon headed on down the river as they paddled much slower than we did.

Only a half hour on the Bell and we entered the Porcupine, a much larger river, where we soon passed the Chestnut canoe. Two caribou came into view and walked upstream along the shore. We stopped paddling and drifted to within a stone's throw before they scampered up over the bank.

Suppertime found us going ashore where Clint made up a special moose stew using potatoes and onions. We poured the stew over the fresh bannock and had wild cranberry sauce for dessert. That was one of our best and most memorable meals. Surprisingly the Chestnut arrived only a half hour behind us and they had seen a large mother wolf with six youngsters along the shore.

We moved along until ten, setting up camp on top of a thirty-foot bank covered with caribou moss and other lichens, interspersed with a few stunted spruce trees. Halfway up the bank was a ledge which made a great place for the campfire.

Monday, 13 September

DAY 150

Two and a half hours of the day were behind us before we embarked. It was certainly slowing us down to have Phil and Tony canoeing along with us. For both breakfast and lunch we continued to feed heavily on moose steaks. It was good to be moving down the Porcupine River.

About twenty miles above Old Crow, we stopped at the tent camp of Ken Nukon. He was forty years old and had only one arm and a lame leg. Living by himself he was building a log cabin near the river.

There were about seven hundred salmon hanging on the rack, drying for winter. Many of those would be used to feed his four sled dogs. We chatted for a while. Asking about Old Crow, we heard about the lazy welfare Indians living in town and the fact that he didn't think very highly of the Canadian government's giveaway program which supported them. He said, "They're crazy people and especially so since they've had liquor in town." He gave us a big salmon and a whitefish, which later we had for supper. In return for his kindness, we gave him some tea.

Seven miles on downriver we encamped for the night. Standing around the fire that evening, I told the others, "I am hoping to be able to buy a new camera tomorrow. It is disturbing to miss out on so many interesting pictures."

"If I had an extra, I'd loan it to you Verlen, but I don't have a spare," Phil replied.

Tony mentioned the fact that Old Crow is the only settlement on the entire six hundred mile long Porcupine River and that nearly all of the river's length was north of the Arctic Circle.

That evening I discovered that my watch was still on Mountain Daylight Saving Time, so I moved it back two hours to Yukon Time. After crawling into our bags, Clint again expressed concern, saying, "It seems to me we need to get in more hours of paddling each day or we will probably fail to achieve our goal before winter sets in!"

And I knew that he was correct.

Tuesday, 14 September

D A Y 1 5 1

"It's time to rise and shine!" I called, just after rolling out at four. "Everyone up!"

Clint followed me out of the tent within a matter of minutes, saying, "Old Crow, here we come!"

Much to our surprise, by the time the fire was burning, Phil and Tony were stirring around in their tent and soon joined us. It was a cold twenty-five degree, cloudy morning so we didn't linger very long except to warm cold hands by the fire. Embarking at six fifteen, we arrived in Old Crow by mid-forenoon. Then Phil told us he had decided to try to rent a motor boat so that he could beat us to Fort Yukon. Clint was overjoyed and later confided to me, "That was the best news I've heard in more than a month. Now we can really move!"

We reported in to the R.C.M.P. so they would know that we had made it over the summit and that we expected to be crossing the border into Alaska within the following two or three days. Then it was to the Co-op store where I was disappointed to learn that they had no cameras. It was a very small place and had operated as a Co-op for only the past year. We did restock with groceries, then before leaving the Indian settlement of about three hundred people, Phil gave us his excess groceries and a big chunk of moose meat. Tony looked around to find an outlet for the surplus meat and dicker for a motor boat ride to Fort Yukon. Then right after lunch Clint and I headed on down the Porcupine.

Ten miles downstream a man in a freighter canoe caught up with us. It was Bill Smith, a resident of the area. He had caught a nice batch of salmon and gave us one. He told us that his old friend Charlie Wolf was only a little more than two days ahead of us and that three men and a woman with a canoe and two kayaks were right behind him. "Traffic is heavy on the Porcupine this fall," he said. Bill also remarked, "We are having colder weather than normal for this time of year. You can expect almost anything in September in these parts." He went on to tell us that a few years earlier, on 8 September, the river froze over solid enough to walk on and remained frozen until early October when it broke up for two weeks. Then it froze up for the winter.

We also learned that he was fifty years of age and first came to Old Crow in 1962 after quitting his job in New Haven, Connecticut. He didn't plan to go back to the States. He was married to an extraordinary Indian woman and used her special hunting and trapping rights. He had shot thirty-five caribou in his nine years in Yukon Territory.

The river was crooked, shallow and full of rock bars that afternoon, but we moved right along. Earlier in Old Crow, we had met two men from the wildlife research team and they invited us to stop at their new camp about thirty-five miles below the settlement. We found their camp on the big bend of the river that evening. It was alongside the old cabin belonging to Steven Frost of Old Crow. We had a good visit with those two New Zealanders and we decided to pitch our tent right there.

While preparing supper in the dark around the campfire, two boat loads of Indian caribou hunters stopped to warm up at our fire. They hunt by cruising up and down the river. That's the easy way to get caribou.

Wednesday, 15 September

D A Y 1 5 2

It was good to roll out in the twenty-five degree temperature and see a bright and sunny day in the making. We again visited with the research team while eating breakfast. They told us the river there had been twenty-nine feet higher during the spring flood than it was while we were there. The water level was at its low for the year. I remarked, "Low water means slow current and sand bars. We've had to exert a lot of extra effort for our mileage due to the adverse weather, wind and water on this trip. It has required persistent determination to keep pushing a little harder to overcome those things, but then, excuses are what failures are made of." We swapped a can of peaches for a good chunk of caribou meat before embarking at six twenty.

Three hours later after moving down a canyon known as The Ramparts, we arrived at Rampart House. That old abandoned post of the Hudson's Bay Company still had some buildings standing but only the wind passed through the doors by the time we were there. Rampart House was built on the Canadian side of the international border when their post at Fort Yukon was moved following the purchase of Alaska by the United States in 1867.

A few minutes later we crossed the border, leaving the Yukon Territory behind and continued down the Porcupine with a better current. I enjoyed the scene immensely. In my observations of trees and vegetation and seeing the past erosion of the high cut banks along the shore, it appeared that time moved slowly in those parts. The various layers of humus and silt with buried logs, vegetation and permafrost being constantly exposed by the river erosion all told a very interesting story of time gone by.

Suddenly in early afternoon my thoughts turned to food. Our journey was either feast or famine. "Clint, it just dawned on me that we have in the canoe with us about thirty pounds of moose meat, ten pounds of fresh salmon and six pounds of choice caribou."

"It's a good feeling to know that we're not

going to have to go hungry," Clint replied. "By the way, when are we going to eat?"

Pulling ashore on a gravel bar, I fried half the salmon and baked a bannock while Clint started another batch of his special moose stew. We really were getting to try out and use food of the various localities through which we traveled.

During the afternoon we left the Upper Ramparts, then entered Howling Dog Canyon as darkness settled in. Sunset occurred at a little after six and it was totally dark by eight. The days and nights were of nearly equal length. With no moon, it was rather hairy paddling on that big, shallow, rock bar infested river in the night. We continued on, rounding Fish Hook Bend where we gave it up for the day at eleven, setting up camp on a rock bar at the head of an island. It had been our best day since we left the Mackenzie, having progressed more than eighty miles.

Thursday, 16 September

DAY 153

The eastern sky was streaked with red when we shoved off at five thirty, anticipating a day of bad weather. A light rain moved in for a while, but before noon the skies had cleared. Earlier, for breakfast we had oatmeal and leftover bannock. We loved bannock. We both made them at different times and it seemed almost impossible to make a bad one. It was also difficult to save any for a later meal. Our bannock were usually eaten as fast as we made them.

Our midday meal was even more substantial, consisting of fried salmon, caribou steaks, fresh bannock and hot cocoa. All in all we did eat pretty well, and after being back on full feed for several days we both noticed a feeling of increased energy.

At eight in the morning we passed the Coleen River flowing in from the north. The country was leveling out and the spruces were thicker and taller than they had been in the higher elevations. After lunch we entered the crooked flatland delta type country with its multiple channels which we would be in for the next one hundred and fifty miles.

We were having a good day and Clint was in a talkative mood. As a matter of fact, so was I. Eventually our talk turned to the early exploration of the area through which we were paddling. Knowing that I had researched our entire route, he asked, "How long ago was this river first discovered by white man?"

"Well, let me think just a minute. It was back in 1846 that the Porcupine was first discovered and explored by John Bell, the Chief Trader of the Hudson's Bay Company. Then during the following year, on June 11, 1847, he sent a young Scotsman, Alexander Murray, down through here to establish a fur trading post on the Yukon River. Even though a young man, this Murray was no stranger to the wilderness. He had worked for the American Fur Company in its outposts in Texas and Louisiana. When he switched to the Hudson's Bay Company, he moved several thousand miles by canoe and overland to reach Fort McPherson on the Peel River. His orders were to establish a post near the junction of the Yukon and the Porcupine. Thanks to John Bell's sketchy map, Murray knew where he was going, but he knew nothing about the Indians in the region, nor whether they might be friendly or hostile. One thing he was sure of, western Canada was producing a great harvest of fine furs and surely Alaska, adjoining it, would prove to be equally profitable."

"That's interesting. That was only one hundred and twenty-five years ago. Tell me more."

"The fact that Alaska was Russian territory, and he had no right to establish a fort or trade there, was ignored. He would take his chances and drain off as many furs as possible before he was forced to move out. With luck, the Russians might even let him alone, and there would be no interruption in the flow of furs to Canada.

"Murray was not to face the wilderness alone. When he left Fort McPherson he was accompanied by a white assistant named McKenzie, a carpenter, and eight half-breeds. One of them would serve as his interpreter with the Indians. Each man carried a forty-pound pack of trade goods, in addition to his personal gear and provisions as they slogged along. The going was difficult; as you see they walked all the way to La Pierre House. In the daily journal he kept of the founding of Fort Yukon, Murray wrote, 'We waded most of the way knee deep, and often to the middle in sludge and water. The mosquitoes had already begun their ravages.'

"After four hours the party reached the top of the nearest hills. Murray and two half-breeds pushed ahead. It was difficult to find a dry campsite. By morning their moss and brush beds were floating in muck. The second day they crossed the mountains. The third day they labored, fought, and waded across the swift, ice-swollen Bell River. None had waterproof clothing. Their thick woolen blanket coats and pants, leggings, knapsacks, and moccasins were soaked. There was no fuss about drying out. All continued through the fourth day to the trading post called LaPierre's House. For a few hours Murray enjoyed shelter and warmth, and relished venison steaks served at a table. Months would pass before he again experienced such comfort and luxury."

"Boy! That certainly is interesting!"

"Earlier that spring, an Indian messenger had brought word to LaPierre's House that Murray would stop there and would need a boat to complete his journey to the Yukon. The crude bark was finished by the time he arrived. It was a combination canoe and barge, about thirty feet long, with the stern covered with birch bark. As soon as it was loaded, the small staff from the trading post fired a farewell salute and sped the boat on its way with hearty cheers. Murray had given the boat a most suitable name. He called it the **Pioneer**. It would be the first white man's craft to stem the upper Yukon.

"The oarsmen brought the **Pioneer** along the many windings of the Bell River. The next day they came to the Porcupine. Six Indian families were camped there. Murray gave each man a three-inch piece of tobacco and invited them to bring their furs down river to the new post. The Indians agreed and hospitably offered to share their muskrat stew, moose fat, and wild onions with the party. Afterward they started to dance. Murray had no time for 'jollification,' as he called it, and left.

"The current in the Porcupine was swift, so the **Pioneer** made good time. Murray charted the river's course with the aid of a compass. He also looked for post sites, in case he met the Russians on the Yukon and had to beat a hasty retreat.

"At several places the Indians showed him where flakes of gold could be washed from the river gravel. It is hard to believe, but he showed no excitement over this. He did not tarry to prospect for more gold. He did make casual note of the gold in his journal and moved on, far more interested in furs than gold. (But thirty years later that small reference to the precious, much-sought treasure would lure gold seekers to the Yukon.)

"On 25 June, eight days' travel and 452 miles west of LaPierre's House, the **Pioneer** nosed into the Yukon. The Indians camped there told Murray that there were no high banks down river. So he moved upstream three miles and chose an open site on the east bank. After the **Pioneer** was unloaded, the men cut willow and small spruce for shelters. Two of the Indian helpers left immediately to contact nearby villages and invite the people in to trade.

"Soon a few Indians showed up. One claimed to be a chief. Through the interpreter, Murray learned that this man had traveled to the lower Yukon and met the Russians there. He said they had many beads, kettles, guns, powder, knives, and tobacco. Murray groaned inwardly. For this first year he had brought only a small supply of trade goods. But what really disturbed him was learning that the Russians planned to explore the Yukon to its source. He knew only too well how they would react to finding British traders camped on their territory.

"He wrote in his journal, 'I kept my thoughts to myself, and determined to keep a sharp lookout in case of surprise. Mr. McKenzie and I divided the night watch between us, a rule laid down and strictly adhered to when Indians were with us.'

"Early the next morning Murray must have thought the Russians had arrived. About 4 a.m. musket shots shattered the quiet. The Britishers grabbed guns and rushed to the waterfront. They watched twenty canoes glide into sight. To Murray's intense relief, the occupants were Indians, all set to offer furs, fresh meat, and dried fish for whatever the white traders had to offer. But first there had to be a ceremonial greeting and the distribution of tobacco, and singing and dancing. This consumed an hour. Then the Indians squatted on the ground and invited Murray to speak. He did, through an interpreter. He explained he was of a different nation from the whites down river who came only once a year to take away their furs and cheat them with shoddy goods. In contrast, he brought only the best quality of goods and would charge less for them. But most important, he would build a large post and live in the country among them. That way they could trade the year around.

"The Indians seemed pleased. They retired briefly, and then reappeared in all their feathered and beaded finery. This included summer costumes of moose and caribou skins ornamented with porcupine quills, shells, beads, and twists of long hair. Men and women alike wore one or more necklaces of red, white, and blue beads. All wore face paint: a black line down the nose, red stripes across the forehead, red and black marks on the chin. Their hair was tied back with thongs and beaded bands. They danced for two hours. Then there was a feast, and more dancing and singing. The Britishers got no sleep that night.

"The next day Murray set his men to building the store. It was twenty-four feet long and fourteen feet wide, of rough logs and bark roof. It was completed by June 30 and the supplies moved inside. One end opened toward the river. Here Murray pitched his tent to prevent any night prowlers from entering. Close by were his men's cabins. Each man slept with a loaded gun at his side.

"The Indians were greatly interested in Murray's pistols. They had never seen a small gun before. A crack shot, Murray waited until a stick came floating down the river. Quickly he drew one pistol from his pocket, fired, and hit the stick. The Indians were astonished and impressed. Their chief offered fifteen marten skins for the pistol, but learned it was not for sale.

"Murray had brought along seed for a crop of potatoes, barley, and turnips. His men spaded an area twelve by eight feet and planted the seeds.

"On July 1 work began on the fort. Almost all the building wood had to be brought in the **Pioneer** from islands in the Yukon. Murray meant to have a stout post.

While this work went on, he commenced trading. He had no difficulty disposing of blankets, axes, powder horns, knives, files, and beads. When the Indians ran out of furs, he asked them to bring in moose skins--which his men would need soon for clothing and boots--and parchment, deerskins, and sinew. Some complied, but others grew bolder. They demanded guns. Murray refused to let them enter the store, and traded from the doorway. But one day, while his back was turned, two Indians slipped inside and grabbed some guns. Murray flashed his pistol and booted them out. They shouted and made threatening gestures.

"The interpreter told Murray worriedly, 'They are saying the Russians treated them badly, too, only they shot some of the Russians and took all their trade goods away from them, and after that they had no trouble.'

"Murray answered sternly, 'Tell them if anyone sets foot in the store again, I will shoot him dead.' He waved his pistol meaningfully. Apparently the Indians understood. There was no more trouble.

"Still, the situation was always tense. At any moment, day or night, Murray knew the Indians might overpower his small band, steal the goods, murder them, and disappear into the wilds. Probably the main reason there was no massacre was that the Indians, now avid for white man's goods, did not want to be cut off from trading year after year. By all odds, Murray should have been a little afraid, and even homesick. Instead he liked the wilderness, the smell of spruce forest and wood smoke. He liked the challenge of establishing a frontier post and building a prosperous trade with sullen aborigines.

"By August 30 the fort was habitable. It was forty-six feet long and twenty-six feet wide and contained five rooms: a center hall with office-sitting room and bedroom in one end, assistants' room and kitchen at the other. It was built of well-squared eight-inch spruce logs. The walls were bullet proof and contained small loopholes neatly fitted with blocks of wood. These plugs could be removed in case of an attack, and a gun barrel inserted in each.

"There still was no time for rest. A boathouse was added, a storehouse for dried fish, two scaffolds for caching meat out of reach of bears and wolves, and long piles of firewood. Knowing that the Russians would not appear this late in the season, Murray did not press for a stockade. But the men did cut and peel enough logs so that a fortifying picket fence could be built around the compound the following summer. Since he was running out of trade goods and having to refuse good furs because of this, he sent two men with five dogs and two sleds back to LaPierre's House. They returned with far less than he needed. He mourned to his diary, 'Without beads, and plenty of them, you can do little or no good here.'

"Murray also reported a comfortable winter. All were warm and dry, and lived well on moose, fish, caribou, wild fowl, rabbits, and cranberries. The garden had yielded only a bushel of potatoes which ranged in size from peas to ptarmigan eggs. He would save them for seed.

"In the spring Murray wrote a letter which would travel long miles to company headquarters at Fort Chipewyan. 'Guns and beads, beads and guns is all the cry in our country. Please to excuse me for repeating this so often, but I cannot be too importunate. The rise or fall of our establishment on the Youcon depends principally on the supply of these articles.'

"After two thirty-eight-foot boats were built, he left McKenzie in charge of Fort Yukon and went back up the Porcupine and Bell to LaPierre's House.

Four months later he returned with an adequate supply of goods––and a wife. All told, several hundred Indians came in to trade. Murray treated them firmly but fairly. They went away satisfied. The Russians never did appear, so the Hudson's Bay Company had no competition in the upper Yukon trade. In time the stockade was completed. Fireplaces, plastered walls, and window glass increased the men's comfort. So well did Murray do that in 1856 he was promoted to the position of chief trader and transferred to larger posts that were closer to civilization. He retired from active trading in 1867."

"Very interesting, Verlen. You certainly do have a remarkable memory."

"Not in everything. History, North American history, was a subject I've always thrived on. Of course, 1867 was the year when the United States purchased Alaska. Then two years later, Captain Raymond of the Corps of Engineers arrived on the steamer Yukon. He presented proof that the Hudson's Bay Company was trespassing on American soil. The resident trader had long expected this, and concluded the sale that saw the British flag come down and the Stars and Stripes rise in its place.

"The new American trading company did well, thanks to its policy of fair trading practices. In time a small band of Yukon Indians settled permanently near the post. But life for them changed very little. They continued hunting, fishing and trading. Missionaries came to live among them and converted them to Christianity. But poverty and hardship remained their lot for many years."

We paddled on into the dark. The river was full of fast winding currents, rock bar islands and dead trees. Progress was risky on such a dark night, so before ten we stopped on a small rock beach along the right shore. There was only space for the tent and campfire and very little fuel but we made out all right.

DAY 154

There was an uprooted spruce tree on our little rock beach which had snagged there in time of high water. I measured it and found it to be sixty feet long and only ten inches in diameter just above the roots. Trees in those flats grow straight and tall.

Following a substantial breakfast we were underway by six on a cloudy morning. The temperature had risen to forty degrees, the warmest morning we had enjoyed since the last week of August. The warm weather brought rain several times during the day. A heavy headwind and rain hit us before noon, driving us off the river for a while, so we climbed the rock and sand bank and went back into the thick spruce woods where we had our lunch. Clint finished preparing his special moose stew with the big pot running over, while I made thirteen bannock. We dined sumptuously, snug in the bush as the storm raged on down on the river.

Earlier we spotted a smoldering campfire on a sand beach. Investigating, we could tell that two men, only a few hours earlier, had spent the night and breakfasted near the fire. One had dug a several-inch-deep depression to sleep in. We assumed it to be Charlie Wolf and his partner.

Ducks and geese were again on the move and we enjoyed a pair of golden eagles which circled overhead in the afternoon. At a rest stop a big bull moose across the river came walking out on a rock bar. He was grunting his mating call. Clint tried to answer, uttering a very off-key note. To me it didn't sound at all like a moose, but the bull thought otherwise. He responded and seemed about to swim the river to get to his answer. That was what I call a strong biological urge.

We encamped at dark in the Six Mile Slough

area about three miles beyond Shuman House.

Saturday, 18 September

DAY 155

The skies had cleared and it was freezing cold again as we rolled out at four. Anxious to cover those final forty miles to Fort Yukon, we embarked at five thirty. We continued to keep a sharp eye out for the two other canoe parties on the river ahead of us as we pulled steadily along through the flat countryside.

In mid-morning we passed the confluence with the Skeenjek River. Then shortly before one, thinking we were still in a channel of the Porcupine, we were surprised to find the current flowing against us. We had entered the Yukon River. We faced the strong Yukon River current for the next couple of miles to the settlement of historic Fort Yukon. It had taken us four days to cover the three hundred miles between Old Crow and Fort Yukon. We had made good time and we were glad to be there.

Phil and Tony had swapped their moose meat for a plane ride on the previous day and were waiting for us as we paddled in. They told us that the German group were about forty-five miles behind us and that Charlie Wolf was even farther upriver. We had passed them both and didn't even know it, probably in one of the multiple channels or in the dark of the night.

We bought a bunch of supplies at the Co-op store including groceries and a pair of felt-lined shoe packs, then did up our laundry. That was the first time some of our things had been dry since leaving Arctic Red River. I picked up my mail and received eight letters from my Honey, two from daughter Nancy, one from daughter Christine and a note from each of our other children. Wow! It was almost too much shock for my emotional system. I must have had an attack of homesickness. Thinking back on it now, I don't know whether it was home-sickness or the 'tent fever' that had the biggest overall effect on me. Certainly those are both diseases which I would wish on no one.

In the excitement of a touch of home I spent a sleepless night. Several hours were required to get off a newsletter to Darwin Gilbert and the rest of the night was spent writing to my sweet Gene-vieve.

19

THE RUSSIAN
FUR TRADE

> *The nameless men who nameless rivers travel,*
> *And in strange valleys greet strange deaths*
> *alone;*
> *The grim, intrepid ones who would unravel*
> *The mysteries that shroud the Polar Zone.*
>
> — *Robert Service,*
> ***To the Man of the High North***

DAY 155

I was anxious to get underway. I roused the others while it was still dark as time was of the essence. It was still eleven hundred miles to the sea. We had our breakfast in the Sourdough Inn where we had stayed overnight. Phil shot several movie sequences of us around Fort Yukon before we finally headed on down the river after saying good-bye to Tony at 10:45 a.m. Phil said he would meet us next where the new Yukon-Prudhoe Highway crosses the river about twenty-seven miles below Stevens Village. In 1971, the road was known as Hickel Highway.

It was a good day for paddling, sunny, no wind and with a good current. We were off on the final leg of our long, long journey. I didn't admit it to Clint then, but I was also beginning to wonder how we were ever going to reach the Bering Sea before it really wintered in. There was no question by then we both felt the urgency of our situation. We would certainly have to make good mileage every day.

The Yukon is a mighty big river. Its headwaters are in northern British Columbia and it flows for more than twelve hundred miles before passing Fort Yukon where we had intercepted it. Then it continues across the very heart of Alaska until finally it pours into the sea just south of Norton Sound. Overall it is one of the great rivers of the world.

We moved right along through the huge area known as the Yukon Flats and by late afternoon were crossing the Arctic Circle heading to the southwest. The current was better than we had hoped for but there were plenty of rock bars and we again found it necessary to stay in the main channel for best speed.

Darkness was settling in by eight when we pitched our tent in a willow thicket, just upstream from Deadman Island. In slightly more than eight hours after leaving Fort Yukon, we had progressed a satisfactory fifty-eight miles. There were fresh bear and moose tracks near our camp. None were sighted while we were there, but at times we had the uneasy feeling that we were being watched.

Monday, 20 September

DAY 156

We continued on through the Yukon Flats during all of the daylight hours except for a three-hour break in midday, during a very strong wind storm. The going had been good that morning but after the storm we had a headwind and choppy waves for the remainder of the day. The river was crooked with lots of islands and multiple channels. Navigation kept us on our toes as the best current was always found in the main channel.

We set up camp on a point of land only a couple of miles beyond Kings Slough Village. The mosquitoes were no problem. Clint and I discussed those nuisances that evening. Neither of us could recall that we had seen a single mosquito since leaving the Mackenzie River. "I'll bet they sure would have been a terror here, back in July."

"That's for sure!" Clint replied.

It had been a good day. We had knocked off another seventy miles.

Tuesday, 21 September

DAY 157

We were up at five and on the river at twenty before seven. There was no wind and it looked like an ideal day for canoeing. "With any luck we should finish with the Yukon Flats today," I quipped.

"That's good! It will be great to have this slough area behind us."

"We won't have to hit it very hard today as Phil isn't due at the crossing below Stevens Village until tomorrow morning," I bravely said. All was quiet for nearly five minutes as we pushed along.

My mind was on other things when Clint finally replied. "I sure hope he is there when we arrive and if he is, that he doesn't hold us up too long."

"Me too!"

On a rocky bar ahead we watched a wolverine playing tag with a raven. Back and forth they went. The raven would fly to the end of the bar, the wolverine would bounce after it and just before catching it the raven would fly about a hundred feet and wait as the animal bounced back for another try. Clint grabbed the 30-30 as we beached the canoe while the little game continued. He attempted to sneak around to get the wolverine, but while running through a willow thicket he nearly stepped on an Arctic fox. Clint stumbled and fell, thus not getting off a shot at either animal. By the time he could again see the rock bar, the game had been discontinued. Returning to the canoe, he told me what had happened. Then he added, "I really didn't want to shoot anything anyway. I don't know what I was thinking of. What in the world would we do with a dead wolverine or a fox, if we had them?"

"Go into the fur trading business," I replied.

Stopping for lunch a few miles above Stevens Village, we enjoyed another big pot of Clint's special moose stew. Then we moved on to the settlement where we met John Betnorf and his wife, who were teaching the sixteen-pupil school there. They had a two-way radio in their quarters but there were no telephones in town. John told us it was twenty-seven miles on downriver to the Hickel Highway, so we left word for Phil to meet us there. Then we headed back to the canoe.

An old Indian had asked where we were heading. Then he told us, "You have one more week of good weather, then ice starts to form in the river and by October 10 it freezes up solidly for the winter."

A couple of hours later we passed old Fort Hamlin. Just below was where the United States was then planning to build a huge dam across the river which would have created the largest man-made lake on earth. It would have been a lake larger than the state of New Jersey. The dam would have flooded seven native villages and displaced more than twelve hundred people. Fortunately for everyone, all that has now changed. Plans for the dam have been discontinued, and instead the area is known as the Yukon Flats National Wildlife Refuge.

At seven thirty we stopped for the day in the canyon where the river swings to the west below old Fort Hamlin, camping high on the right bank across from an old cabin. We had moved only fifty-two miles.

Wednesday, 22 September

DAY 158

Two hours of paddling and we arrived at the construction site for the crossing of the Yukon-Prudhoe Highway. At that time considerable grading and roadbed work had been done on the south side of the river. Phil was not there as we had hoped. "But after all," I told Clint, "it's still early forenoon. He probably stayed overnight in Fairbanks and will be here in a little while." So we waited.

Mel Williamson and his wife drove up while we were there. They had managed to get through the gate where the new road began, some sixty miles to the southeast. We had a good visit with them and learned that they were from Fairbanks and on vacation. In the course of our conversation I mentioned our upset on the Rat River and the fact that we had both lost our cameras, and was lamenting how badly I felt in not being able to get pictures of this fantastic part of our journey. They very generously loaned us their camera to use during the remainder of our descent of the Yukon. We would mail it back to them the following month. Boy! Were we happy! That was our lucky day!

We prepared a good substantial meal, but still no Phil. So we waited some more. I could sense that Clint was growing impatient to move on, but he didn't say a word about it. I, too, was anxious to be underway, so finally I said, "Let's go! We have wasted another four hours of valuable time waiting for Phil and that's enough. I don't know when or where he will catch us, but we just can't wait any longer."

So we shoved off, taking pictures like crazy! We made up for some lost time that afternoon. Finally as darkness settled in, we set up camp at the big bend only about a dozen miles north of the village of Rampart.

Thursday, 23 September

DAY 159

It was a cold, foggy morning on the Yukon. We rolled out at four thirty in an attempt to put more miles behind us. Embarking at six it was an eerie feeling moving along in the heavy, pea soup fog. We followed close to the shoreline until the fog lifted. By ten the sun came out and melted the ice which had built up on the canoe. By that time we were already well past the settlement of Rampart.

Lunch time found us just below Garnet Island.

SEWARD

PENNINSULA

166   164   KOTZEBUE SOUND   160
DEERING
KIWALIK

+4714
KIGLUAIK MTS.
65
COUNCIL
KOYUK
NOME
WHITE
MOUNTAIN
ELIM
NORTON BAY
REINDEER
HILLS
KOYUKUK
NULATO
KALTAG

64
NORTON
SOUND
BERING
SEA
STUART
I.
UNALAKLEET

KWIKPAK
ST. MICHAEL
BLACKBURN
63
JOURNEY'S
END
CHANILIUT
GRAYLING

YUKON RIVER
KAIYUH RIVER

ANVIK

ALAKANUK

62
YUKON
ILIVIT MTS.
HOLY
CROSS

MOUNTAIN
VILLAGE
PILOT
STATION
PAIMIUT
ST. MARY'S
PITKAS POINT
MARSHALL
RUSSIAN
MISSION
CROOKED
CREEK

CHOGAMIUT
KALSKAG
RIVER
ANIAK
61

KUSKOKWIM

BETHEL
164   H. KLEIN '84   162   160

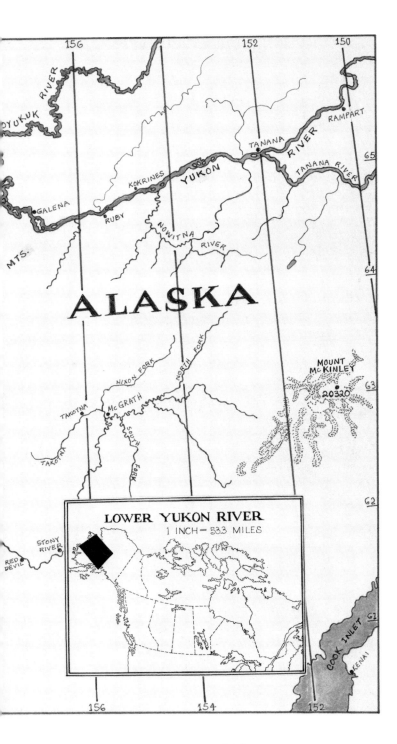

ALASKA

LOWER YUKON RIVER
1 INCH = 53.3 MILES

Then pressing on as we listened to the howling of the wolves in the nearby hills, we noticed black clouds moving in from the west. Shooting right on through the fast water near Senatis Mountain, we were passing Moosehead Rack as the frontal system and accompanying storm hit us. Battling a headwind with sheets of rain, we continued on until seven thirty, stopping for the night only eight miles above the mouth of the Tanana River.

After preparing supper in the cold rain and eating inside the tent, the storm let up so we could relax by the fire for a while before crawling into our bags. I recalled that the Tanana River is the second longest river in Alaska and that its junction marks the division between the Upper and Lower Yukon. Then I also remembered reading about all of the steamboat traffic on the Yukon during the days of the big gold rush. In 1897 a parade of sixty steamboats were seen chugging up the Yukon towards the Klondike. Now, of course, there is almost no river traffic other than the local people with their motor boats and the twice a year supply barge which services the villages.

Friday, 24 September

DAY 160

The storm continued all night and it was after six before we were once more on the water. It was rough going into the face of the cold, heavy head-wind. We arrived in the village of Tanana by eight thirty and found a good store, cafe and post office. In talking with the store keeper we learned that a year earlier on 24 September, ice was forming in the river, and that his supply barge became

Fish wheel on the Yukon River

caught in the ice on 8 October and there it stayed all winter. He told us that about four hundred people were then living in Tanana and that John Ball had canoed the river earlier in the year, making a travelogue movie of the Yukon River from Whitehorse to the ocean. That project was taking two years to film.

We inquired about Phil, wanting to know if he had tried to contact us, but no one there knew anything about him. I called home and it was a great boost to my morale but it also increased my problem of homesickness.

We pushed on into very strong headwinds and waves, and got soaking wet. Along the way we passed several fish wheels but very few of them were turning. Apparently most people had already laid in their supply of salmon for the winter. There were huge quantities of fish, however, on drying racks at nearly every Indian tent or shack all along the river.

At our lunch break we went up into the forest to get out of the wind and blowing rain, where we built a campfire and warmed up a little. "I hope and pray that this doesn't turn into one of those three day winds," I said.

"Me too! But I'm afraid winter is closing in on us."

In the afternoon we saw a fox along the shore cleaning up where there had been a moose kill. Clint shot at it twice but those shots didn't seem to worry that fox very much!

Then late in the afternoon we met an open power boat heading up the river. They stopped and talked with us. Drifting along we learned that it was John Pine, his wife and their three children. He was a missionary at the Tanana Bible Church and from the Independent Fundamental Churches of America, out of Portland, Oregon. The Pine family had moved to Tanana from Kaltag, Alaska, only a few weeks before. They were on their return to Tanana from a Bible Camp they had held, sixty-seven miles downstream.

John answered many of our questions. "Last fall ice started forming in the river at Kaltag on October 9 and froze over solidly by October 23," he said.

"How far is Kaltag from here?" Clint asked.

"It's two hundred and fifty-seven miles from Tanana. I think the river up here usually freezes over a couple of weeks earlier than it does down there," John replied.

It was certainly like a ray of sunshine to meet a real brother in the Lord, on such an otherwise miserable canoeing day. They gave us a dried salmon and a lot of information about the river before John started his engine and they headed up the river.   The Pines were certainly a wonderful family.

Struggling on until seven thirty we set up camp in the trees back from the river at Grant Creek, opposite Darvin Island.   The wind blew on throughout the evening but calmed down shortly after we crawled into our sacks.

Saturday, 25 September

DAY 161

We were underway by seven thirty.   The days were growing shorter and shorter.   While passing Cronin Island the strong headwind picked up again and made progress slow and difficult for the remainder of the day.   The wind-blown waves were so rough that we were unable to take advantage of the good flow of the river.   The strong wind coming up against the current really whipped up the water making sharp, steep waves and white caps with splashing, blowing water which made canoeing impossible.   A condition of that kind makes a normal river current look like a bad rapids and it has the same loud roar.   To keep going we had to stay tight along a shore, out of the current.   There, many times we found ourselves in a backwater or eddies which made for slow progress.

We took our lunch break at the abandoned settlement of Birches.   Exploring, we found many old relics including an old dog team sledge.   Before re-launching, I checked the thermometer and it stood at forty-six degrees, the warmest day in quite some time.   While there we were surprised to be attacked by a swarm of black flies.   Clint said,

"This must be the fall hatch."

"You're probably right," I replied. There was no question about it. I found Clint to be very knowledgeable on all forms of flora and fauna. That, no doubt, was the result of his training and work with the U. S. Forestry Service. He often answered my questions about plants and wild life. I learned a lot from him during our journey.

The rains returned in the afternoon. We gave it up for the day at seven thirty after making only forty-five miles of difficult progress. Our camp was made in the trees along the south shore just below Edith Island.

Following supper, I said, "If this wind slacks off, we should make it down past Ruby tomorrow."

"I sure hope so. Maybe your lost cameraman will be there waiting for us."

"We'll have to check it out. By the way, Clint, Ruby was at one time a gold camp and there they turned up one of the world's largest gold nuggets. The nugget weighed in at ninety-six ounces."

"Wow! That's six pounds. That was one huge chunk of gold!"

Sunday, 26 September

DAY 162

There had been a light freezing rain overnight and it was a bit unpleasant getting started but we did manage to head on downriver by first light. An hour later we bypassed the settlement of Kokrines. By mid-forenoon the wind once more became a problem with heavy swells rolling up the river.

The Yukon resembled a mile-wide lake giving me the impression that the west end had dropped out of my imaginary lake and all of the water was pouring out somewhere ahead. It certainly was a big river and in a strong wind those large lake-type waves and swells did roll.

By two in the afternoon we had arrived in the town of Ruby. Hurriedly we checked around the settlement for any word from Phil. No one had seen or heard about him. "Maybe he has given it up and gone back to Michigan," Clint chided. "He's probably had his belly full of the north by now."

"I agree that this weather isn't too pleasant, but I'm sure we'll find him somewhere along here."

Two hours later we again headed on into the wind and rain. At seven we encamped up on the Sandstone Bluffs, opposite the west end of Big Island in a clump of trees overlooking the river. We were cold, wet and miserable. It was tough getting a fire going. Everything was wet including the tent and sleeping pad. Once camp was set up and we had polished off a big batch of pancakes fortified with wheat germ, our outlook improved. At about that time the rain stopped and we sat out around the fire for a while as we dried things out.

We were comfortably relaxing when Clint said, "I keep thinking about those deserted villages we have seen along the river. This area must have a lot of interesting history. Verlen, do you know anything about how and when this Lower Yukon was first discovered?"

"Certainly. I've studied Alaskan history quite a bit and I still have copies of a few pages from the book **The Yukon** in my personal pack. You've probably heard of Vitus Bering?"

"Yes. The Bering Sea was named after him, wasn't it?"

"That's right. Alaska was discovered by Bering, a Dane exploring for a Russian ruler. The Russians had penetrated eastward across Siberia in the sixteenth century, and reached the Pacific Ocean in the seventeenth century. Rumors of fabulous lands beyond and an interest in expanding

ONE INCREDIBLE JOURNEY

Russian trade led the Russian rulers to authorize an exploring expedition. After incredible difficulty and delay, Bering sailed from the Kamchatka River in July, 1728. He discovered St. Lawrence Island and the Diomedes Islands. He navigated the icy strait which now bears his name and entered the Arctic Ocean. The next year he charted the coast and discovered that Asia and America were not connected. On another voyage, in 1741, Bering named Mount St. Elias, rising from the southern coast of a new land mass. He learned that natives called the region **Alyasca,** meaning 'the great land.' Bering claimed it for Russia and called it Alaska. Let me dig those pages out of my pack."

"Good! That will be interesting."

"Here they are. Let me sit here near the fire. Several years after Bering's 1741 voyage to Alaska, it says——

> *Russian hunters began shoving off from Siberian ports in search of the prized sea otter, whose breeding grounds were along the Bering seacoast and around the Aleutian Islands. The luxuriant fur of the sea otter brought the highest price on the fur markets of the world. In searching for more of the animals, Russian ships moved along the shore line of western Alaska, and by 1829 had located the mouth of a great river. They noted this on their charts, but neither named it nor crossed the treacherous sandbars to stem its current. Their great river turned out to be what is now known as the Yukon.*
>
> *Two years later Lieutenant Michael Tebenkov, a naval officer, was sent to make a reconnaissance of the Bering coast. In the course of doing so he was told by Eskimos of a large river reaching the sea just north of the Kuskokwim. The Eskimos called it the Kuikpak, 'kuik' for large or great, 'pak' for river.*

It was the Yukon they were referring to, and the Russians adopted their name for it. In 1833 Tebenkov returned to the region to establish a base for the penetration of the big river he still had not seen. Near the Yukon delta the coast is low and harborless; the best site that Tebenkov could find was a barren wind-swept island just offshore. There, sixty miles northeast of the Yukon's mouth, he built a fortified post and named it St. Michael.

Then, early the next year, Andrei Glazanoff and four others with two sleds trudged eastward overland from St. Michael to the head of the Anvik River. They soon ran out of food. Fortunately they stumbled onto an Eskimo igloo and were treated to an ample meal of rotten fish. Their energies renewed, the party followed the Anvik down to its confluence with the Yukon. Thus the Yukon, which Glazanoff named the Kwikpak, actually was first discovered by white men on January 24, 1834.

"Goodness, that is interesting. That was only about a hundred years before I was born."

The Eskimos at Anvik vacated an igloo and turned it over to the Russians. Glazanoff met with them in their big underground house and distributed tobacco. The men were much pleased and presented the visitors with fish, blubber, and bear meat. They also marveled at Glazanoff's metal knife and kettle. Through an interpreter, he made them understand that they could have such articles by exchanging furs for them. The natives were surprised. They hunted only to obtain food and clothing. Now they could hunt for another reason, to carry on trade with the white men.

ONE INCREDIBLE JOURNEY

However, Glazanoff was no trader. He had no trade goods. His job was to explore the country and learn whether it would be profitable for traders to come there regularly. Apparently he found it was. His party suffered much hardship as it explored the Yukon delta. At one point the white men were obliged to eat their dog harnesses, boots, and sealskin provision bags. Only with the help of natives were they able to return eventually to St. Michael.

In the years following Glazanoff's visit, Russian fur traders representing the Russian American Trading Company ventured five hundred miles up the Yukon. Above Anvik they met the Indians of the interior Yukon basin. These Indians stemmed from the subgroup called the Athapascans. Perhaps as recently as two thousand years earlier the last of their forebears may have crossed the Bering Strait and drifted onto the New World. Since there never was enough game and fish along the Yukon to support a large population, these people remained small in numbers. Glazanoff estimated there might be no more than thirteen hundred of them all told. But they were a hardy people to have survived through centuries of eking out a living from the Yukon and its valley.

Although they ranged the middle Yukon and were jealously protective of their individual hunting areas, occasionally these Indians ventured down river and encountered Eskimos. Or, an Eskimo band, weary of the ceaseless toil and bitter winds off the Bering Sea, sought a more protected location up the river. Inevitably, when the two peoples came together there was considerable bloodshed. The ill feeling between the two lasted many years.

The Indians of the middle Yukon basin

lived by hunting, fishing, and trapping. They holed up in dwellings made of brush, tree bark, and skins during the severe winters, and spent their summers in tent camps wherever the fishing and hunting was good. Salmon was their staple diet, both for people and dogs. However, those who settled back from the river ate caribou, bear, rabbit, and ptarmigan meat.

These people clung to small tribal organizations that took their names mostly from the rivers they frequented—for instance, the Anviks, the Koyukuks, and the Tananas. As a people they were taller and swarthier than Eskimos, had high cheek bones and dark eyes and hair. Each little band or group was headed by a man who acted as a sort of chief, but without real power. The older men did the advising and made all the decisions. The men shared the work with the women. In the summer they moved about in bark canoes. In winter, they used dog sleds and snowshoes.

After the Russian traders contacted them, the Yukon Indians began swapping furs and dried salmon for kettles, tobacco, cloth, needles, beads, and many other items. They quickly grabbed up any boxes or cans discarded by the traders. The cans made fine stoves. Getting hold of a small barrel in which to melt snow water was cause for a celebration. Later the natives acquired steel traps, matches, axes, and finally guns.

In 1838 an employee of the Russian Fur Company named Malakoff built a small fort and trading post in Nulato. When he returned overland to St. Michael for supplies, Indians burned his buildings. In 1842 another fort was built under the direction of a Lieutenant Zagoskin. A trader named Derzhavin was placed in charge, and for several years carried on a thriving business with the Indians. But in

ONE INCREDIBLE JOURNEY

1851 a neighboring tribe, the Koyukuks, swooped down on the fort and massacred Derzhavin, his helpers, and several others. But in 1854 still another, larger fort was built and maintained until they withdrew in favor of the Americans in 1867.

Meanwhile, hundreds of miles up river from Nulato, the British traders for the Hudson's Bay Company fur posts were also contacting the Yukon Indian hunters. They treated them better than the Russians did and gave them a much better return in goods for their furs. But after the United States purchased Alaska in 1867, both the Russians and British withdrew from trading along the Yukon. An American trading firm took over supplying the Indians and did a good business in this moneyless land.

Acquiring articles such as kettles, knives, and steel traps made life a little easier for the Yukon Indians. But by a civilized white man's standards, they remained desperately poor. Theirs was the hardest physical existence lived by man anywhere on earth. They lived like animals in dens. Hunger was always a threat. And yet, by some miracle, these people--who were not too far removed from their Stone Age ancestors--became a friendly, happy people. Still, life remained very difficult for many years until missionaries and teachers began coming to the Yukon to help them achieve a better existence. Nowadays, of course, the various government agencies provide assistance. The children go out to boarding schools and are furnished with medical and dental care, clothing, books, and instruction in trade skills. Every effort is made to help them attain a higher standard of living and become a part of Alaska's bigger communities. The adults receive medical and

*dental care, too, and monthly welfare checks.
Some manage their money well, live in neat
houses, and supplement their income by working
on construction jobs, in canneries, and by
making Indian craft articles. But many squan-
der their money in drinking and gambling, will
not work, and are destitute. Fewer and fewer
educated teenagers return to their villages.
They prefer to work at better paying jobs in
the larger towns like Fairbanks, Anchorage,
and Juneau. The villages along the Yukon grow
smaller and smaller. Perhaps some day they
will disappear altogether.*

"Very interesting! Thanks for sharing it with
me."

Monday, 27 September

DAY 163

The days were getting shorter and shorter,
giving us more hours of darkness than daylight. We
were on the river at sunrise, a few minutes after
seven following a big breakfast of pancakes and hot
cocoa. The temperature was twenty-five degrees, it
was partly cloudy and the wind still came out of
the west but with less velocity than on the previous days.

We moved right along passing Whiskey Creek,
Fish Island, Louden, the Cave Off Cliffs and by two
in the afternoon, had arrived in the settlement of
Galena. The population was about four hundred
people, plus those stationed at the nearby airforce
base, where there was lots of activity at that
time. We picked up a few supplies in one of the
two stores and tried to find Phil. Once more it
was the same old story. No one there knew anything

about him. We even checked with the Alaska State Trooper stationed there, but to no avail. We had rolls and coffee in the local cafe and before leaving town, I called home. That call made my day.

Late in the afternoon we moved on through Jimmy Slough and passed the old settlement of Yistletaw, continuing on until eight thirty, when we set up camp on the west end of Bishop Rock Island. It was a very cold evening. We huddled near the fire as we talked and enjoyed the clear sky, bright stars and northern lights. Earlier I had noticed that sunset came at seven ten, and twilight lingered until nearly eight o'clock. At our rest stops that day, I started the practice of running up and down along the shore line for a half mile or more. It felt good to stretch the legs and besides, it was a good way to drive away the chill.

Bishop Rock is really a small mountain with a sheer face dropping right into the river. There was a great whirlpool at its base with a slow swirl measuring nearly a quarter mile across.

Tuesday, 28 September

DAY 164

When we started out at sunrise the temperature was twenty-five degrees and we enjoyed a light tail wind out of the northeast. "This could be our lucky day," said Clint. "This is the first tail wind we have had in a long, long time."

"It sure is unusual. If this continues all day, we could really knock off some miles."

Working those paddles with power, before nine we were passing the settlement of Koyukuk and the mouth of the river with the same name. It was a cold day with ice still forming on the canoe at midday, but with the wind at our backs and the sun shining, we didn't notice the cold as much as we did on those headwind days. It was noon when we arrived at the settlement of Nulato. We inquired about our lost cameraman but no one knew anything about him. There were several fish wheels operating nearby. We picked up a nice salmon from one of them for a dollar and it tasted delicious at our lunch break.

In the early afternoon we noticed a large halo, or ring, around the sun, so anticipated that bad weather was once more in store for us. The thing that we didn't anticipate, however, was just how soon the frontal system would arrive.

We were still seeing numerous birds as we moved along that day, including another bald eagle, ducks and gulls. Then of course the gray jays and ravens were common all along the way. Nearly all of the summertime birds had long since departed for the warmer climates.

Late in the afternoon the skies clouded over and the wind increased in velocity out of the northeast. An hour later we were caught in a deluge of rain. Keeping along the west shore, the big waves rolling down the river helped to push us along. Several islands such as Ninemile and Halfway offered protection from the heavy rollers. Then as darkness settled in and we came out of the protection of Sevenmile Island, we were hit by some huge waves. Slowly we eased along the right shore with the wind pushing us along. In the heavy gusts it was a struggle to keep the canoe off the rocks and still not be swamped by being too far off shore. It was almost impossible to keep going, and yet there was no way we could turn back in those heavy, rolling seas. We were in a very tight situation there in the dark. It was much too rough to attempt to go ashore over those big rocks.

We tried to keep the canoe about one canoe

length from shore but sometimes the huge waves picked us right up and set us over. Several times I pushed off the shore rocks with my paddle. If we'd hit shore even for an instant, we'd surely have been swamped. We kept at it while I did some praying and by the Grace of God, we finally reached the protection of a small island just upstream from the village of Kaltag. By flashlight we made camp on the wet, sloping shoreline as the rain became mixed with snow and the storm raged on.

We had no protection from the wind. Everything was soaking wet. I unrolled my sleeping pad and the water ran out of it. Finally the tent was up and we had a cold supper inside the tent. We had moved sixty-four miles and that evening in our flapping, soggy tent we were about as miserable, wet and cold as we had ever been.

Wednesday, 29 September

DAY 165

The storm died down shortly after midnight but not before it threatened to tear the tent apart. I peeked out of the tent and my morning greeting to rouse Clint ran about as usual but this time it may have been a little ridiculous: "It's a beautiful day!" I always look forward to each new day in the spirit of adventure. There is no day so dismal that there isn't something to enjoy.

We were slow to get started. There was a half inch of snow and slush on the ground and no firewood around, as we were only about a mile north of the settlement. Everything was wet and cold. It was about as unpleasant a morning as you could imagine, with fog and light drizzle but no wind. Rolling up our wet pads and bags, we made room to have a cold breakfast in the tent, consisting of a can of pears, beans with beef, cookies, hardtack and the warm tea, still in our thermos jugs from the previous day.

Shortly before nine we packed everything up wet and paddled down to Kaltag. The village had three small stores for the population of less than four hundred people. We checked around about Phil. Once more it was the same old story, no one had seen or heard anything of him. Perhaps Clint was right. Maybe Phil had actually gone back to Michigan. I decided to find out. By radiophone, I placed a call to my home, but no Jenny. Then I placed a call to Bob McGee, but no Bob. Finally, in desperation, I placed a call to Judy Pemberton, Phil's wife in Grand Rapids, Michigan. Phil was not at home and Judy had no idea where he was, so the mystery was still unsolved.

We bought a few groceries and chatted with the storekeeper, who remarked, "This is the worst storm we have had this year."

"Wherever we go we seem to attract the worst of the weather," Clint replied.

A few minutes later we headed on down the river. The light rain continued throughout the day. In early afternoon we crossed the sixty-fourth parallel as we moved to the southwest. At seven in the evening we found a place to camp in a willow thicket along the left shore opposite Steamboat Slough. We soon had a good fire going but with the rain continuing all evening, drying our wet things was impossible. We were both taking the ordeal in surprisingly good spirits.

20

WINTER CLOSES IN

> God moves in a mysterious way,
> His wonders to perform;
> He plants his footsteps in the sea,
> And rides upon the Storm.
>
> — William Cowper,
> **Light Shining out of the Darkness**

Thursday, 30 September

DAY 166

The wind was calm as we rolled out at five thirty to be ready to again tackle the Yukon River at daybreak. It was another of those foggy mornings with a light drizzle keeping everything wet. Embarking at the first sign of dawn, we hugged the shoreline in the fog. Thirty minutes later the fog

406

became even more dense, engulfing us in a white shroud. We were paddling on instruments. I watched the built-in compass to make certain we were heading south. Suddenly the huge, sheer face of a hill loomed up out of the fog. We had to backpaddle to keep from hitting it head on. Then we veered down along the shore, passing Eagle Slide.

The fog began to lift by noon but the rain continued. Moving past Bullfrog Island a flock of geese passed overhead, the first we had seen in many days. Ducks were still plentiful. I found some birch bark at our shore break and would try to keep some handy for starting fires, for it had been difficult to get our fires going during that streak of bad weather.

It warmed up that day and we were beginning to see some greenery and color. The trees and brush were still holding most of their leaves where we were then paddling. The black flies were another surprise. Whenever we were ashore they gave us a bad time. Not just a few but swarms of those vicious, biting little creatures.

We tented close against a high bank near the top of a long, sloping mud beach near Alice Island, and were hoping for better weather on the morrow.

Friday, 1 October

DAY 167

We spent a very damp night as our sleeping bags had been getting a little wetter day by day. A strong wind was blowing from the northeast as we shoved off at first light. We soon crossed to the east shore for a little protection from the wind. Even though we had a tail wind we didn't get much assistance from it as the river was so rough. It was another cloudy day with intermittent snow showers.

Hugging the left shore we passed Fox and Eagle Islands. Opposite the latter on the west bank we could plainly see the new settlement of Grayling, which had been founded in 1963. "Visibility has certainly improved today. Maybe some good weather is on the way," said Clint.

Arriving in Anvik at five, we again checked for any news of our lost cameraman. Once more all response was negative. I had planned to call home but we soon learned it was impossible as the radio-phone hours ended at three in the afternoon and would not reopen until nine the next morning. We were surprised to find a coffee shop backed up against Hawk Bluff where we enjoyed our supper. The place was operated by an interesting, middle-aged white woman who was married to an Indian. Her husband was the preacher at the Episcopal church. The lady told us, "About a hundred people now live in Anvik, there are twenty-nine pupils in our school and we have two teachers." We enjoyed a nice visit as we told her what we were doing. She also told us that the mouth of the Yukon was only three hundred miles downstream. She also directed us to the storekeeper, who opened the store for us.

Heading on downriver in improving weather, we listened to the haunting cries of a common loon flying on to the south. We encamped before nine, up on the shelf of a cut bank along the west shore opposite Elkhorn Island. We soon had a good fire going and rigged up a system of lines between stakes to dry out some of our wet things.

For the next three hours we stood or sat near the fire, keeping it burning, turning the wet bags and discussing our situation. Eventually our talk again turned to the fur trading activities along the Yukon when Clint asked, "Didn't you tell me that Anvik was the place where the Russian explorers first arrived on the Yukon?"

"That's right."

"Did they set up a fur trading post there?"

"No. I don't think so, even though it was seriously considered. They set up their first post along this river down at Russian Mission in either 1836 or 1837. For two or three years prior to that the natives took their furs out to St. Michael Island, across the long portage trail from the Yukon to Unalakeet, and then across the sea ice of Norton Sound to the post at St. Michael."

"That must have been a long haul."

"It was. The trail was nearly sixty miles long, over the hills and then another fifty miles across the sea ice. Clint, you might also be interested in hearing a little more about Andrei Glazunoff and his first meeting with the natives at Anvik."

"I sure would. Tell me about it."

"Better yet, I'll read it to you from these pages from **The Yukon—**"

> *Glazunoff had come with Lieutenant Michael Tebenkov to establish St. Michael, and after the lieutenant had left, late in the summer of 1833, he remained there. That winter he was given command of an exploring party consisting of five Russians and three natives. His orders were to penetrate inland to the region where the Kuikpak was thought to flow and to chart a portion of its course. Following this, he was to traverse nearly a third of Alaska, all of it completely unknown, to the head of Cook Inlet, the site of present day Anchorage. Though Glazunoff would not accomplish the second part of his mission, his journey was to be the first significant penetration of the interior of western Alaska. He kept a journal of the expedition, which, before it was lost, was published in a para-*

phrased French translation.

In January 1834, Glazunoff and his men set out from St. Michael by dogsled. They carried a supply of trade goods to barter for food and native goodwill, but they took little actual food, an omission that would cost them dearly. The midwinter journey, in almost perpetual darkness, was extremely difficult.

After nearly two weeks they reached the crests of the low tundra hills that separate the Bering Sea from the forested interior. On the eastern slope of these hills they came to the sources of the Anvik River and they followed this stream down about a hundred miles. At dusk on February 4, 1834;, as they drew near the mouth of the Anvik, they sighted in the distance a large Indian village, the first they had seen. Just beyond it lay the Kuikpak — the Yukon—a white ribbon of snow-covered ice a mile across. No white man had seen this river before. Nor had the people of this village, or any other along the river, yet seen white men.

Glazunoff had felt it advisable to wait till next morning to enter the village. His party, however, had already been observed.

As soon as the inhabitants had seen them [according to Glazunoff's journal] they went out in large numbers from their houses and climbed on the rooftops while shouting loudly and holding bows and arrows in their hands. But Glazunoff took care to stop out of range of the arrows and to send one of his companions to the Indians to show them that they had nothing to fear from such a small number of strangers, adding that, if they [the

Indians] refused to deal with them, the Russian party would pass by the village without even entering. This discourse quieted the savages, who lay aside their bows and arrows, and sent toward the newcomers ten old men who invited them to come and rest in the village.

Glazunoff installed his men, their guns loaded in case of trouble, in the proffered shelter and went himself to the kashim, the underground communal house of the village men. He was given the place of honor; from it, in the dim light of the fish-oil lamps, he counted 240 men; they had just finished their daily sweat baths and were stark naked. Through an interpreter he delivered a speech in which he told the assembled men of the village of Anvik that he had been sent by his chiefs to invite them to come and trade with the Russians at St. Michael. In exchange for their furs, he said, they would receive many things of great value. After the discourse Glazunoff passed out tobacco and snuff, and it is a wonder that amicable relations did not cease at once. For some of the Indians 'were so much dazed by the smoke that they fell unconscious' while others 'inhaled such a quantity [of snuff] that they could not stop sneezing.'

After the meeting in the kashim the Indians said to Glazunoff, 'Tell us what you need, and we will be eager to furnish it to you, now that we are persuaded of the good intentions of the Russians.' During the rest of his stay in Anvik they supplied him and his party with all the food, wood and water they could use.

The reaction of the people in the second

Yukon village Glazunoff visited was much the same. At first sight of the Russians, they 'took flight immediately and sent their women and children to a nearby mountain.' But they were coaxed back, and again Glazunoff was invited to the kashim. He gave his speech inviting them to trade at St. Michael, and again they responded favorably. One of the men of the place confided to Glazunoff, 'Now we shall no more believe what has been said to us of the Russians, that their nails and teeth are of iron; we see that the Russians are men like us, and we are thankful to know the truth. We will come to visit your forts and are all disposed to trade with you'.

"That certainly is interesting!" Clint commented. "I never heard anything about that while I was in school."

Our sleeping bags were dry when we finally crawled into the tent. With good weather we wanted to get an early start the next morning.

Saturday, 2 October

DAY 168

"Verlen! Let's be up and at 'em. It's six thirty! And it's such a beautiful morning. Let's get going."

Clint's cheerful but urgent words brought me out of the dream world. Jumping out of my comfortable sleeping bag, dry for the first time in several days, we soon had a fire going and breakfast ready. Quickly I checked the thermometer. It stood at eighteen degrees and that fire felt good.

We embarked at sunrise, just after eight, Alaska Daylight Savings Time. We took special notice of the time of sunrise as we had seen so little of it for the past month and a half. It was a fine canoeing day. We moved right along past Cement Hill and between the Long Mountains and Carlo Island. Those mountains are only along the west side of the river, the east being rather flat bush country. I wanted a picture but the camera I had borrowed from Mel Williamson had quit working a few days before.

By mid-afternoon we had made it into the village of Holy Cross, a settlement of about two hundred people made up of Indians, Eskimo and whites. Located at the foot of the Holy Cross Hills along the west shore of Walker Slough, it is a scenic little town. Directly across from the settlement, the Innoko River joins the Yukon behind Salmon Island. We needed no supplies so the only thing we did was to inquire around about Phil. It was the same old story. No one had seen him.

Paddling on until nearly an hour after the seven p.m. sunset, we found a nice level campsite in a willow thicket up on a sand beach along the south side of Horse Island. Before disembarking to look the spot over, a bright full moon came up in the east. I stepped out into the soft, muddy silt just above the water line. Clint said, "It's such a nice night. We really should keep at it for another hour or two, don't you think?"

"Let me check this one. Good campsites have been hard to find. This may be a good one." I ran up to the high water shoreline and looked around. "This is great! Let's camp here. You'll like it!" So without further discussion we encamped.

While setting up camp we heard a bull moose grunting and snorting his mating call as he wandered around the island all evening, scouting and on the prowl. It was a little uncomfortable, sharing an island with a sex crazy moose. We soon

413

decided on our battle strategy in case he came too close or mistook us for a female moose.

It was such a nice moonlight night that before turning in, I went for a long walk while Clint kept the campfire burning.

Sunday, 3 October

DAY 169

Shortly after five thirty we rolled out and built a campfire to prepare breakfast. It was an invigorating-type morning, with full moon and stars shining brightly and the thermometer standing at twenty degrees. We were on the water an hour before sunrise and before nine had rounded the bend, passing Tabernacle Mountain. While moving through Summer Slough a strong, gusty wind began to whip up from the northeast which later in the day gave us crosswind problems.

We stopped at the fish camp of Paimut and talked with a native and his wife. They told us that two other canoe parties had preceded us that summer, heading for the ocean. We wondered who they were and why anyone else would be canoeing down the Lower Yukon.

At lunch time we were on a scenic rocky ledge along the Paimut Hills at the foot of a steep mountain. Sheltered from the wind we built a rock fireplace and made a double batch of bannock and heated a large can of pork and beans. We were warm and comfortable there in the sunshine. Otherwise it was cold, not getting above the freezing point as ice continued to form on the canoe and paddles throughout the day.

Late in the afternoon we had been paddling along in serene silence for a couple of hours, enjoying the sun and beauty of the wilderness, when suddenly my partner was attacked by another bad case of 'tent fever.' It had something to do with the fact that I was not properly paddling in the bow end of the canoe. I didn't reply as I didn't know what to say. I just sat there stunned, listening and thinking for the next sixty seconds or so as Clint, paddling frantically by himself, promptly ran into a sand bar. I still didn't say anything. Helping him back off the sand bar, we may have exchanged a few more unpleasantries, before we again headed on down the river.

Thinking back on it now, I undoubtedly was not paying ample attention to my paddling that afternoon and I may not be the easiest man on earth to get along with over an extended period of time.

Just after sundown we found a nice campsite close beside a high hill along the Ilivit Mountains only a couple of miles above Dogfish Village. After supper in the bright moonlight as we sat by the fire, we talked out our problems. Then before crawling into the tent we both went for a lengthy walk and a run along the dry river bottom well back from the water.

Monday, 4 October

DAY 170

Slowly my mind awakened at five but it took me fifteen minutes to build up the courage to get going. It was cold, with the temperature in the teens. Since it had turned so cold, we had been sleeping with most of our clothes on. I built the fire and made breakfast by moonlight as Clint packed up the bags, pads and tent. Thanks to the full moon, we slid the canoe back into the river and headed downstream more than an hour before sunrise. The shore ice had been freezing harder each night, becoming more and more of a problem but we had made it again.

Our beards and mustaches iced up that morning. My beard was so long and thick that I hadn't been able to comb it out for more than a week. My mustache was so long that it kept getting into my mouth, especially while eating, and it was also a good soup strainer and food collector.

Arriving at the settlement of Russian Mission before ten, we again checked for Phil. He was still among the missing. The village had a population of about one hundred and sixty people, most of whom were Eskimo. There were two stores where we bought a few groceries and some smoked, dried salmon before again heading down the river.

Lunch time found us at the foot of the mountains, just above Grand Island. Before leaving the place we climbed to the top of the tallest hill, an eight hundred foot peak, and had an exceptional view in all directions. That climb gave us a very good workout. It was a good day for paddling and by nine in the evening, we had passed the short bend around Roundabout Mountain and headed north through Cross Slough. We encamped on a point eleven miles beyond the Eskimo fish camp of Ohogamut.

That was a good campsite, dry and level with a good supply of wood for fuel nearby. There we discovered that we had lost our camp axe which Phil had given us at Fort Yukon. We had only begun to use it during the most recent spell of bad weather, and must have left it behind at our midday stop above Grand Island.

Clint was still having persistent problems with circulation in his hands, which bothered him a lot while trying to sleep. Then on the cold mornings, even though wearing two pairs of woolen gloves his hands would swell and be so cold that we sometimes had to stop paddling to give him a chance to rub some circulation back into them.

Before turning in, once more we went for a run on the dry part of the river bed.

Tuesday, 5 October

DAY 171

It was our coldest morning with the wind out of the southeast and a pair of sundogs clearly visible in the eastern skies. Sundogs are certain portenders of bad weather. We had overslept and by the time our fuel tanks were filled with pancakes and hot cocoa and we had broken camp, it was nine o'clock.

We headed for Marshall which is located along the right shore. Approaching Arbor Island, we chose to take the shortcut known as Wilson Creek Slough. There is where our troubles began. Only a small volume of water was moving through the Slough and we were hardly able to get past the numerous sandbars. Then after a couple of miles we hit ice from shore to shore which kept getting thicker and thicker as we went along. Paddling soon became impossible but not before we had made some progress by backing up and ramming forward several times. Finally the canoe slid up on top of the ice and we scooted to the shore.

"I guess it would have been better to have taken the long way around," said Clint.

"That's for sure!" I replied. "Ice problems again! As it was in the beginning, so shall it be in the end."

From there we lined the canoe over the ice while walking along or near the shore for the next three miles before we again found canoeable water. In some places, the ice was an inch and a half thick.

It was early afternoon when we arrived in Marshall. We were met near the shore by a fine young priest, Chuck Peterson, who had for his parish the settlements of Russian Mission, Bethel and Marshall. He was very friendly and helpful. He had heard that Phil was on downriver at St. Marys. He tried to put us in touch by radio but no luck. I wanted to call Jenny but there was no radiophone operator in town. We bought a few groceries and a new flashlight before we again slid the canoe back into the water.

It was a cold day. Ice built up on the canoe to a half inch in thickness. The river below Marshall is very crooked, so during the afternoon the strong southeast wind hit us from every quarter. It was tough going. Then in early evening it started to snow. At camping time, we couldn't find a place to take out along the steep cut banks. We were in some very rough water along the shore as darkness settled in. We began to get wet but finally found a place to get ashore. Fortunately, right there was an excellent campsite. We soon had a nine o'clock supper only four miles above the Dogtooth Bend. It had been one difficult, forty-mile day.

Wednesday, 6 October

DAY 172

By morning the wind had calmed down and there was an inch of snow covering everything. We were back on the river by seven and arrived in the Eskimo village of Pilot Station by nine. It was soon apparent that we had arrived at a bad time. There had been a big wedding the previous day and the whole settlement was suffering from a hangover. Both storekeepers, who were also the radio operators, were drunk. The groom, who was a government social worker, was also in a bad way. We were unable to get a message out to find Phil, nor could I call home. There was nothing to do but move on and hope for better results in the next town.

Heading back to the canoe we talked with a

Mr. Polty, who was busy building a new house. He insisted that we take time to go to his house for a cup of coffee and some food. A light headwind picked up as we paddled on, blowing snow in our faces most of the remainder of the day.

Two miles downriver from Pilot Station comes Hills Island. Recalling our experience of the previous day, we avoided Hills Slough by taking the long route in the main channel around the south side of the island.

At three thirty we arrived at the settlement of Pitkas Point, located on the north shore where the Andreafsky River joins the Yukon. The town of St. Marys is situated four miles up that river. We were wondering if we were going to have to paddle up the Andreafsky to find Phil. The radio operator in Pitkas Point, John Tinker, was very helpful. He made several calls to St. Marys but never did contact Phil. His sister insisted that we have coffee and lunch with them while we waited. She wouldn't take no for an answer, saying it was a tradition that they so welcome all visitors to the Point.

I called Jenny and made a date with her for Anchorage on 11 October, believing that we could easily be there by then. Clint and I also purchased airline tickets for that same afternoon from St. Marys to Anchorage. Phil finally showed up at five thirty in a power boat with two motors. He would follow along for the final ninety miles out to the ocean. He briefly told us what he had been doing since we had last met. Mainly he had been trying to catch up with us and doing research work in Fairbanks.

It was getting late so we paddled on until darkness settled in, then found a good spot to camp considering the wind and snow, five miles short of Mountain Village. Then after supper, while Clint went for a walk, Phil and I had a talk around the campfire.

Nearing the end, in Mountain Village, Alaska

Thursday, 7 October

DAY 173

The magnetic urge to finish our journey was very strong. I could almost smell the Bering Sea so we were up nearly two hours before daylight. We were delayed by Phil, who wanted to do another sequence. The north wind began to blow before we embarked just before eight. By the time we hit the small channel three miles below Mountain Village, the wind really began to whip up the water. Even in the small channel the wind would often slow us to a standstill and the cold, raw north wind continued all day. We battled our way by sheer force to where the channel widened. The wind whistled and howled up the river, whipping the water to a froth. Going any farther was an absolute impossibility. We were blown off the river at three thirty as we pulled into a small cove off the slough in an attempt to make camp in an alder thicket.

Inasmuch as Phil was to follow us in the power boat, we had put our tent, cook kit and most of our food in his boat that morning because it was handy and that was our mistake. So there we were, trapped in the Yukon River delta in a raging winter storm, twenty miles from nowhere with no tent and little food for the coming night.

"What are we going to do if your camera man doesn't show up this time?" Clint inquired worriedly. We stood and discussed our situation and decided that judging from the way the wind was blowing, Phil just might not be able to get to us that day. Analyzing our situation we decided that we should start making plans to get by as best we could.

We were as excited and happy as a couple of school boys on an overnight camping trip, with the prospect of making do with what we had. Taking stock of our resources we found two small, ultra-light tarps, one poncho, our sleeping gear and clothing. In the food department there were ten pounds of flour, baking powder and salt, a pound of lard, a can of pears, two pounds of brown sugar, a small bag of macaroni, a quart of powdered potatoes, two Lipton soup mixes, three Kool-Aids and ten Snickers bars. We could make it.

Clint went to work making a lean-to out of our tarps and some poles while I busied myself gathering a big pile of dead tag alders and willows, the only fuel in the vicinity. Bannock would be our main food. We built a comfortable arrangement for our griddle and made four big batches of bannock using half of the flour. Spreading a little lard and brown sugar on them, along with cups of hot

Kool-Aid, made us a good supper.

We leveled our sleeping spots under the lean-to with small sticks of wood and would sleep with all of our clothes on except boots and pants. At sleeping time I also slipped into my down jacket and clean dacron pants.

I had hung my orange rain coat on three sticks out near the river as a signal for Phil when and if he came along. In the early evening a native spotted the coat and came over near it but didn't stop. He wouldn't have been able to make it into our little cove with his motor boat.

That evening as we kept warm near the fire, I wondered how difficult it would be for me to re-learn certain good manners which would be expected once we returned to civilization. Things such as washing and combing my hair, and not scratching and belching. I was also having very strong thoughts of my home and family and my ever loving sweetheart back in Michigan.

Friday, 8 October

DAY 174

We lay in the sleeping bags watching and listening to the cold wind whip and twist the tops of the twenty-foot tag alders. On the ground it was only a mild, gusty wind, but it was hitting those tops with force making them snap and crack as they crashed into each other. Clint remarked, "That's why they're called tag alders."

They were miserable-looking trees, crooked, twisted and bent every which way, but they certainly did defuse the strong wind which was whipping down out of the Arctic barrens at gale force. As we watched, certain small, red capped birds picked seeds out of the alders. Clint, who understood his birds, identified them right away as common redpolls.

It was another real windbound day so we breakfasted in mid-forenoon on more bannock and peaches. Then Clint went exploring downriver as far as a deserted cabin and I went upriver to look around. The area had only a fringe of brush and small trees along the river banks. Behind that we were in the barrens, endless muskeg and tundra as far as the eyes could see. Out there we felt the full effects of the cold wind.

Here is a quote from my diary, written late that afternoon when it became obvious that we would have to spend another cold night in our makeshift lean-to:

The wind is as strong and violent as it was when we were blown off the river twenty-four hours ago. What a time to be windbound! Only two more days and we would have crossed the finish line. In fact, with good weather we would have been out to the ocean today. It looks like this storm could go on for days. We have lots of available firewood and are quite comfortable but still no Phil. It's probably too rough even for power boats today. We could very well be here for several days while the river freezes completely over. There goes my date with Jenny in Anchorage. Darn it!

We baked up another batch of bannock biscuits, eating several for supper along with an emptied peach can full of Lipton soup fortified with powdered potatoes, and hot lemonade. Then at nine in the evening, two seal hunters stopped by and warmed up by our fire. We gave them each a bannock and a cup of hot tea. They promised to spread the word as to where we were pinned down.

Saturday, 9 October

DAY 175

Still lying in my sleeping bag and trying to build up enough courage to brave the early morning cold, I looked out from under our little lean-to and saw a large grey timber wolf staring me in the face, less than ten feet away. Fortunately, the bright moon was shining and I had a good look at him. As soon as I moved, he bounded away.

We discovered that the wind had shifted to the northeast. We would have a go at it, for the right shore should offer some protection from the heavy blasts. Right after breakfast and two hours before sunrise, we again took off down the mighty Yukon. Progress was slow but at least we were moving ever nearer our goal.

In the early afternoon we had just started a fire to prepare the last of our food when we heard a motor boat coming down the river. It turned out to be Phil in an eighteen-foot boat, powered by two forty horsepower Johnson motors and operated by a seal hunter, Cookie Kies from Mountain Village. We were happy to see Phil and to meet Cookie, and were especially pleased to learn they had brought some food. We prepared a little bigger meal and they joined us.

Phil told of his experiences since we had last met. Attempting to catch up with us on Thursday, he had swamped his rented power boat and once ashore had made an emergency camp before being rescued that evening by Cookie Kies. While discussing the magnitude of our journey with Cookie around the campfire, he said, "That kind of a trip is not for me. I'm not a hardcore outdoorsman." He also told us about four men from St. Marys who were hunting above Pitkas Point and had drowned in the recent storm. "Every year," he continued, "the Yukon claims the lives of some of the local people."

We also learned that Cookie was the same seal hunter who had almost stopped at our camp on Thursday evening.

Arriving at the Head of Passes that afternoon, we crossed over into Kwikluak Pass flowing out to the west. Nothing interested us except reaching the ocean as quickly as possible. The canoe and paddle heavily iced up and we had to keep breaking off the ice to keep the weight down. We had several difficult stretches in strong crosswinds working our way around the shallow sandbar shore lines. It turned out to be one of the most difficult days of the journey.

Phil and Cookie had gone on ahead to set up camp as Clint and I continued on in the dark, desperate to knock off as many miles as possible. Just before midnight we became entrapped in an ice jam in the middle of mile-wide Kwikluak Pass while trying to work our way around a sandbar. Once free of the ice jam we were forced farther out into the main current in the center of the channel where the windblown waves were very rough and tricky. Finally we skirted the sandbar going miles out of our way and made it back to the protection of the right shore. The river was running with ice preliminary to the winter freeze up. Winter was definitely nipping hard at our heels.

It was nearly midnight when in the distance we could see a campfire flickering. Heading for it, we were pleased to find Phil and Cookie deep in their sleeping bags on a tarp, spread over the snow, near the fire. We set up our tent and soon crawled in. It had been a difficult fifty-five mile day and we were at the place where Kwiguk Pass splits off to the right from Kwikluak Pass.

Sunday, 10 October

DAY 176

We broke camp and embarked with a strong north wind blowing in a temperature of twenty-four degrees. We were having a real sense of anxious urgency to get to the Bering Sea. After all of those months and miles of obstacles we were so close. We could hardly wait to cover those final twenty miles. We would be taking the Hwiguk Channel out to the ocean.

It was a battle of crosswinds until midforenoon. We tried to take a short cut, starting up a small channel filled with slush ice. Finding dead water we turned back to the main channel. Both canoe and cover iced up until the ice was four inches thick on the bow. It stuck to the bottom like glue and even built up on our paddle blades, bogging us down like an anchor, making the canoe heavy and sluggish. If we had stayed in that water much longer, we would have been encased inside of a floating iceberg.

Rounding a point into the face of the north wind we had to turn on full power to make any headway at all. Then heading west came a crosswind and we were only a few miles from the sea. Already we were straining our eyes looking about five miles down the long channel and imagining we could see ocean water. Tension and anticipation were building up with almost every stroke of the paddle. The elements seemed to resist us as though we were being put to a final test of settling for a few miles short of our original goal.

About two miles from the ocean a huge sand bar island almost choked off the channel. Along the right on the wind-protected side, the channel was ice jammed. There was no way to get through. Going far around to the left put us miles out of our way, and into the full, unprotected fury of the fierce north wind. We would settle for nothing less than going all the way, so we dug in and fought the wind and waves and shallow sand bar all the way around.

Fortunately by then the buildup of ice on the canoe below the water line melted as we neared the sea. Phil and Cookie had gone to Alakanuk to pick up some groceries that morning as our food had nearly all been used up. They came back, passed us, and Phil set up his camera on the right shore on a point of land where Kwiguk Pass meets the Bering Sea. There they waited for us.

An island about a mile straight out from the mouth of Kwiguk Pass is what Clint and I headed for. We wanted the feeling of paddling in the Bering Sea. When Phil discovered where we were heading, he quickly packed up and with outboard whining, moved to the island where his camera was grinding away as we came paddling in. The time was twelve noon, Alaska Daylight Savings Time. We had accomplished our mission. The journey was completed. We had reached the Bering Sea.

All praise and glory to God!

In a rainbow of mixed emotions, and a deep sense of personal satisfaction, Clint and I paddled that last stroke, laid our paddles across the canoe and just sat there looking out over the Bering Sea for a few minutes. We reveled in the moment and the accomplishment that was ours alone, soaking up hard-earned salt spray, as the canoe bobbed in the rough seas from a strong cold wind out of the north. We had accomplished what we had set out to

We arrive in the Bering Sea

do, against nearly impossible odds and had arrived
on the exact date estimated in our Time and Distance Schedule. This was as far as we were
going--and it was far enough! It had been a tremendous experience.

We celebrated with a big lunch and were jubi-
lant. "Now to get home," I said. "Many things are
yet to come out of all this. All is not yet over.
More than likely there will be a complete change in
our life patterns and I don't believe things will
ever again be quite the same."

EPILOGUE

Our return to civilization is another story. Early Sunday afternoon we loaded everything including the canoe into Cookie Kies' eighteen-foot power boat and headed for Mountain Village, eighty-five miles up the river. It was a cold, rough and wet ride but we made it, arriving an hour after dark. We spent the night in the armory which was also being used as a school room.

The three of us were nearly out of money. We had difficulty in finding transportation from Mountain Village to St. Marys but by noon had caught a ride in a fifteen-foot boat which was really overloaded. About eight miles short of Pitkas Point, they realized they didn't have enough gasoline to make it with the overload, so Clint and I volunteered to lighten the load by putting our canoe back into the water. We would paddle towards the village. About halfway there we were hit by a sudden blinding snow storm with heavy winds. Phil had said he would send a power boat right back to pick us up, if they made it into town.

We were blown ashore below and across the river from Pitkas Point. The wind and waves were just too big to attempt to cross over. So there we were, stranded on a sandbar on the wrong side of the Yukon River in a raging blizzard with no tent and no food, with only our canoe. We tipped it up against a driftwood tree stump to make a windbreak from the driving wind and snow. Then huddling under the canoe we hoped that rescue would soon come.

Then we heard it above the roar of the storm. The plane was circling to land at St. Marys airport. The one upon which we were ticketed to fly to Anchorage. The next scheduled flight was not until three days later. Twenty minutes passed and we heard it again as it departed. Two hours later, we heard the whine of a motor boat coming upstream. Frantically we waved our arms. They were nearly past when they saw us and came back to see what the problem was. It was an Eskimo and his mother on their way to Pitkas Point. Those good people hauled us into town where Phil had been unable to get anyone to come to our rescue.

The following day we made it to the St. Marys airport where they allowed us to sleep on the floor of the terminal. We arranged to send our canoe C.O.D. to Detroit. The next day we flew to Bethel and there connected with a flight to Anchorage, where Jenny was still waiting. The three of us had less than five dollars left between us.

Seven thousand miles is a long ways when measured by a canoe paddle, one stroke at a time. By a close mathematical calculation, our journey required about 5,184,199 strokes of the paddle by each of us. There were one hundred and thirty-three portages totaling one hundred and fifty-three miles, including the unexpected ones to get around the ice in April. Then there was an additional fifty-four miles of towing the canoe while lining up the Richardson Mountains. There were seventeen dams along the entire route, six on the Ottawa River and seven on the Winnipeg. Our final dam to cross was the Grand Rapids dam on the Saskatchewan River as we left Lake Winnipeg.

Most of our route was still unchanged from what the fur traders were familiar with. But even the changes did not really detract from the overall magic of the impressions we received. It's all a part of the realities of life in an ever-changing world.

Apparently as a side effect we did set some kind of a record or two. We are the only two people in history to paddle the full route by man-power only, in less than six months. We also hold the record for the most miles ever traveled in a two-man canoe in less than six months.

Our Time and Distance Schedule worked out very well. We arrived in Flin Flon on the exact date proposed. At Summit Lake, we were only three days behind schedule. The biggest surprise was the planned finish date of 10 October. Almost as though gifted with prophetic powers, we reached the Bering Sea on the exact date the schedule called for.

Clint Waddell came home from our journey and a month later married Beverly Renko. They now live in the Minneapolis suburb of Brooklyn Park, where he operates a construction business specializing in log homes. Clint is also the successful manufac-turer of the Waddell canoe paddle.

Clint still canoes frequently and paddled along with Valarie Fons and me for a day in April of 1984, while doing the Eddie Bauer Mississippi River Challenge. In 1980 while on the Ultimate Canoe Challenge, Clint paddled along with us for a while, and in December of 1971, Jenny and I canoed with Beverly and Clint for a couple of days as they honeymooned in the swamps of Florida.

Phil Pemberton now lives in Petoskey, Michigan and is still into adventure movie making. The movie of our journey, entitled **Never Before –– Never Again,** is an excellent film. The response from the public has been exceptional wherever it has been test marketed. I regret that a shortage of capital is the reason this spectacular film has not been distributed for viewing by the general public.

ONE INCREDIBLE JOURNEY

To conclude, here is a little information on myself. Some would say I've done a lot of canoeing since our Cross Continent Canoe Safari in 1971, about 43,500 miles of it, making a total of 59,200 miles since I first seated myself in a canoe back in 1963. Jenny and I now have twenty-two grand-children. We sold our plumbing business in 1979 to my brother, Lawrence Kruger and my son-in-law, Terry Norris. Since that time I've been a canoe bum.

The 28,000-mile Ultimate Canoe Challenge with Steven Landick was my biggest adventure, but that's another story. Most recently it was the record-breaking descent of the Mississippi River with Valarie Fons, completed on May 20, 1984 in 23 days, 10 hours and 20 minutes.

Presently I am busy on the travelogue circuit with showings to audiences across the North American continent.

BIBLIOGRAPHY

B O O K S

Browning, Peter. **The Last Wilderness.** San Francisco: Chronicle Books, 1975.

Campbell, Marjorie Wilkins. **The North West Company.** New York: St. Martin Press, Inc., 1957.

Davidson, Gordon Charles. **The North West Company.** New York: Russell and Russell, 1967.

Edwards, Samuel. **The Magnificent Adventures of Alexander Mackenzie.** London: A. Redman, 1964.

Henry, Alexander. **Travels and Adventures in Canada.** Edmonton: M. G. Hurtig, Ltd., 1969.

Innis, H. A. **Peter Pond — Fur Trader and Adventurer.** Toronto: Irwin and Gordon, 1930.

Keating, Bern. **Alaska.** Washington: National Geographic Society, 1969.

Longfellow, Henry Wadsworth. **The Song of Hiawatha.** Chicago: Smith-Andrews Publishing Co., 1898.

Mackenzie, Sir Alexander. **Voyages from Montreal Through the Continent.** Toronto, Alerton Press – The Radisson Society of Canada, 1927.

Mathews, Richard. **The Yukon.** New York: Holt, Rinehart & Winston, 1968.

McGuire, Thomas. **99 Days on the Yukon.** Anchorage: Alaska Northwest Publishing Company, 1977.

Morse, Eric W. **Fur Trade Routes of Canada.** Ottawa: Queen's Printer of Canada, 1969.

Olson, Sigurd F. **The Lonely Land.** New York: Alfred A. Knopf, 1961.

–––. **Listening Point.** New York: Alfred A. Knopf, 1963.

–––. **The Singing Wilderness.** New York: Alfred A. Knopf, 1963.

Place, Marion T. **The Yukon.** New York: Ives and Washburn, Inc., 1967.

Roberts, Leslie. **The Mackenzie River.** New York: Rinehart Press, Inc., 1949.

Sevareid, Eric. **Canoeing with the Cree.** St. Paul: Minnesota Historical Society, 1968.

Service, Robert. **The Complete Poems of Robert Service.** New York: Dodd, Mead and Company, 1947.

Smith, James K. **The Mackenzie River.** Toronto: Gage Publishing, Ltd., 1977.

Weber, Sepp. **Wild Rivers of Alaska.** Anchorage: Alaska Northwest Publishing Company, 1976.

Bibliography

A R T I C L E S

Armstrong, James B. "The Train to Hay River." **The Beaver,** Winter, 1975.

Benoit, Barbara. "The Mission at Ile-a-la-Crosse." **The Beaver,** Winter, 1980.

Branson, Branley Allen. "Messages of the Clouds." **Canoe,** April/May, 1980.

Brown, Bern Will. "The Hare Indians." **The Beaver,** Autumn, 1974.

Bruemmer, Fred. "The Tree Line." **The Beaver,** Autumn, 1978.

Christensen, Deanna. "Steamboat Bill of Cumberland House." **The Beaver,** Winter, 1974.

Connelly, Dolly. "Mackenzie River Cruise." **The Beaver,** Spring, 1973.

Eddington, Bryan. "The Great Hall at Old Fort William." **The Beaver,** Summer, 1981.

Jacobson, Cliff. "Kosdaw's Revenge." **Canoe,** November, 1979.

–––. "Rainy Days Make Me Smile." **Canoe,** April/May, 1980.

Johnston, Thomas F. "The Hi'O Ceremony." **The Beaver,** Spring, 1976.

Leggett, Robert F. "Permafrost." **The Beaver,** Winter, 1972.

Letourneau, Roger. "The Grand Rapids Tramway." **The Beaver**, Autumn, 1977.

McDonald, Bill. "Peter Pond." **Canoe**, March, 1984.

Nute, Grace Lee. "Jehu of the Waterways." **The Beaver**, Summer, 1960.

Rogers, E. S. and Lee Updike. "Alexander Mackenzie as Surveyor." **The Beaver**, Winter, 1959.

Tessendorf, K. C. "George Simpson: Canoe Executive." **The Beaver**, Summer, 1970.

Vickery, Jim Dale. "A Bluejay Calling." **Canoe**, February, 1980.

Williams, Glyndwr. "The Hudson's Bay Company and the Fur Trade: 1670-1870." **The Beaver**, Autumn, 1983.

INDEX

Index

439

Index

Index

Wilderness **H**ouse **B**ooks
P. O. Box 968
Fowlerville, MI 48836

Please send _____ copies of **One Incredible Journey** at $16.95 $ _____
($21.95 Canadian)

Please send _____ copies of **Cold Summer Wind** at $13.95 $ _____
($18.95 Canadian)

(Postage will be paid by the publisher.)

Send check or money order - no cash or C. O. D.   Autographed - Yes<>   No<>

Mr./Mrs./Ms._____

Street_____

City_____   State/Province_____   ZIP_____

Wilderness **H**ouse **B**ooks
P. O. Box 968
Fowlerville, MI 48836

Please send _____ copies of **One Incredible Journey** at $16.95 $ _____
($21.95 Canadian)

Please send _____ copies of **Cold Summer Wind** at $13.95 $ _____
($18.95 Canadian)

(Postage will be paid by the publisher.)

Send check or money order - no cash or C. O. D.   Autographed - Yes<>   No<>

Mr./Mrs./Ms. _____

Street _____

City _____ State/Province _____ ZIP _____